Aims and scope

The *European Journal of Developmental Psychology* is an official publication of the European Society for Developmental Psychology. It publishes innovative original theoretical, empirical, methodological and review papers dealing with psychological development and developmental psychopathology during infancy, childhood and adolescence. It also publishes papers on social policy, based on developmental science and which are relevant to education, health or well-being in infancy, childhood and adolescence. It is keen to receive papers that are relevant to European developmental psychology in that they take account of topics such as European history, European policy or cultural diversity and their relevance to developmental matters. The Journal aims to cover the areas of cognitive and social development and the development of the person (self, identity and personality) and to do so from a disciplinary and/or an interdisciplinary perspective. On occasions, issues will be devoted to a special theme, under the editorship of an invited expert.

All subscription orders should be addressed to Psychology Press, c/o T&F Customer Services, Informa UK Ltd, Sheepen Place, Colchester, Essex, CO3 3LP, UK; Tel: +44 (0)20 7017 5544; Fax: +44 (0)20 7017 5198; E-mail: tf.enquiries@tfinforma.com. Send notices of change of address to the offices of the publishers at least six weeks in advance. Please include both old and new addresses.

The *European Journal of Developmental Psychology* (USPS 022251) is published six times a year (in January, March, May, July, September, and November), by Psychology Press, 27 Church Road, Hove, BN3 2FA, UK. The 2010 US Institutional subscription price is $620.00. Periodicals Postage Paid at Jamaica, NY 11431 by US Mailing Agent Air Business Ltd, C/O Worldnet Shipping USA Inc., 149-35 177th Street, Jamaica, New York, NY 11434, USA. **US Postmaster:** Send address changes to *European Journal of Developmental Psychology* (PEDP), Air Business Ltd, C/O Worldnet Shipping USA Inc., 149-35 177th Street, Jamaica, New York, NY 11434, USA.

EUROPEAN JOURNAL OF DEVELOPMENTAL PSYCHOLOGY
2010, 7 (1), 1–16

Ψ Psychology Press
Taylor & Francis Group

Theory of Mind: Specialized capacity or emergent property?

Elisabeth H. M. Sterck

Utrecht University, Utrecht, and Biomedical Primate Research Centre, Rijswijk, The Netherlands

Sander Begeer

VU University Amsterdam, Amsterdam, The Netherlands

Theory of Mind (ToM), the cognitive capacity to attribute emotions, intentions and knowledge to oneself and others, has been claimed a hallmark of human cognition. Nonetheless, ToM is considered limited in young children and people with autism. Moreover, its presence in animals is much investigated, and hotly debated. For cross-disciplinary discussions and real insight in this unique capacity it is essential to know what constitutes ToM. We aim to tackle this question by combining insights from three different scientific fields that study ToM: animal behaviour, typical child development and developmental disorders such as autism and AD/HD. In this introductory paper, we will first discuss different theoretical views of ToM: that it can be considered a specialized capacity or an emergent property. Essential features of these views will be deduced and predictions will be derived. Subsequently, we review how ToM is studied in the three discussed fields and how this relates to these theoretical views. After that we will review the contributions to this special issue and discuss how they relate to the different predictions. Last, we will combine the evidence and propose our view on what constitutes ToM. The data are more consistent with the view that ToM is an emergent capacity. The employment of ToM appears to depend on the functioning of its constituting capacities, represented mental states and context factors. A focus on the ingredients that

---

Correspondence should be addressed to Elisabeth H. M. Sterck, Behavioural Biology, Padualaan 8, NL-3584 CA Utrecht, The Netherlands. E-mail: e.h.m.sterck@uu.nl

We thank the Cognition and Behaviour Program from the Netherlands Organisation for Scientific Research (NWO) for financially supporting the 2006 meeting "Theory of Mind: module or emergent property?" in Wageningen, the Netherlands, with an Advanced Study Initiative 2006 Grant to EHMS.

This special issue is based on contributions to and discussions during this meeting. We also thank the co-organizers, Richard van Wezel and Juliane Cuperus, and all participants of the meeting for sharing their ideas. Finally, we are indebted to Sonja Koski and Mark Meerum Terwogt for their helpful comments on an earlier version of this manuscript.

---

http://www.psypress.com/edp   DOI: 10.1080/17405620903526242

contribute to and allow the expression and employment of ToM will enable us to start understanding when and how individuals, whether human or non-human, deal with the minds of others.

Keywords: Theory of Mind; Animal behaviour; Human development; Autism; Emergence.

Humans pride themselves in being the species with the most advanced cognitive capacities. One of these advanced capacities is Theory of Mind (ToM), the ability to attribute emotions, intentions and knowledge to oneself and others (Flavell, 2004). Nevertheless, not all humans are equipped with this capacity. ToM is traditionally considered limited in young children (Wellman, Cross, & Watson, 2001) and people with autism (Baron-Cohen, Leslie, & Frith, 1985), and recent studies even question the use of ToM skills by normal adults (Keysar, Lin, & Barr, 2003). Moreover, its presence in animals is much investigated (Call & Tomasello, 2008; Premack & Woodruff, 1978), and hotly debated (Bolhuis & Wynne, 2009; Penn, Holyoak, & Povinelli, 2008; Povinelli & Vonk, 2003, 2004). However, research on the capacity for ToM in humans and non-human species has proceeded relatively independently, resulting in different methods to prove its presence and different conceptualizations to define its nature. This is unfortunate, because the interdisciplinary study of ToM in different species forces a sharpening of methodological and conceptual choices. For example, if animals show ToM skills, then language may not be a necessary component of ToM. Therefore, for cross-disciplinary discussions and real insight in this unique capacity, it is essential to determine what constitutes ToM in a species-independent way.

We aim to tackle this question by combining insights from three different scientific fields that study ToM: animal behaviour, typical child development and developmental disorders such as autism and AD/HD. This interdisciplinary approach highlights human versus non-human and typical versus pathological development. In this introductory paper, we will first discuss different theoretical views of ToM. Essential features of these views will be deduced and predictions will be derived. Subsequently, we review how ToM is studied in the three discussed fields and how this relates to these theoretical views. After that we will review the contributions to this issue and discuss how they relate to the different predictions. Last, we will combine the evidence and propose our view on what constitutes ToM.

TWO DIFFERENT VIEWS ON THEORY OF MIND

Two different theoretical views on what constitutes ToM will be examined. First, one may consider ToM a specialized capacity (Saxe, 2005) or module (Fodor, 1983). This idea has been put forward by scholars in the field of psychology, biology and philosophy, and is considered consistent with the idea that human cognition is unequalled and distinct from animal cognition (Macphail & Bolhuis, 2001). Alternatively, ToM may require a number of different, independent capacities (Tomasello, Carpenter, Call, Behne, & Moll, 2005), the combination of which leads to the emergence of ToM (Barrett, Henzi, & Dunbar, 2003). The theoretical implications of these two views will be explored and compared to the empirical and theoretical evidence.

The specialized capacity or modular view considers ToM an innate cognitive module (Scholl & Leslie, 1999) or mechanism (Baron-Cohen, 1995) with a unique conscious cognitive nature (Barrett et al., 2003). This conception features domain specificity, i.e., ToM only operates on certain kinds of input, specifically meta-representations of propositional attitudes (Gerrans, 2002). Moreover, modules are fast, offer constrained outputs and can be selectively impaired by neural damage. Therefore, ToM will be either present or absent—however, see Leslie, Friedman, and German (2004) for a modular, yet gradual view on the developmental of ToM. The operation of a specialized capacity is considered mandatory, i.e., it is impossible not to interpret situations as involving intentional agents (Scholl & Leslie, 1999). It can be selectively impaired by neural damage and the capacity disappears entirely when any of its constituent parts fail to operate. While the modular approach has been an effective way of distinguishing the concept of ToM as a social skill, the approach may be less helpful in the exploration of the nature of ToM. It should be noted that considering ToM a specialized capacity or module is independent from evidence for or against neural localization, since a single capacity might also be based on distributed neural architectures (and vice versa—an emergent property may operate on a network of tightly defined neural substrates).

The view of ToM as an emergent property provides a framework to explore the constituent parts of ToM. An emergent property is a new property that results from the combined action of a number of features (Grimm & Railsback, 2005). An example of an emergent property is a conversation: it is the result of two (or more) people talking in interaction with each other. The verbal output from a single person cannot be considered a conversation, but is a crucial constituent part of it. An emergent outcome is not deducible to one of the constituting features and, in turn, may lead to new processes and outcomes. Considering ToM an emergent property would entail that it includes multiple capacities that alone do not lead to ToM. This approach allows for different levels of complexity of ToM abilities. ToM will show gradual emergence when one of the constituting cognitive capacities becomes available at an advanced enough stage. Likewise, it will show gradual decline when the constituent parts fail. How these multiple capacities are combined may be a crucial feature. This approach assures that the constituent parts are separate, distinct abilities, rather than simpler versions of the same construct.

While some people may find the above presentations cartoon-like, we aim to provide a clear contrast between the view of ToM as a special capacity or an emergent property.

THE VIEW OF THEORY OF MIND IN ANIMAL RESEARCH

In animal research ToM was initially treated as one advanced capacity that could be measured with single tests. A ToM test was designed where chimpanzees had to understand the intentions and situation of others (Premack & Woodruff, 1978). Mirror recognition tasks assessed whether animals may have a concept of self (Gallup & Capper, 1970). These tests were criticized, since alternative explanations were possible, such as previous associative learning yielding the correct outcome of a presented sequence (Heyes, 1993) or co-ordinated reactions to mirror images that could have represented co-movement with an other instead of exploring own movements (Povinelli, 1993). Moreover, chimpanzees did not pass the hallmark test of ToM (see below), the false-belief task (Call & Tomasello, 1999), presumably because they failed to understand the content of others' beliefs (Povinelli & Eddy, 1996b). These critiques and failures led some to conclude that animals do not have ToM (Macphail & Bolhuis, 2001; Wynne, 2004) and that we do not proceed in understanding animal's cognition by squeezing them into this anthropocentric cognitive framework (Barrett & Henzi, 2005). Others continued investigating ToM by developing new approaches.

The new approach dissects the capacity and assumes that ToM consists of different capacities that can have simpler components. For example, one important prerequisite for ToM is that an animal understands the visual perspective of another individual (Emery, 2000; Povinelli & Eddy, 1996b). This can range from a simple co-orientation with the looking direction of the other based on associative learning (Burkart & Heschl, 2006), to understanding that the other is looking at a particular location, even if its own view is blocked (Brauer, Call, & Tomasello, 2005; Povinelli & Eddy, 1996a), to the advanced capacity to form a mental representation of the visual knowledge of the other (Hare, Call, & Tomasello, 2001; Dally et al., 2010 this issue). This approach has resulted in the proposal that ToM emerges from a suite of other cognitive capacities. One proposal postulates that its constituting capacities are causal reasoning, analogous reasoning, episodic memory, inhibition and a large processing capacity to combine information (Barrett et al., 2003). These capacities are also considered cognitively advanced, but they can be investigated separately. Evidence for these constituting capacities indicates that these animals may have ToM or components thereof.

Crucial for determining ToM and other advanced capacities in animals is to show that the evidence does not allow an alternative, cognitively simpler interpretation, since cognitively simpler explanations should be preferred over those requiring cognitively advanced ones for the principle of parsimony (Lloyd Morgan's canon, e.g., Shettleworth, 1998). These simpler explanations include solving the problem via learning or understanding the situation or behaviour without a mental state representation. The outcome of tasks assessing advanced cognitive capacities in animal research has to be distinguished from cognitively simple associative learning: where one (combined) stimulus is linked to one behavioural outcome. Training on the final task is not allowed, since this would provide the animal the opportunity to form a simple association between one feature and an outcome. However, training on behaviour that has to be used in a novel situation is allowed. In the novel situation, the predicted novel behaviour has to be produced through combining different strands of information for the first time (see Clayton, Bussey, & Dickinson, 2003, for episodic-like memory). This novel situation is ensured by providing unique, or only a few, trials to the tested animal. It should be impossible to solve the problem with a simple rule (e.g., long vs. short time for episodic-like memory), but only through abstraction from earlier experiences (triangulation; Heyes, 1993). Therefore, the flexible combination of information is an essential feature of tasks assessing advanced cognitive capacities, including ToM, in animal research. ToM paradigms have also been criticized for not proving that animals may interpret behaviour without a cognitive representation of other's mental states (i.e., "behaviour reading"; Povinelli & Vonk, 2003), which has led to improved testing of various control conditions to exclude behaviour reading as an explanation. The requirement to explicitly exclude such alternative behaviour reading explanations has been evoked less often in human studies. However, it could be argued that flexible and spontaneous application of skills may also be required as evidence for human ToM (see below). Altogether, animal research has advanced from viewing ToM as a singular capacity to viewing at a capacity composed of several capacities. This marks a crucial difference in approach.

THE VIEW OF THEORY OF MIND IN DEVELOPMENTAL PSYCHOLOGY

Much like the research in animal behaviour, ToM research in developmental psychology started out highlighting the false-belief task (Wellman et al., 2001), though the essentials of ToM may be traced back to Piaget (1929). To date many textbooks and scientific papers still equate ToM with false-belief reasoning, and consequently state that the ability has a clear stage-like onset, leaving little room for further development. Indeed, false-belief reasoning is one of the most researched topics in child development, resulting in clear developmental stages: most 3-year-olds do not pass the false-belief task, and most 5-year-olds do (Wellman et al., 2001). This evidence favours the specialized capacity perspective; once ToM is acquired, the skill may be fine-tuned, but its presence is indisputable, much like learning to walk. However, studies using adaptations of the same false-belief test contrast this account. Better skills than expected were shown in infants, with 13-month-olds showing a preliminary understanding of false beliefs (Onishi & Bailargeon, 2005). At the same time, normal adults show poorer skills than expected, since many well-known experiments from the domain of social psychology challenge an overly optimistic view of adult ToM (Saxe, 2005).

Indeed, adolescents and adults, who show a conceptual understanding of meta-representations, may still fail more complex and behavioural measures. This aspect is illustrated extensively in the contributions by Roeyers et al. and Begeer et al. (2010 this issue). Studies on human development increasingly take a broader perspective on ToM, with a strong focus on its components in young children, such as imitation, shared attention, social referencing, but also delineating the constituent parts of ToM, highlighting the role of imagination, executive functions and pragmatic language skills (Geurts et al., 2010 this issue) and the difference between competence and performance (Begeer et al., 2010 this issue). Furthermore, going beyond the childhood years, recent studies increasingly target ToM skills across the adult life span, including its decline in older age (Sullivan & Ruffman, 2004). This endeavour is a promising route for a truly comprehensive perspective on the development of ToM.

THE VIEW OF THEORY OF MIND IN DEVELOPMENTAL DISORDERS

The atypical development of ToM has been studied in a variety of mental and physical disorders, such as schizophrenia, psychopathy, deafness and blindness, but, by far, most studies have focused on autism, a disorder that is sometimes defined as an impairment in ToM or "mind blindness". In general, school-aged children with autism have a well-established limitation on ToM tasks (Wellman et al., 2001), but when children with autism are normally intelligent or "high functioning", they often score adequately on most elementary and many advanced measures of their ToM understanding (Senju, Southgate, White, & Frith, 2009). In his book entitled *Mindblindness*, Baron-Cohen (1995) attempted to differentiate between underlying mechanisms of ToM and its impairment in autism. Two of these are often presented as precursors of ToM: the ability to share attention and the ability to detect eye directions. The third mechanism, the "intentionality detector", refers to the ability to interpret self-propelled motion stimuli in terms of volitional mental states of goal and desire. Finally, the somewhat homuncular term "theory of mind mechanism" is evoked to explain the ability to attribute epistemic mental states such as pretending, thinking, knowing, believing, while the ToM ties the volitional, perceptual and epistemic mechanisms together (Baron-Cohen, 1995). While individuals with autism were initially presented as impaired on all four domains, recent studies increasingly show that high-functioning individuals were able to conceive of mental representations and are even quite eloquent and aware about ToM. Nevertheless, they generally failed to apply this conceptual understanding in their daily life interactions (Begeer, Rieffe, Meerum Terwogt, & Stockmann, 2003; Frith, Happé, & Siddons, 1994; Senju et al., 2009).

The increasing focus on the adequate performance of individuals with autism and average or above average IQ levels challenges the boldness of the mind-blindness hypothesis. Many individuals with autism even state that they are in fact the only humans with a ToM, referring to their theoretical approach to other minds. Those without autism use less theory and more intuitive simulation in their attempts to make sense of others' subjective experiences (Gallese, 2007). Without trivializing the limitations of individuals with autism, these contrasting perspectives call for a better conceptualization of the construct.

Studies on autistic individuals have also highlighted the role of other information-processing impairments such as their tendency to miss the big picture and focus too much on detailed information (weak central coherence; Frith & Happé, 1994). Central coherence and executive functions are often presented, together with ToM, as the three main explanatory theories on autism. However, ToM in itself is not a scientific theory. Rather, it should be conceived of as an ability that can to some extent be explained by central coherence and executive functioning. Longitudinal studies on the development in these domains will have to shed more light on the causal relationships between them. Thus, while autism research first focused on the modular approach to ToM, the adequate conceptual abilities of individuals with autism and average or above IQ levels undermines the ideas of an impaired module.

CONTRIBUTIONS TO THE CURRENT SPECIAL ISSUE

Non-human theory of mind

Research on ToM capacities in non-human animals combines the results of multiple behavioural experiments to deduce the nature of applied cognitive capacities. The contribution of Dally, Emery, and Clayton to this issue reviews evidence for a mental representation of visual knowledge in scrub jays. Scrub jays are a food-hoarding corvid species. Wild scrub jays store food in many places and can recover it at a later stage. Conspecifics, however, can exploit food stored, "stealing" it from the individual that stored it. The reviewed behavioural experiments investigate how scrub jays react when conspecifics know where they hid food. Observed jays recovered and cached food in new locations. Re-caching of food, however, depended critically on the subject's own experience of stealing hoarded food from another bird. Moreover, the subject's actions depended on the identity of the observing bird, not its behaviour. Since the correct behaviour of a subject jay depended on a combination of information, not on one cue, the authors argue that they have a mental representation of the knowledge of other jays: namely whether they observed the hoarding of food at a particular location or not.

This study indicates that scrub jays combine different strands of information to guide their behaviour when they can re-cache food. First, an animal translates its own actions in the past into the appropriate action against this action, namely stealing of food translates into hiding of food. This may represent a degree of causal (if hoarding is seen, then food can be stolen) and analogous (if I can steal after seeing hoarding, so can an observer when I hoard food) reasoning. Second, it forms a memory of a particular event, the location where food was hidden in combination with the observation of this action by a particular individual, and this memory can be considered an episodic-like memory of a past unique event. These two strands of information are combined with the current presentation of the hoarding tray and the presence of a particular conspecific now. A simple explanation, one cue or reading the behaviour of the observing bird, cannot explain the reaction. Therefore, the alternative, that jays use a mental representation of the observing bird's knowledge, is the best explanation of the results. This indicates that the formation of this mental representation consists of different constituent parts.

It has been argued that chimpanzees form mental representations of others' knowledge, intentions and goals (see Call & Tomasello, 2008, for a review), but not of false beliefs (Kaminski, Call, & Tomasello, 2008). This conclusion was based on the combined results of multiple experiments, analogous to the approach on scrub jays, and has been taken by Koski and Sterck (2010 this issue) as a starting point to investigate chimpanzee's empathic concern for others, a capacity related to ToM. The paper proposes at what cognitive level chimpanzees may express empathy. Although empathy has been linked to advanced cognitive processing in emotional state representation, it may also be based on cognitively simpler mechanisms (Preston & de Waal, 2002), as empathy is based on two partially distinct components, namely emotional and cognitive processing. Koski and Sterck propose that chimpanzee processing of others' emotions depends on the combined action of emotional contagion, some level of the cognitive distinction between own and other's emotional states and the ability to inhibit own emotions. The first, emotional contagion, makes it possible to feel what the other feels. The later two capacities determine whether an individual understands the emotional state to be other's rather than their own, and potentially how the co-feeling with the other is translated in behaviour beneficial for the other. Following the evidence from chimpanzees' capacity for representing some mental states of others and of inhibiting own responses (Dufour, Pele, Sterck, & Thierry, 2007), they propose that chimpanzees may have the capacity for veridical empathy, which is cognitively simpler than full cognitive (ToM) empathy, but more advanced than mere emotional contagion. Thus, the partial capacity for ToM in chimpanzees is used as a constituting component determining the ascent of cognitive complexity of chimpanzee empathy.

Human development

In both humans and non-humans, the definition of ToM often mistakenly includes a one-sided focus on attributing mental representations to others, neglecting the ascription of mental representations to oneself. Consequently, most research to date—focusing on humans, from the traditional false-belief tasks to the more recent advanced ToM measures, employs a similar focus on mental representations of other individuals rather than those of oneself (see Begeer et al., 2010 this issue; Roeyers et al., 2010 this issue). The contribution of Mitchell, Bennett, and Teucher includes a perspective on children's acknowledgment of their own mental representations. When considering our own minds or mental representations, it is often taken for granted that *we* know best what is on our mind. The privileged access to one's own experiences is assumed to result in direct knowledge about the content of our own mind. Interestingly, when children are asked who knows best about their (the children's) own interior states, they often denote others, such as their parents or a teacher, rather then themselves. Mitchell et al. discuss this phenomenon in a review of findings on typical development from preschool age to preadolescence. While children seem to start out thinking they may not be best qualified to know their own minds, they increasingly acknowledge their own authority. This development depends not only on the type of knowledge at hand, but also on cultural background. Individualistic cultures seem to focus more on the individual itself, while collectivist cultures focus more on the context. The developing understanding of own and other people's access to subjective mental representations offers an intriguing aspect of the broader understanding of ToM, which encompasses a much overlooked awareness of our own inner states.

Following the more traditional focus on attributing mental representations to others, Ketelaars et al. present a much-needed longitudinal approach. Their research investigates the development of different aspects of ToM in normally developing children between 5 and 7 years. They highlight the understanding of mental representations that differ in complexity, from simple emotions to understanding more complex processes of emotion display rules, mixed emotions and false beliefs. While emotion attribution remained relatively stable, all other measures improved with age. Moreover, performance of these tasks, and also language ability, at a particular age was correlated and predictive of performance at a later age. Confirming earlier studies, children were generally able to perform the simpler tasks at a younger age than the more advanced tasks, indicating that the mental representations become more complex with age. In addition, the ability to perform simpler tasks likely functioned as a prerequisite for performing more complex tasks. However, what is the precise cognitive change that allows children to perform more complex tasks remains unclear.

Pathological human development

The section on pathological human development has a strong focus on autism, which is unsurprising, given that difficulties with ascribing mental representations to others can be seen as one of the core features of autism. The section starts with a contribution by Begeer, Malle, Nieuwland, and Keysar, describing two new instruments that measure the application of ToM skills during the representation and partaking in social interactions. Highlighting normally intelligent, or high-functioning children and adolescents with autism spectrum disorders (HFASD), the authors argue for a strong need for new ways of measuring ToM in complex, real-life settings. This is important because, from preadolescence, most traditional ToM tests do not target the problems of individuals with HFASD, who seem to grasp the elementary principles from ToM on a theoretical level, but primarily fail to apply this understanding in practice. Tackling this problem, a task was designed where participants are asked to retell a story about an interaction between two people. The HFASD group showed a diminished tendency to represent the social interactions in mentalistic terms. Second, participants were tested in a direct perspective-taking task. Both the typically developing and HFASD participants performed at similar—though quite poor—levels on this task. Apparently, even structured interactions are filled with perspective-taking errors, including in normal adults. Interestingly, the performance was positively correlated to chronological and mental age in the HFASD group only. Therefore, their ToM skills are probably not systematically deficient but may dependent on cognitive abilities, suggesting different processing styles in typically developing individuals and HFASD.

The role of intelligence in the performance on ToM tasks likely indicates that individuals with HFASD use more cognitive, rule-based strategies in social situations. While this may be helpful in highly structured situations, the more dynamic social reality in daily life interactions often presents unexpected situations, which can result in sudden failures in perspective taking that are often highly confusing to others. Typically developing individuals, on the other hand, seem to employ more intuitive or heuristic approaches, which provide them with the ability to improvise and respond in a more flexible way to changing environments.

Indeed, the clear structure of many traditional false-belief-type tasks may have overestimated the performance of the HFASD individuals. This argument is closely related to the rationale of the contribution of Roeyers and Demurie, who review various approaches to advancing ToM measures, specifically for adolescents and adults with HFASD. A first series of tasks presented static social stimuli to infer mental states, but varied the modality of the stimuli by using voices or parts of faces. This provided widely varying results. For instance, the use of eye-region pictures to infer their mental states has yielded mixed results with respect to group differences between HFASD participants versus matched controls. A second series has aimed to approach the dynamics of real-life interactions using film fragments. This approach has indicated limitations of individuals with HFASD, though large individual differences were found. Interestingly, the performance of HFASD individuals improved when the interaction was more structured (i.e., involving a well-known situation such as getting acquainted). The roles of structure and the ability of HFASD individuals to use explicit social scripts in well-known situations are further discussed. Both Roeyers et al. and Begeer et al. (2010 this issue) note that in real-life situations structure may help HFASD individuals to use of ToM skills.

Geurts, Broeders, and Nieuwland provide a wider perspective on ToM by highlighting the link with two related domains of functioning: executive functioning and pragmatic language abilities. Executive functioning provides a clear explanatory framework for ToM functioning. Executive functions, defined as the cognitive control processes that enable us to monitor behaviour in a dynamically changing environment, can be said to fundamentally underlie ToM in pragmatic language use. Alternatively, deficits in ToM and executive functioning could be caused by another cognitive deficit. This hypothesis is investigated by reviewing the evidence for ToM deficits in children with a disorder known to be related to impaired executive functioning: AD/HD.

While the bottom line of the empirical findings is that children with AD/ HD are overwhelmingly impaired in executive functioning, limitations in ToM are not convincingly found, suggesting that impairments in executive functions do not automatically result in ToM deficits. When considering the relation of both capacities with pragmatic language use, the relatively unimpaired ToM abilities of children with AD/HD can be contrasted with their poor pragmatic language skills. Interestingly, the task discussed as measuring pragmatic language use, the strange stories task, is also often put forward as an advanced ToM task (Roeyers et al., 2010 this issue), showing the need for a better conceptualization of the construct of ToM. In short, the Geurts et al. paper shows that the research on ToM will benefit from a longitudinal focus on multiple domains in multiple disorders to disentangle why some children develop impairments in specific aspects of their social cognitive functioning.

DO CURRENT CONTRIBUTIONS SUGGEST SPECIALIZED CAPACITY OR EMERGENT PROPERTY?

Perspectives from non-human development (Dally et al., 2010 this issue; Koski & Sterck, 2010 this issue) give credence to the interpretation that animal ToM consists of multiple constituting capacities. Both chimpanzees (Call & Tomasello 2008) and scrub jays (Dally et al., 2010 this issue) entertain mental representations of other's knowledge, goals, desires and intentions. However, chimpanzees do not seem to entertain mental representations of false beliefs (Kaminski et al., 2008), a capacity not tested in scrub jays. In particular the chimpanzee data suggest that entertaining one type of mental representation does not automatically imply that other mental representations are formed, indicating a gradual emergence of ToM. Animal research, however, does not provide information on whether ToM is mandatory to use once present, since research aims at investigating whether it is actually present, not whether it is present and is not employed.

Perspectives from human development also seem to suggest a gradual emergence, differentiating between various different tools (Malle, 2005) that ToM is comprised of, in keeping with the emergent property hypothesis. Children show a gradually increased awareness of their own mental representations (Mitchell et al., 2010 this issue) and an increasing ability to pass ToM tasks (Ketelaars et al., 2010 this issue) with age. Also, the waning of the initial confusion about who has most access to one's own mental states during development is inconsistent with ToM as a mandatory process (Mitchell et al., 2010 this issue). Moreover, the evidence for perspective-taking failures in normal adults is in full contrast with the idea that ToM is a capacity that will be used when present in an individual (Begeer et al., 2010 this issue). In addition, Ketelaars et al. (2010 this issue) highlight the large individual variance in children's performance on a range of tasks related to ToM skills. Their evidence for a correspondence between belief reasoning and emotion understanding emphasizes ToM as a dynamic construct, suggesting separate but connected skills that broaden over time to later insights. Furthermore, following Geurts et al. (2010 this issue), it could be argued that cognitive flexibility and inhibitory control are skills that are required for passing ToM tasks, on both conceptual and applied levels.

Perspectives from pathological development show even more strongly that the idea of ToM as one specialized capacity is not tenable when considering more able and older human individuals, whether typically developing or with autism. Different outcomes of ToM tasks using different methodology, whether conceptual versus practical, or unstructured versus explicit and structured tasks, suggest a strong context dependency in the performance. Moreover, the findings that normal adults often fail to act according to ToM, despite the fact that they have been found to pass every single method of measuring ToM in its official definition, shows that there may not be a specialized capacity that we can define as ToM (Begeer et al., 2010 this issue), but rather a variety of situated capacities that may allow us to deal with other minds, if applied in the adequate way.

It is intriguing to contrast the rule-based, theoretical approach of ToM of individuals with HFASD with the strict criteria from studies in non-human species that prohibit training animals on ToM. In behavioural biology, the possibility that an animal's behaviour relies on rule-based, associative learning disallows this behaviour to be considered ToM. The criteria for using rule-based responses in human studies are less clear. These contrasting approaches raise the question of whether flexibility and spontaneity of behaviour should be considered necessary and sufficient components of ToM, and whether overly learned or rule-based responses should be excluded.

Language skills have been considered mandatory for ToM (Astington & Jenkins, 1999). While Ketelaars et al. (2010 this issue) indeed found a relationship between language skills and performance in ToM tasks in normally developing children, Geurts et al. (2010 this issue) found that AD/HD children with poor language skills performed well on ToM tasks. Moreover, animals lack language (Pinker, 1994), but show some aspects of ToM. This gives rise to the question of whether language is required for ToM. Tomasello et al. (2005) argued for the idea that language is an important by-product of ToM, rather than a necessary ingredient. The studies on animals suggest that language may not be an essential constituent part of ToM, but a critical view of the limited results with regard to animal ToM skills do leave the option that language is indeed a necessary ingredient to form particular mental representations or to put them to particular use.

This finding can also have a bearing on how ToM is tested in humans. Psychological measures of ToM usually rely heavily on language skills (see Ketelaars et al.; Begeer et al.; Roeyers et al., all this issue). The inconsistent findings with these measures regarding autism may show that—IQ independent—non-verbal or behavioural assessments may provide a closer account of the core problems of ToM skills of adults with HFASD (Senju et al., 2009). Altogether, the precise role of language skills in employing ToM remains to be investigated.

In conclusion, the data are more consistent with the view that ToM is an emergent capacity than the view that it is a special capacity. Therefore, whether an individual has a ToM cannot be answered with yes or no, as this concept is not a dichotomous one. The employment of ToM appears to depend on the functioning of its constituting capacities, the type and level of represented mental states and context factors. To determine what allows its use in particular situations is the challenge for the future. We hope this introduction and the contributions to this special issue have peaked interest in not just testing whether ToM is present according to some criterion, but that the focus will be on the ingredients that contribute to and allow (or prevent) the expression and employment of ToM in a particular setting. Only this will allow us to start understanding when and how individuals deal with the minds of others.

REFERENCES

Astington, J. W., & Jenkins, J. M. (1999). A longitudinal study of the relation between language and theory-of-mind development. *Developmental Psychology, 35*, 1311–1320.

Baron-Cohen, S. (1995). *Mindblindness: An essay on autism and theory of mind.* Cambridge, MA: MIT Press.

Baron-Cohen, S., Leslie, A. M., & Frith, U. (1985). Does the autistic-child have a theory of mind. *Cognition, 21*, 37–46.

Barrett, L., & Henzi, P. (2005). The social nature of primate cognition. *Proceedings of the Royal Society: B-Biological Sciences, 272*, 1865–1875.

Barrett, L., Henzi, P., & Dunbar, R. (2003). Primate cognition: From "what now?" to "what if?" *Trends in Cognitive Sciences, 7*, 494–497.

Begeer, S., Malle, B. F., Nieuwland, M. S., & Keysar, B. (2010). Using Theory of Mind to represent and take part in social interactions: Comparing individuals with high-functioning autism and typically developing controls. *European Journal of Developmental Psychology, 7*(1), 104–122.

Begeer, S., Rieffe, C., Meerum Terwogt, M., & Stockmann, L. (2003). Theory of mind-based action in children from the autism spectrum. *Journal of Autism and Developmental Disorders, 33*, 479–487.

Bolhuis, J. J., & Wynne, C. D. L. (2009). Can evolution explain how minds work? *Nature, 458*, 832–833.

Brauer, J., Call, J., & Tomasello, M. (2005). All great ape species follow gaze to distant locations and around barriers. *Journal of Comparative Psychology, 119*, 145–154.

Burkart, J., & Heschl, A. (2006). Geometrical gaze following in common marmosets (*Callithrix jacchus*). *Journal of Comparative Psychology, 120*, 120–130.

Call, J., & Tomasello, M. (1999). A nonverbal false belief task: The performance of children and great apes. *Child Development, 70*, 381–395.

Call, J., & Tomasello, M. (2008). Does the chimpanzee have a theory of mind? 30 years later. *Trends in Cognitive Sciences, 12*, 187–192.

Clayton, N. S., Bussey, T. J., & Dickinson, A. (2003). Can animals recall the past and plan for the future? *Nature Reviews Neuroscience, 4*, 685–691.

Dally, J. M., Emery, N. J., & Clayton, N. S. (2010). Avian Theory of Mind and counter espionage by food-caching western scrub-jays (*Aphelocoma californica*). *European Journal of Developmental Psychology*, *7*(1), 17–37.

Dufour, V., Pele, M., Sterck, E. H. M., & Thierry, B. (2007). Chimpanzee (*Pan troglodytes*) anticipation of food return: Coping with waiting time in an exchange task. *Journal of Comparative Psychology*, *121*, 145–155.

Emery, N. J. (2000). The eyes have it: The neuroethology, function and evolution of social gaze. *Neuroscience and Biobehavioral Reviews*, *24*, 581–604.

Flavell, J. H. (2004). Theory-of-mind development: Retrospect and prospect. *Merrill-Palmer Quarterly Journal of Developmental Psychology*, *50*, 274–290.

Frith, U., & Happé, F. (1994). Autism: Beyond Theory of Mind. *Cognition*, *50*, 115–132.

Frith, U., Happé, F., & Siddons, F. (1994). Autism and theory of mind in everyday life. *Social Development*, *3*, 108–124.

Fodor, J. (1983). *The modularity of mind*. Cambridge, MA: MIT Press.

Gallese, V. (2007). Before and below "theory of mind": Embodied simulation and the neural correlates of social cognition. *Philosophical Transactions of the Royal Society: B-Biological Sciences*, *362*, 659–669.

Gallup, G. G., & Capper, S. A. (1970). Preference for mirror-image stimulation in finches (*Passer domesticus domesticus*) and parakeets (*Melopsittacus undulatus*). *Animal Behaviour*, *18*, 621–624.

Gerrans, P. (2002). The theory of mind module in evolutionary psychology. *Biology & Philosophy*, *17*, 305–321.

Geurts, H. M., Broeders, M., & Nieuwland, M. S. (2010). Thinking outside the executive functions box: Theory of Mind and pragmatic abilities in attention deficit/hyperactivity disorder. *European Journal of Developmental Psychology*, *7*(1), 135–151.

Grimm, V., & Railsback, S. F. (2005). *Individual-based modeling and ecology*. Princeton, NJ: Princeton University Press.

Hare, B., Call, J., & Tomasello, M. (2001). Do chimpanzees know what conspecifics know? *Animal Behaviour*, *61*, 139–151.

Heyes, C. M. (1993). Anecdotes, training, trapping and triangulating—Do animals attribute mental states. *Animal Behaviour*, *46*, 177–188.

Kaminski, J., Call, J., & Tomasello, M. (2008). Chimpanzees know what others know, but not what they believe. *Cognition*, *109*, 224–234.

Ketelaars, M. P., Van Weerdenburg, M., Verhoeven, L., Cuperus, J. M., & Jansonius, K. (2010). Dynamics of the Theory of Mind construct: A developmental perspective. *European Journal of Developmental Psychology*, *7*(1), 85–103.

Keysar, B., Lin, S., & Barr, D. J. (2003). Limits on theory of mind use in adults. *Cognition*, *89*, 25–41.

Koski, S. E., & Sterck, E. H. M. (2010). Empathic chimpanzees: A proposal of the levels of emotional and cognitive processing in chimpanzee empathy. *European Journal of Developmental Psychology*, *7*(1), 38–66.

Leslie, A. M., Friedman, O., & German, T. P. (2004). Core mechanisms in "theory of mind". *Trends in Cognitive Sciences*, *8*, 528–533.

Macphail, E. M., & Bolhuis, J. J. (2001). The evolution of intelligence: Adaptive specializations versus general process. *Biological Reviews*, *76*, 341–364.

Malle, B. F. (2005). Three puzzles of mindreading. In B. F. Malle & S. D. Hodges (Eds.), *Other minds: An interdisciplinary examination* (pp. 26–43). New York: Guilford Press.

Mitchell, P., Bennett, M., & Teucher, U. (2010). Do children start out thinking they don't know their own mind? An odyssey in overthrowing the mother of all knowledge. *European Journal of Developmental Psychology*, *7*(1), 67–84.

Onishi, K. H., & Bailargeon, R. (2005). Do 15-month-old infants understand false beliefs? *Science*, *308*, 255–258.

Penn, D. C., Holyoak, K. J., & Povinelli, D. J. (2008). Darwin's triumph: Explaining the uniqueness of the human mind without a deus ex machina. *Behavioral and Brain Sciences, 31*, 153–178.

Piaget, J. (1929). *The child's conception of the world.* New York: Brace.

Pinker, S. (1994). *The language instinct: How the mind creates language.* New York: William Marrow & Company.

Povinelli, D. J. (1993). Reconstructing the evolution of mind. *American Psychologist, 48*, 493–509.

Povinelli, D. J., & Eddy, T. J. (1996a). Chimpanzees: Joint visual attention. *Psychological Science, 7*, 129–135.

Povinelli, D. J., & Eddy, T. J. (1996b). What young chimpanzees know about seeing. *Monographs of the Society for Research in Child Development, 61*, 1–152.

Povinelli, D. J., & Vonk, J. (2003). Chimpanzee minds: Suspiciously human? *Trends in Cognitive Sciences, 7*, 157–160.

Povinelli, D. J., & Vonk, J. (2004). We don't need a microscope to explore the chimpanzee's mind. *Mind & Language, 19*, 1–28.

Premack, D., & Woodruff, G. (1978). Does the chimpanzee have a theory of mind? *Behavioral and Brain Sciences, 1*, 515–526.

Preston, S. D., & de Waal, F. B. M. (2002). Empathy: Its ultimate and proximate bases. *Behavioral and Brain Sciences, 25*, 1–20.

Roeyers, H., & Demurie, E. (2010). How impaired is mind-reading in high-functioning adolescents and adults with autism? *European Journal of Developmental Psychology, 7*(1), 123–134.

Saxe, R. (2005). Against simulation: The argument from error. *Trends in Cognitive Sciences, 9*, 174–179.

Scholl, B. J., & Leslie, A. M. (1999). Modularity, development and "theory of mind". *Mind & Language, 14*, 131–153.

Senju, A., Southgate, V., White, S., & Frith, U. (2009). Mindblind eyes: An absence of spontaneous theory of mind in Asperger syndrome. *Science, 325*, 883–885.

Shettleworth, S. J. (1998). *Cognition, evolution and behavior.* New York: Oxford University Press.

Sullivan, S., & Ruffman, T. (2004). Social understanding: How does it fare with advancing years? *British Journal of Psychology, 95*, 1–18.

Tomasello, M., Carpenter, M., Call, J., Behne, T., & Moll, H. (2005). Understanding and sharing intentions: The origins of cultural cognition. *Behavioral and Brain Sciences, 28*, 675–691.

Wellman, H. M., Cross, D., & Watson, J. (2001). Meta-analysis of theory-of-mind development: The truth about false belief. *Child Development, 72*, 655–684.

Wynne, C. D. L. (2004). The perils of anthropomorphism: Consciousness should be ascribed to animals only with extreme caution. *Nature, 428*, 606.

EUROPEAN JOURNAL OF DEVELOPMENTAL PSYCHOLOGY
2010, 7 (1), 17–37

Ψ Psychology Press
Taylor & Francis Group

Avian Theory of Mind and counter espionage by food-caching western scrub-jays (*Aphelocoma californica*)

Joanna M. Dally

University of Cambridge, Cambridge, UK

Nathan J. Emery

*University of Cambridge, Cambridge, and Queen Mary,
University of London, London, UK*

Nicola S. Clayton

University of Cambridge, Cambridge, UK

Food-caching scrub-jays hide food for future consumption and rely on memory to recover their caches at a later date. These caches are susceptible to pilfering by other individuals, however. Consequently, jays engage in a number of counter-strategies to protect their hidden items, caching most of them behind barriers, or using shade and distance as a way of reducing what the potential pilferer might see. Jays do not place all their caches in one place, perhaps because unpredictability provides the best insurance against pilfering. Furthermore, after being observed by a potential pilferer at the time of caching, jays re-hide food in new places. Importantly, however, jays only re-cache food if they have been observed during caching and only if they have stolen another bird's caches in the past. Naïve birds that have no thieving experience do not do so. The inference is that jays with prior experience of stealing others' caches engage in experience projection, relating information about their previous experience as a pilferer to the possibility of future cache theft by another bird. These results raise the intriguing possibility that re-caching is based on a form of mental attribution, namely the simulation of another bird's viewpoint.

Keywords: Avian cognition; Corvids; Food-caching; Scrub-jays; Theory of Mind.

Correspondence should be addressed to Nicola S. Clayton, Department of Experimental Psychology, Downing Street, Cambridge CB2 3EB, UK. E-mail: nsc22@cam.ac.uk

http://www.psypress.com/edp   DOI: 10.1080/17405620802571711

INTRODUCTION

When faced with a novel problem, humans are able to assess whether or not they have the requisite knowledge for its solution. For example, although no two games of cards are ever alike, participants in a one-deck game of poker might assess their chances of winning by considering the cards in their hand, the cards which have been played, and the cards which are still unaccounted for. To do so participants must not only evaluate what they know, but also what others do and do not know, and update this information to inform their future behaviour.

The ability to attribute others with specific knowledge states is a facet of high-level social cognition known as Theory of Mind (ToM). In brief, ToM refers to the ability to attribute other individuals with mental states, such as seeing and knowing, and to know that the mental states of others may differ to your own. Humans are endowed with a unique means of communicating the possession of this cognitive ability, namely language. Consider our poker players: if at the end of the game we were to ask them why they played the cards they did, we would undoubtedly be given a verbal report of the judgements they had made. Even if our players were not adept at remembering which cards others had or had not *seen* being played, and therefore which cards others did or did not *know* about, they might purport to have been successful by basing their game on a "feeling of knowing".

One of our primary research interests is the extent to which a very different species, the western scrub-jay (*Aphelocoma californica*), is also capable of social cognition. One reason we might expect western scrub-jays to be socially astute is that they are members of the corvid (or crow) family, a group of songbirds that often live in large social groups (Goodwin, 1986). Rather than populations of spatially aggregated individuals, however, corvid social life is typified by a high degree of social complexity (see Clayton & Emery, 2007, for a recent review). For example, rooks and jackdaws are colonial and known to form life-long monogamous pair bonds, with individuals forming long-term alliances with other members of their group, and understanding "third-party" relationships (Emery, von Bayern, Seed, & Clayton, 2007).

While western scrub-jays are generally considered to be semi-territorial, they are often embroiled in prolonged social interactions (Curry, Townsend Peterson, & Langen, 2002). For example, although mated jays commonly defend their territory, pair members frequently interact with neighbouring birds and, outside of the breeding season, tolerate the presence of non-breeders in their territory (Curry et al., 2002). Moreover, like their close relative, the Florida scrub-jay (*Aphelocoma coerulescens*), specific populations of western scrub-jays engage in a system of co-operative breeding where several closely related family members share the responsibility of raising the young (Burt & Peterson, 1993; Curry et al., 2002). This has led to the speculation that western scrub-jays might have "more complicated social networks than appears superficially" (Curry et al., 2002, p. 18).

The complex social life of primates has been invoked as an explanation for their advanced cognitive abilities (Humphrey, 1976; Jolly, 1966). In the social function of intellect hypothesis, Humphrey (1976) argued that "social primates are required by the very nature of the system they create and maintain to be calculating beings" (p. 309), and went on to liken the strategies involved in social manipulation to the plots and counterplots involved in a game of chess. The capacity for primates to socially manipulate one another has since been termed "Machiavellian intelligence" (Byrne & Whiten, 1988).

While the social function of intellect hypothesis (Humphrey, 1976) was developed to provide a context for the advanced intelligence of primates, Whiten and Byrne (1997, p. 14) subsequently suggested that "an evolutionary selective pressure towards greater social intelligence must surely apply to any species meeting the basic criteria, of living in large, semi-permanent social groups of long lived individuals". As Clayton, Dally, and Emery (2007) have discussed, these parameters are wholly applicable to corvids. Consequently, we might expect species such as the western scrub-jay to possess socio-cognitive abilities on a par with the great apes. Although this review focuses specifically on the western scrub-jay, we suspect that many other corvids may also possess these complex socio-cognitive skills, and indeed there is very strong evidence to support the case for ravens (e.g., Bugnyar & Heinrich, 2005, 2006; Bugnyar & Kotrshal, 2002, 2004; Bugnyar, Schwab, Schloegl, Kotrschal, & Heinrich, 2007; see Bugnyar, 2007, for a review).

The notion that a bird may possess ToM, a cognitive ability supposedly unique to humans, may at first sight appear preposterous. Many researchers would argue that if any non-human animal would be predicted to possess ToM or at least the precursors of ToM, surely it would be a chimpanzee (Premack & Woodruff, 1978). But as we have argued, corvids demonstrate cognitive skills on a par with the great apes, and in many cases surpass them, suggesting convergent evolution of intelligence in these two distantly related families (Emery & Clayton, 2004). Until recently, the avian brain was thought to be unable to support complex cognition because the forebrain was largely comprised of areas devoted to species-specific or survival behaviours, such as feeding and mating (e.g., striatum), compared to the largely cortical mammalian forebrain devoted to learning and cognition. However, recent studies of avian neural connectivity, neurochemistry and phylogenetic analyses have found that the avian forebrain is more cortical like than previously thought, with few striatal areas (Jarvis et al., 2004). Indeed, part of the avian forebrain called the nidopallium is structurally, neurochemically and functionally equivalent to the mammalian prefrontal cortex (Güntürkün, 2005). Furthermore, corvid and ape forebrains are the same relative size (Emery & Clayton, 2004). These new findings therefore provide an empirical neural basis for any suggestion of complex cognitive abilities such as mental time travel, causal reasoning and ToM, as well as executive functions that are processed within the prefrontal cortex of humans, and presumably other apes (e.g., Waltz et al., 2002). We will turn our attention to the question of whether some birds, notably food-caching western scrub-jays, may also possess complex social reasoning skills.

FOOD-CACHING AND SOCIAL COGNITION

When observing jays, Aristotle noted that when "acorns are getting scarce, it [the jay] lays up a store of them in hiding" (translated by Balme, 1991, p. 275). While food-hiding behaviour is by no means unique to jays (Vander-Wall, 1990), Aristotle's observation encapsulates the idea that sequestering food has evolved to enable the food-cacher to survive periods of temporal food scarcity (Roberts, 1979).

We now know that a number of corvids, including western scrub-jays, not only store food, but also use observational spatial memory to steal caches that they have observed others make (Bednekoff & Balda, 1996a, 1996b; Clayton, Griffiths, Emery, & Dickinson, 2001; Heinrich & Pepper, 1998; Watanabe & Clayton, 2007). Cachers and pilferers (birds who steal others' caches) can therefore be considered opposing sides of what has been termed an "evolutionary arms race" (Bugnyar & Kotrschal, 2002), a metaphorical race in which the "arms" in question are the tactics that cachers should develop to thwart the pilfering attempts of their competitors, and that pilferers should perfect to facilitate cache theft. Consequently, we might expect individuals to engage in behaviours to outmanoeuvre their conspecifics and maximize their own access to resources. As the same individuals play the dual role of storer and stealer, however, the division between the two sides is far from clear cut.

Protecting hidden caches

While at the University of California Davis, one of us (Clayton) noticed that western scrub-jays commonly took food scraps discarded by humans during their lunch hour and cached them in the surrounding grounds. After hiding their spoils, storers tended to fly off to a nearby perch and wait. These birds were colour-banded and therefore individually recognizable, and, once other jays had left the scene, it was possible to observe the storer returning to recover their hidden items. Rather than eating their caches, however, the storer would typically move most of the recovered items to new sites. The inference from these field observations is that by re-caching items in new sites when competitors had left the scene, storers prevented potential pilferers from using observational spatial memory to accurately steal their caches. It is possible, however, that the presence of other birds at the point of caching was coincidental to, and not the motivation for, the storer's re-caching behaviour.

To determine whether re-caching behaviour constitutes a protection behaviour, scrub-jays were presented with two locations in which to cache. As illustrated in Figure 1, top panel, jays cached in one tray while being observed by a conspecific (Observed tray), before caching in the second tray when the observer's view was obscured (In Private tray), or vice versa. Three hours post-caching, the Observed and In Private caching trays were returned to the storer together with a third previously unseen (new) tray, and the birds were allowed to recover their caches. To ensure that the birds' recovery behaviour was dependent on a memory for the social context of the caching episode, as opposed to being guided by behavioural cues from potential thieves, cache recovery always occurred In Private. If re-caching functions as a cache protection strategy, storers would be predicted to re-cache items hidden in the presence of observers, and to move these caches specifically to sites in the new tray as these would be unbeknown to their competitor.

As shown in Figure 1, bottom panel, the jays re-cached significantly more items from the Observed tray relative to the In Private tray (Emery & Clayton, 2001). Furthermore, while the few items re-cached from the In Private tray were placed in new and old sites alike, caches from the Observed tray were moved specifically to sites in the new tray. By re-caching items from the Observed tray in sites unbeknown to prior observers, storers preclude potential thieves from using memory to facilitate cache theft. The results of these experiments therefore accord with those expected if re-caching functions as a cache protection behaviour.

Who is watching

The previous experiment demonstrated that scrub-jays adjust their recovery behaviour as a function of whether or not they were observed during a specific caching event. What is not clear is whether a storer's re-caching behaviour is governed by the presence of a live conspecific at caching, or whether the moving image of a conspecific would be sufficient to motivate the storer to re-cache.

In a second experiment, we allowed our jays to cache food in each of three social contexts; Observed, In Private and in the presence of a mirror. The Mirror condition acted as a control, providing the image of a moving bird without the increased risk of cache theft provided by the presence of a real observer. Cache recovery always took place In Private. The experimental set-up is illustrated in Figure 2, top panel.

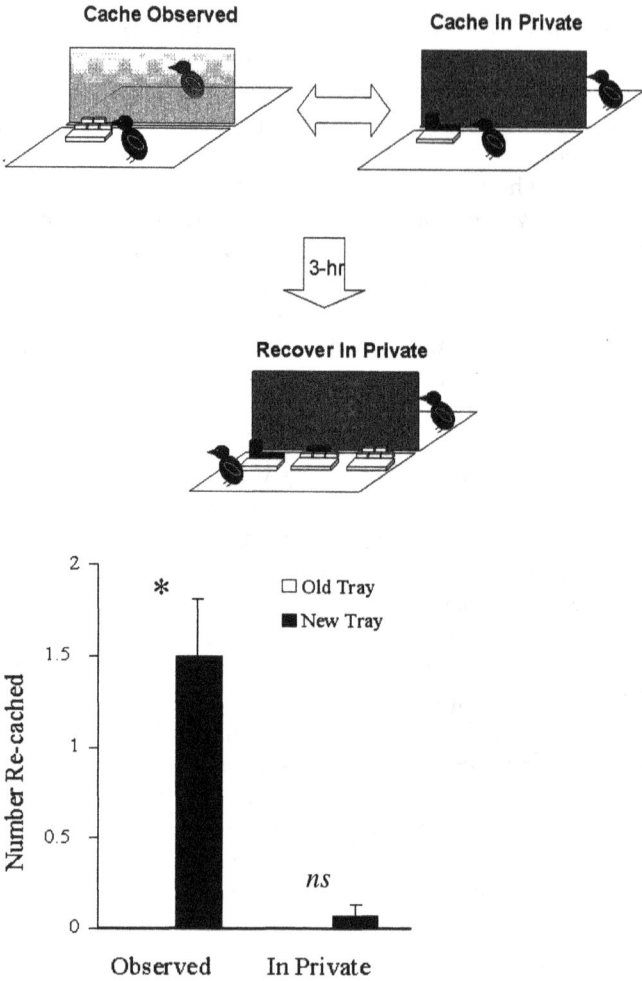

Figure 1. *Top panel*: The experimental set-up of the caching and recovery conditions for the Re-caching experiment. Storers cached in one tray watched by a conspecific (⬚ = Observed tray) and in a second tray when the observer's view was obscured by an opaque divider (⬛ = In Private tray). At recovery, which occurred In Private, storers received the trays in which they had previously cached plus one "new" tray (⬚). *Bottom panel*: The mean number of items (+ *SEM*) re-cached in the new and old trays after the Observed and In Private caching conditions. $*p < .05$.

Based on the results of the previous experiment, the birds' recovery behaviour was predicted to differ between the three caching conditions. If the presence of a moving image was sufficient to elicit re-caching behaviour, we predicted that jays should re-cache items at a similar level after caching in the Mirror and Observed conditions and that in both these conditions

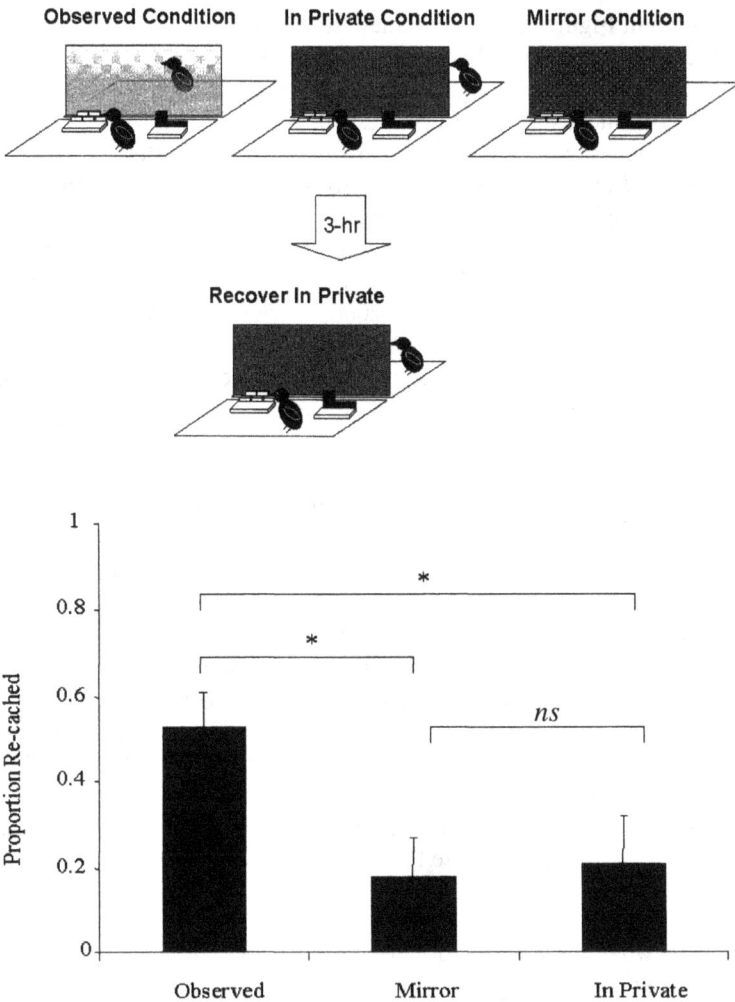

Figure 2. *Top panel*: The experimental set-up for the Mirror experiment. Storers cached either Observed by a conspecific, In Private, or in front of a mirror. Irrespective of caching condition storers recovered their caches In Private. *Bottom panel*: The mean proportion of items (+ *SEM*) re-cached after the Observed, In Private and Mirror caching conditions. *$p < .05$; $ns =$ non-significant.

re-caching should occur at a higher rate than after caching In Private. By contrast, if the presence of a live conspecific is necessary to stimulate re-caching at recovery, the storers' recovery behaviour after caching in the Mirror condition should be similar to when In Private, but significantly different from when Observed.

As shown in Figure 2, bottom panel, the birds re-cached many items after the Observed condition whereas few items were re-cached after the In Private condition. Intriguingly, the birds' recovery behaviour after the Mirror condition was similar to that exhibited after the birds had cached In Private with few items being re-cached in new and old sites.

A variety of avian species have previously been exposed to their mirror image, and in all but one case their reaction suggested that they treated their reflection as a social stimulus (parrots, *Psittacus erithacus*, Pepperberg, Garcia, Jackson, & Marconi, 1995; jungle crows, *Corvus macrorhynchos*, Kusayama, Bischof, & Watanabe, 2000; towhees, *Pipilo fuscus petulans*, Ritter & Benson, 1934; chickens, *Gallus gallus*, Gallup, 1991). Perhaps it is not at all surprising that the one exception concerns a fellow corvid, the magpie. In a recent study, Prior and colleagues argued that magpies may indeed be capable of recognizing themselves in a mirror, for rather than attacking their mirror image, they pass the mark test, i.e., using the mirror to investigate marks placed on parts of their body they would otherwise be unable to see (Prior, Schwarz, & Güntürkün, 2008).

Our jays, like the magpies and unlike the other avian species that have been subjected to mirror tests, are clearly responding to more than the distinction between the presence and absence of a visual image of another bird, because they did not respond to the mirror image in the same way as a live observer. The birds' re-caching behaviour therefore raises the possibility that scrub-jays, like magpies (Prior et al., 2008) and like the highly encephalized mammals, namely apes (chimpanzees, *Pan troglodytes*, Povinelli et al., 1997; Suarez & Gallup, 1981; orangutans, *Pongo pygmaeus*, Miles, 1994; Suarez & Gallup, 1981) and dolphins (*Tursiops truncatus*, Reiss & Marino, 2001), may recognize that the reflection in the mirror is an image of themselves.

An understanding of "self" has been proposed as a key cognitive skill for monitoring what we do and do not know, a prerequisite for attributing others with knowledge or ignorance, as it requires an assessment based on personally unique information. It is not necessary to invoke a self-concept, however, to explain the differences in the scrub-jays re-caching behaviour in the Observed and Mirror conditions. It is possible that the jays may simply have habituated to the mirror image, and might therefore have ceased to respond to it as a competitor. It should be noted, however, that while the jays had been exposed to a mirror for a period of 12-hours prior to this experiment (Emery & Clayton, 2004), many species fail to habituate to a mirror image even when exposed to a mirror for over 20,000 hours (Anderson, 1983, 1984; Gallup, 1979). Alternatively, the storer might perceive the "conspecific" in the mirror to be preoccupied by their own caching behaviour, and therefore to pose little threat as a potential thief. Indeed, Kalländer (1978) noted that rooks storing walnuts were not secretive if nearby conspecifics were also storing. Finally, like parakeets (*Melopsittacus undulates*) the storer may have differentiated between the live and reflected "observer" because of the perfect contingency between the storer's own movements and those of the "conspecific" (Gallup & Capper, 1970).

Cache site choice

Irrespective of the specific discrimination being made the results of the Mirror experiment add further support to the hypothesis that scrub-jays engage in re-caching behaviour to minimize cache theft from potential thieves. In the wild, however, waiting until potential thieves are no longer present before engaging in cache protection behaviour may not always be possible, as observers have constant access to the storer's caches. Perhaps a storer's most effective tactic would be to cache in sites that others cannot see.

There are three lines of converging evidence to suggest that scrub-jays are sensitive to the visual perspective of potential thieves (what they can and cannot see), and that storers use this information when engaging in cache protection. First, when allowed to cache in two trays, one of which was in view of a potential thief and one of which was positioned behind a barrier such that it was out of view of the observer, jays preferentially cached in sites their competitor could not see (Dally, Emery, & Clayton, 2005a). Second, when unable to cache out of view of potential thieves, jays cached primarily in sites that were, in relative terms, harder for observers to see. For example, when given the opportunity to cache near or far from a conspecific, storers preferentially cached in far sites (Dally et al., 2005a). Similarly, when cache sites differed in that one was well lit and the other in shadow, storers preferred to cache in the "shady" tray (Dally, Emery, & Clayton, 2004). Critically, the birds' selectivity to cache out of view of conspecifics, or in far or shady sites, was only exhibited when they were observed during caching; when caching occurred In Private all sites were used with indifference. This suggests that storers engage in strategies to prevent or reduce the transfer of visual information to potential thieves during a caching event, a behaviour which might serve to reduce the accuracy with which competitors are able to use memory to locate the storer's caches.

The final line of evidence to suggest that jays are sensitive to the visual perspective of others comes not from their behaviour at caching but from their behaviour at recovery. As we described earlier, one way in which storers might reduce the likelihood that their caches will be stolen is to re-cache items hidden in the presence of observers when alone. Indeed, after each of the experiments we have just described (Barrier, Distance, Shade), re-caching levels were greatest after the birds had been observed during caching relative to when caching occurred In Private (Dally et al., 2004,

2005a). Particularly pertinent to our current discussion is that during the Observed condition this re-caching behaviour was directed specifically at those sites to which the observer had the best visual access (near, in view, well lit). Because, irrespective of caching condition, cache recovery always occurred In Private these differences in the birds' recovery behaviour must depend on a storer's memory for the social context of caching (i.e., the absence or presence of an observer jay) and the specific attributes of the two trays (i.e., in view vs. out of view). One potential benefit of re-caching items to which prior observers had the best visual access is that those caches most at risk of theft are conferred an additional degree of protection.

Access all areas

Until now we have focused on the capacity for storing jays to reduce the pilfering accuracy of potential thieves by implementing visually based cache protection strategies. In the wild, however, these tactics might be impractical as potential thieves would be able to constantly reposition themselves in order to maximize their view of a caching event. Indeed, Bugnyar and colleagues found that in the presence of storing conspecifics, ravens often altered their position relative to structures that would have otherwise blocked their view (Bugnyar & Kotrshall, 2002), and actively lead competitors away from the true cache locations (Bugnyar & Kotrshall, 2004), as well as keeping track of knowledgeable and ignorant competitors in their role as both cacher and pilferer (Bugnyar & Heinrich, 2005, 2006).

To determine how our jays would cope when the position of observers was unpredictable, we allowed them to cache in two trays in two very different conditions. The first condition was a replicate of the Barrier experiment, in that one of the storer's trays was constantly in view and one constantly out of view of a potential thief (Constrained condition). By contrast, in the Free condition, a partial barrier was placed in the observer's home cage such that the observer could see the tray on the left-hand side of the storer's cage by moving to the left of the barrier (which then occluded the right-hand tray), and the tray on the right of the storer's cage by moving to the right of the barrier (which then occluded the storer's left-hand tray). Consequently, while the observer was potentially able to see both of the storer's trays, it was only able to view one tray at any one moment in time. The experimental set-up is illustrated in Figure 3, top panel.

Irrespective of caching condition storers preferentially cached when observers were out of view; a finding that accords with that of the Barrier experiment we described previously (Dally et al., 2005a). When caching in the Free condition, storers recovered their cached items and re-hid them elsewhere. As shown in Figure 3, bottom panel, however, items the observer had seen being cached were not simply moved to a new hiding place and left

(i) Free condition

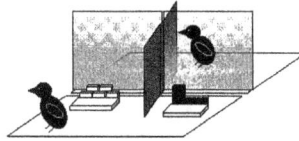

(ii) Constrained condition

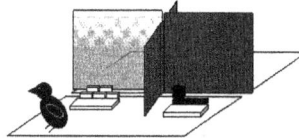

(i) Free condition

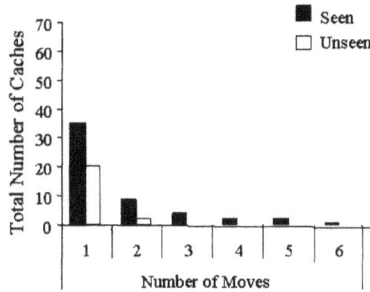

(ii) Constrained condition

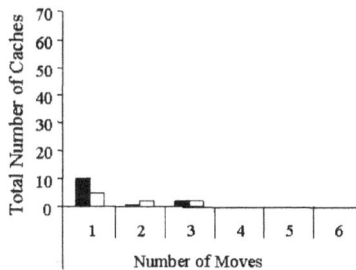

Figure 3. *Top panel*: The experimental set-up for (i) the Free condition and (ii) the Constrained condition (redrawn from Clayton et al., 2007). In the Free condition, the cages of both the storer and observer were partially divided with opaque dividers, which restricted the visual access of both birds to one side of the opposite cage. In the Constrained condition, the storer's cage was partially divided, and the observer's cage fully divided, with opaque screens. The observer therefore had visual access only to one side of the storer's cage. Irrespective of condition, recovery took place In Private (solid dividers attached to both sides of the storer's cage). *Bottom panel*: The total number of times individual caches from seen and unseen sites were moved during the caching period of (i) the Free condition and (ii) the Constrained condition (redrawn from Clayton et al., 2007).

there. Instead, many were moved up to six times, movements that occurred specifically in view of their competitor. By contrast, when cache sites were consistently in view or out of view of potential thieves (Constrained condition), few items were moved.

The repeated movement of caches in the Free condition appears to be a response to the unpredictability of the observer's position, and consequently what they could and could not see. By moving items the observer witnessed being cached, storers might reduce the accuracy with which their competitors are able to relocate hidden caches as the observer's memory for past cache sites should interfere with their memories for the current location of caches. Importantly, storer's were able to recover moved and unmoved caches with a comparable degree of accuracy.

In all the experiments we have described thus far, storers have been responding to the *potential* risk posed by an observer. That is, the observer was positioned behind a transparent barrier such that it could not immediately access the storer's caches. Yet in the wild observers would have constant access to the area in which the storer cached. To investigate the caching behaviour of scrub-jays in a more naturalistic context, we placed groups of seven birds into each of three aviaries. Each aviary was provisioned with a bowl of waxworms and the birds caching behaviour observed.

In each aviary, all birds gained access to, and ate from, the bowl of waxworms. Notably, however, only the most dominant male and/or his partner cached (Dally, Emery, & Clayton, 2005b). Like several other corvids, dominant jays used aggression to drive potential thieves away from cache sites (Eurasian jays, *Garrulus glandarius*, Bossema, 1979; Goodwin, 1986; Wilmore, 1977; rooks, *Corvus frugilegus*, Goodwin, 1986). What is of particular interest is that aggressive defence was used in conjunction with another strategy, namely moving caches multiple times.

While the multiple movements of caches appears to represent a cache protection tactic, it may represent little more than an "automatic" response to the presence of mobile observers. Closer analysis of the birds' movement behaviour renders this explanation unlikely, however, as the number of times birds moved caches around on any given trial increased relative to the number of times conspecifics attempted to steal their caches. This suggests that repeated cache movement is expressed flexibly depending on the degree of risk posed by observers.

The risk of cache theft was not the only factor to influence whether or not storers engaged in cache protection behaviour. Although jays aggressively defended cache sites from potential thieves, storers tolerated their partner moving their caches from one site to another. Moreover, partners often aggressively defended one another's caches from pilfering conspecifics. These two lines of evidence suggest that, like ravens (Heinrich & Pepper, 1998), scrub-jays do not perceive their partner to pose a risk to cache safety.

To investigate the effect of social relationships on the propensity for jays to engage in cache protection tactics, we conducted a replicate of the Distance experiment. In this study, storers were once again given the opportunity to cache in each of two trays, one of which was further from an observing conspecific than the other. To determine whether a storer's social relationship with an observer impacted upon their caching behaviour, birds cached in each of four conditions; observed by their partner, a dominant bird, a subordinate bird or In Private.

Intriguingly, the birds engaged in a distance strategy in the Dominant and Subordinate conditions but did not do so after caching in view of their partner or In Private (Dally, Emery, & Clayton, 2006). Moreover, during a private recovery period, storers re-cached items hidden in the tray to which the observer had the best visual access (near tray) after caching in view of a subordinate or a dominant bird. Yet no such preference was exhibited if the cacher hid the caches in view of their partner. Cachers also appeared to differentiate between the relative risk the subordinate and dominant birds posed to their caches, as re-caching levels were highest after caching in view of a dominant bird suggesting they do not perceive their partner to pose a risk to cache safety (Dally et al., 2006).

Assessing observer risk

The jays' behaviour in the aviary study provided some insight into the cache protection behaviour of jays in a group situation. In the wild, however, the same birds might not always be present at caching and recovery. For example, some observers might leave the area in which a storer cached only to be replaced by previously absent conspecifics. Consequently, a storer might become surrounded by birds that had, or had not, witnessed a prior caching event. Our most recent experiment provided an analogue of this situation (Dally et al., 2006). Specifically, storers were given the opportunity to cache in the presence of two different observers in two consecutive caching events, and then to recover their caches either when In Private, watched by one of the prior observers (Observed condition), or watched by a naive bird that had not witnessed either caching event (Control condition). The experimental design is shown in Figure 4, top panel.

As predicted by our previous findings, storers re-cached hidden items in new sites when they recovered their caches In Private. By contrast, in the Observed condition, storers moved caches the observer at recovery had seen them make multiple times. This result accords with the birds' behaviour in two earlier experiments (Free vs. Constrained experiment and the aviary study; Dally et al., 2005a, 2005b) in which storers were unable to engage in behaviours that conferred their caches with a degree of visual protection. As shown in Figure 4, bottom panel, items that the observer at recovery had not

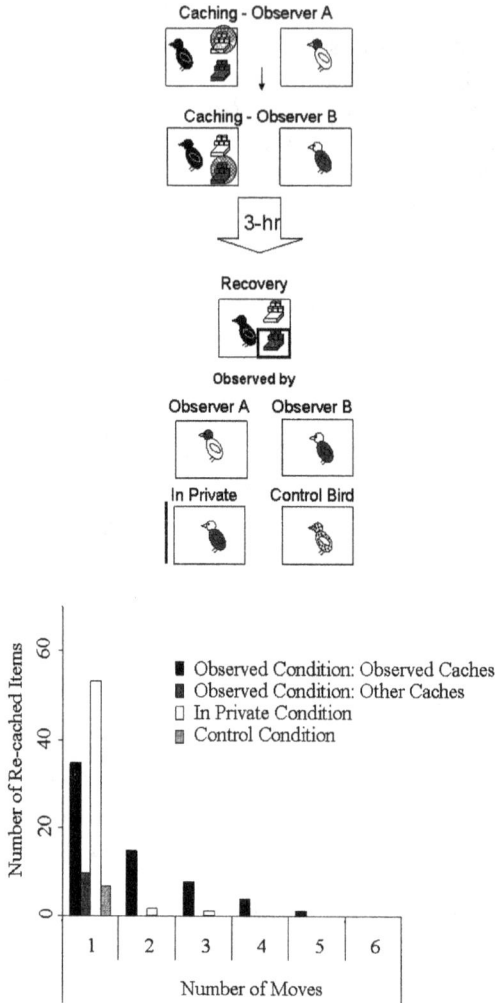

Figure 4. *Top panel*: The caching and recovery conditions of the "who was watching" experiment. 🐦= storer, 🐦= observer A, 🐦= observer B, 🐦= control-observer, ○= Perspex strips, ☐= "observed" tray (redrawn from Clayton et al., 2007). *Bottom panel*: The total number of times individual caches were moved from the observed and other trays in the Observed condition, and from both trays during the Control and In Private conditions.

seen cached were rarely moved, a finding illustrated most clearly by the storers' propensity to move very few items during the Control condition. Indeed, moving caches observers had not witnessed being cached, would only have served to provide currently uninformed observers with the observational information necessary to facilitate accurate cache theft.

These findings may be taken to suggest that the jays' are capable of one of the key skills of high-level social cognition, understanding what others do and do not know, and that they remembered *who* saw *which* caches being hidden and took appropriate action to protect their caches during a subsequent recovery period. A simpler explanation is that storers may have responded to behavioural cues exhibited by the potential thief. Consider the storers propensity to repeatedly move caches the observer at recovery had witnessed being hidden. It is possible that this behaviour constituted a response to the observers' propensity to preferentially attend to sites in which they had observed items being cached, and to spend little time attending to the tray in which they had not observed the storer cache.

To determine whether scrub-jays differentiate between observers on the basis of what they do and do not know, or whether they simply responded to behavioural cues exhibited by the observer, we ran a further experiment (Dally et al., 2006). This experiment comprised an Observed condition, a direct replicate of the Observed condition in the previous experiment, and an Observer-Control condition (Figure 5, top panel). The two conditions were similar in that storers cached successively in two trays, each in view of a different observer. In the Observer-Control condition, however, a control-observer also witnessed a control-cacher caching in one of the two trays. Consequently, two observers and one control-observer had each witnessed food being hidden in one of the two trays. At recovery, both observer and control-observer saw a storer (not a control-storer) recover its caches. As a result, storers in the Observed condition were observed by the same observer at caching and recovery, whereas storers in the Observer-Control condition, cached in view of an observer, but recovered their caches in the presence of the control-observer.

Based on the previous experiment, we predicted that cachers in the Observed condition would predominantly re-cache items from the tray in which the observer at recovery had seen them cache (observed tray) and not from the other tray. If this re-caching behaviour represents a capacity for social cognition, storers should re-cache few items from either tray in the observer-control condition, because the control-observer was not present when the storer cached and is therefore ignorant of the location of cache sites. If, however, storing birds base their recovery behaviour on behavioural cues emitted by competitors (e.g., differences in the degree to which observers attend to sites they have and have not observed being cached in) storers should re-cache items from the observed tray in both conditions, as although the control-observer was not present when the cacher cached, it would be attending to the tray in which it had previously observed the control-storer cache.

As shown in Figure 5, bottom panel, the birds' behaviour was consistent with a cognitive explanation, and not with an explanation based in terms of

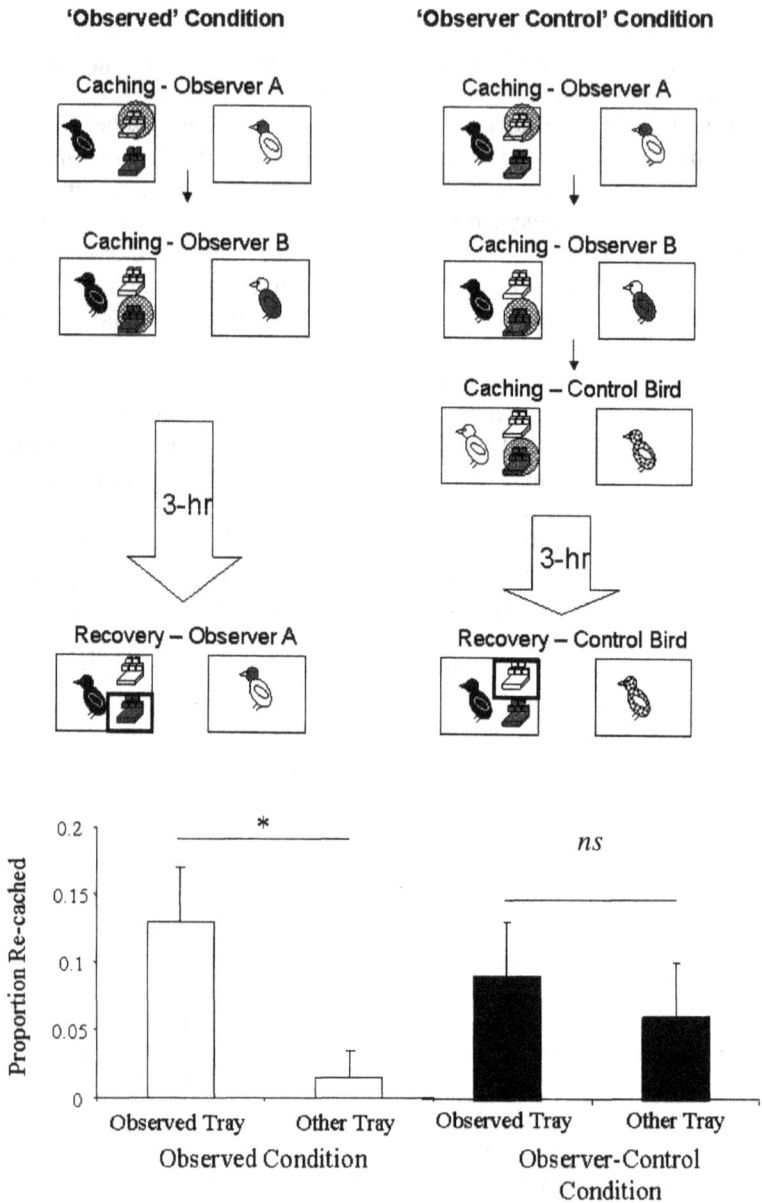

Figure 5. *Top panel*: The experimental set-up of the "Observed" and "Observer-Control" conditions. 🐦 = storer in "Observed" and "Observer-Control" conditions, 🐦 = control-storer, 🐦 = observer A, 🐦 = observer B, 🐦 = control-observer. O = Perspex strips, ☐ = "observed" tray (redrawn from Clayton et al., 2007). *Bottom panel*: Mean proportion (+ *SEM*) of items re-cached from the "observed" and "other" trays in the "Observed" and "Observer-Control" conditions. *$p < .05$; ns = non-significant.

behavioural cueing. In the Observed condition, items were predominantly re-cached from the tray in which the observer at recovery had seen them cache, whereas both trays were treated alike in the Observer-Control condition.

Our findings suggest that scrub-jays remember who was present during particular prior caching events, and use this information when engaging in behaviours to minimize cache theft. At first glance, this behaviour appears to necessitate the birds to be able to attribute their conspecifics with unobservable states such as "knowing". It is necessary to point out, however, that rather than requiring a human-like "theory-of-mind", the birds' behaviour may have arisen from a combination of behavioural predispositions and conditional discriminations.

Theory of Mind and experience projection

In a social environment, the outcome of any given interaction depends not only on your own behaviour, but also on the behaviour of others. The capacity for attributing others with knowledge states appears to represent a cognitive cornerstone in predicting how others might behave. Indeed, we have suggested that food-caching jays might tailor their use of cache protection behaviours to reflect a competitor's knowledge state (Dally et al., 2006). Yet in humans, social behaviour is shaped not only by the events of the present, but by the consequences of past experiences.

To investigate whether scrub-jays were able to draw upon the experiences of their past to mitigate a socially induced problem, that of cache theft, Emery and Clayton (2001) allowed two groups of jays to cache either Observed or In Private and to recover their caches three-hours later In Private. Critically, only one of these two groups had prior experience of stealing others' caches.

As predicted by the "Re-caching" experiment we described earlier, jays only re-cached hidden items after being observed during caching, and re-cached items were placed specifically in new sites. Critically, however, this re-caching strategy was specific to birds that had previously been thieves. Birds without this experience consistently failed to re-cache many items, irrespective of having previously cached in view of observers or of witnessing cache theft, and those few items that were re-cached were often placed in old sites (Figure 6).

The finding that storers need first-hand experience of pilfering the caches of others in order to know which items to re-cache, and where to re-cache them, suggests that scrub-jays are capable of a high level of social understanding called "experience projection" (Emery & Clayton, 2004). Specifically, storers appear to relate information about their previous experience as a pilferer to the possibility of future theft by another bird, and

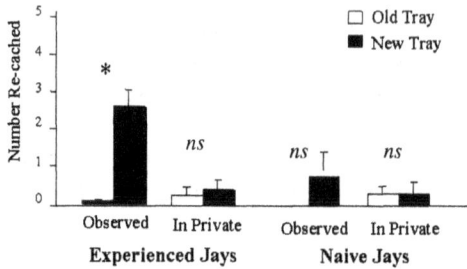

Figure 6. The mean number (+ *SEM*) of items re-cached in new and old sites at recovery after the Observed and In Private caching conditions for (*left*) birds that had previously stolen the caches of others (experienced birds), and (*right*) birds that had not experienced stealing others' caches (naïve birds). *$p < .05$; ns = non-significant.

adjust their recovery behaviour to ameliorate the effects of the thieving behaviour in which they previously engaged.

CONCLUSION

Common to all the cache protection behaviours we have discussed is that they function to reduce the quality of a competitors' informational, or epistemic, environment. For instance, by caching in sites that conspecifics cannot see, storing jays prohibit informational/knowledge transfer to their competitor. Yet the jays not only act to reduce a conspecifics access to factual information (i.e., cache location), but they also engage in behaviours that function to misrepresent the informational environment. This ability to "muddle" the epistemic environment of competitors (Proust, 2006), is perhaps best evidenced by the jays' propensity to re-cache hidden items when prior observers are no longer present, resulting in potential thieves being misinformed as to cache location.

When considering behaviours that function to muddle the epistemic environment, it is immediately apparent that they need not be underpinned by any form of complex socio-cognitive process. Consider the propensity for plovers to perform a broken-wing display in the presence of a predator (Ristau, 1991). Rather than an intentional act to draw a knowledgeable competitor away from their nest, the plovers display might simply represent a response to the stimulus "predator". The use of cache protection behaviours by scrub-jays cannot be explained in such terms, however. Instead, the finding that tactics are employed flexibly, as a consequence of the cacher's social relationship with the competitor, the likelihood of cache theft, and the specific caching episodes the observer has witnessed, suggests that the birds' behaviour is grounded in social cognition. Moreover, the finding that jays appear capable of experience projection, using their own past experience of being a thief to predict how another individual might behave in the same situation, provides evidence for a form of Theory of Mind yet to be demonstrated in any of the great apes, other than humans.

REFERENCES

Anderson, J. R. (1983). Responses to mirror image stimulation and assessment of self-recognition in mirror and peer raised stump tailed macaques. *Quarterly Journal of Experimental Psychology, 35B*, 201–212.

Anderson, J. R. (1984). Monkeys with mirrors: Some questions for primate psychology. *International Journal of Primatology, 5*, 81–98.

Aristotle. (1991). *The history of animals 9.13*. (Loeb Classical Library, D.M. Balme trans.). Cambridge, MA: Harvard University Press.

Bednekoff, P., & Balda, R. (1996a). Social caching and observational spatial memory in pinyon jays. *Behaviour, 133*, 807–826.

Bednekoff, P., & Balda, R. (1996b). Observational spatial memory in Clark's nutcrackers and Mexican jays. *Animal Behaviour, 52*, 833–839.

Bossema, I. (1979). Jays and oaks: An eco-ethological study of a symbiosis. *Behaviour, 70*, 1–117.

Bugnyar, T. (2007). An integrative approach to the study of ToM-like abilities in ravens. *Japanese Journal of Animal Psychology, 57*, 15–27.

Bugnyar, T., & Heinrich, B. (2005). Food-storing ravens differentiate between knowledgeable and ignorant competitors. *Proceedings of the Royal Society of London Series B, 272*, 1641–1646.

Bugnyar, T., & Heinrich, B. (2006). Pilfering ravens, *Corvus corax*, adjust their behaviour to social context and identity of competitors. *Animal Cognition, 9*, 369–376.

Bugnyar, T., & Kotrschal, K. (2002). Observational spatial learning and the raiding of food caches in ravens, *Corvus corax*: Is it tactical deception. *Animal Behaviour, 64*, 185–195.

Bugnyar, T., & Kotrschal, K. (2004). Leading a conspecific away from food in ravens, *Corvus corax*. *Animal Cognition, 7*, 69–76.

Bugnyar, T., Schwab, C., Schloegl, C., Kotrschal, K., & Heinrich, B. (2007). Ravens judge competitors through experience with play caching. *Current Biology, 17*, 1804–1808.

Burt, D. B., & Peterson, A. T. (1993). Biology of co-operative-breeding scrub jays (*Aphelocoma coerulescens*) of Oaxaca, Mexico. *Auk, 110*, 207–214.

Byrne, R. W., & Whiten, A. (1988). *Machiavellian intelligence: Social expertise and the evolution of intellect in monkeys, apes and humans*. Oxford, UK: Clarendon Press.

Clayton, N. S., Dally, J. M., & Emery, N. J. (2007). Social cognition by food-caching corvids: The western scrub-jay as a natural psychologist. *Philosophical Transactions of the Royal Society, 362*, 507–522.

Clayton, N. S., & Emery, N. J. (2007). The social life of corvids. *Current Biology, 17*, R652–R656.

Clayton, N. S., Griffiths, D. P., Emery, N. J., & Dickinson, A. (2001). Elements of episodic-like memory in animals. *Philosophical Transactions of the Royal Society London B, 356*, 1483–1491.

Curry, R. L., Townsend Peterson, A., & Langen, T. A. (2002). Western scrub-jay. In A. Poole & F. Gill (Eds.), *The birds of North America* (No. 712, pp. 1–36). Washington DC: American Ornithologists' Union.

Dally, J. M., Emery, N. J., & Clayton, N. S. (2004). Cache protection strategies by western scrub-jays (*Aphelocoma californica*): Hiding food in the shade. *Proceedings of the Royal Society of London Series B Biological Letters, 271*, S387–S390.

Dally, J. M., Emery, N. J., & Clayton, N. S. (2005a). Cache protection strategies by western scrub-jays: Implications for social cognition. *Animal Behaviour, 70*, 1251–1263.

Dally, J. M., Emery, N. J., & Clayton, N. S. (2005b). The social suppression of caching by western scrub-jays (*Aphelocoma calfornica*). *Behaviour, 142*, 961–977.

Dally, J. M., Emery, N. J., & Clayton, N. S. (2006). Food-caching western scrub-jays keep track of who was watching when. *Science, 312*, 1662–1665.

Emery, N. J., & Clayton, N. S. (2001). Effects of experience and social context on prospective caching strategies by scrub jays. *Nature, 414*, 443–446.

Emery, N. J., & Clayton, N. S. (2004). The mentality of crows. Convergent evolution of intelligence in corvids and apes. *Science, 306*, 1903–1907.

Emery, N. J., von Bayern, A. M. P., Seed, A. M., & Clayton, N. S. (2007). Cognitive adaptations of avian sociality, neural mechanisms and the evolution of social bonding in birds. *Philosophical Transactions of the Royal Society, 362*, 489–505.

Gallup, G. G. (1979). Self-awareness in primates. *American Scientist, 67*, 417–421.

Gallup, G. G. (1991). Towards a comparative psychology of self-awareness: Species limitations and cognitive consequences. In J. Strauss & A. Goethals (Eds.), *The self: Interdisciplinary approaches* (pp. 121–135). New York: Springer Verlag.

Gallup, G. G., & Capper, S. A. (1970). Preference for mirror-image stimulation in finches (*Passer domesticus domesticus*) and parakeets (*Melopsittacus undulates*). *Animal Behaviour, 18*, 621–624.

Goodwin, D. (1986). *Crows of the world*. Bury St Edmunds, UK: British Museum (Natural History).

Güntürkün, O. (2005). The avian "prefrontal cortex" and cognition. *Current Opinion in Neurobiology, 15*, 686–693.

Heinrich, B., & Pepper, J. (1998). Influence of competitors on caching behaviour in the common raven (*Corvus corax*). *Animal Behaviour, 56*, 1083–1090.

Humphrey, N. K. (1976). The social function of intellect. In P. P. G. Bateson & R. A. Hinde (Eds.), *Growing points in ethology* (pp. 303–317). Cambridge, UK: Cambridge University Press.

Jarvis, E. D., Güntürkün, O., Bruce, L., Csillag, A., Karten, H. J., Kuenzel, W., et al. (2004). Avian brains and a new understanding of vertebrate brain evolution. *Nature Reviews Neuroscience, 6*, 151–159.

Jolly, A. (1966). Lemur social behaviour and intelligence. *Science, 153*, 501–506.

Kalländer, H. (1978). Hoarding in the rook (*Corvus frugilegus*). *Anser Supplement, 3*, 124–128.

Kusayama, T., Bischof, H.-J., & Watanabe, S. (2000). Responses to mirror-image stimulation in jungle crows (*Corvus macrorhynchos*). *Animal Cognition, 3*, 61–64.

Miles, H. L. W. (1994). Me Chantek: The development of self-awareness in a signing orangutan. In S. T. Parker, R. W. Mitchell, & M. L. Boccia (Eds.), *Self-awareness in animals and humans* (pp. 254–273). Cambridge, UK: Cambridge University Press.

Pepperberg, I. M., Garcia, S. E., Jackson, E. C., & Marconi, S. (1995). Mirror use by African grey parrots (*Psittacus erithacus*). *Journal of Comparative Psychology, 109*, 182–195.

Povinelli, D. J., Gallup, G., Eddy, T. J., Bierschwale, D. T., Engstrom, M. C., Periloux, H. K., et al. (1997). Chimpanzees recognise themselves in mirrors. *Animal Behaviour, 53*, 1083–1088.

Premack, D., & Woodruff, G. (1978). Does the chimpanzee have a theory of mind? *Behavioural and Brain Sciences, 1*, 515–526.

Prior, H., Schwarz, A., & Güntürkün, O. (2008). Mirror-induced behaviour in magpies: Evidence of self-recognition. *Public Library of Science Biology, 6*(8), e202.

Proust, J. (2006). Rationality and metacognition in non-human animals. In S. Hurley & M. Nudds (Eds.), *Rational animals?* (pp. 247–274). New York: Oxford University Press.

Reiss, D., & Marino, L. (2001). Mirror self-recognition in the bottlenose dolphin: A case of cognitive convergence. *Proceedings of the Natural Academy of Sciences, 98,* 5937–5942.

Ristau, C. A. (1991). *Cognitive ethology.* Hillsdale, NJ: Lawrence Erlbaum Associates, Inc.

Ritter, W. M. E., & Benson, S. B. (1934). "Is the poor bird demented?" Another case of shadow boxing. *The Auk, 51,* 169–179.

Roberts, R. C. (1979). The evolution of avian food storing behaviour. *American Naturalist, 114,* 418–438.

Suarez, S. D., & Gallup, G. (1981). Self-recognition in chimpanzees and orangutans, but not gorillas. *Journal of Human Evolution, 10,* 175–188.

Vander-Wall, S. B. (1990). *Food hoarding in animals.* Chicago: University of Chicago Press.

Waltz, J. A., Knowlton, B. J., Holyoak, K. J., Boone, K. B., Mishkin, F. S., de menses Santoa, M., et al. (2002). A system for relational reasoning in human prefrontal cortex. *Psychological Science, 10,* 119–125.

Watanabe, S., & Clayton, N. S. (2007). Observational visuospatial encoding of the cache locations of others by western scrub-jays (*Aphelocoma californica*). *Journal of Ethology, 25,* 271–279.

Whiten, A., & Byrne, R. W. (1997). *Machiavellian intelligence II: Extensions and evaluations.* Cambridge, UK: Cambridge University Press.

Wilmore, S. B. (1977). *Crows, jays, ravens and their relatives.* London: David & Charles.

EUROPEAN JOURNAL OF DEVELOPMENTAL PSYCHOLOGY
2010, 7 (1), 38–66

Ψ Psychology Press
Taylor & Francis Group

Empathic chimpanzees: A proposal of the levels of emotional and cognitive processing in chimpanzee empathy

Sonja E. Koski

*University of Cambridge, Cambridge, UK, and University of Jyväskylä,
Jyväskylä, Finland*

Elisabeth H. M. Sterck

*Utrecht University, Utrecht, and Biomedical Primate Research Centre,
Rijswijk, The Netherlands*

Chimpanzees are arguably capable of empathizing with others' emotional states. Understanding emotional states is closely associated with understanding non-emotional mental states, thus, with Theory of Mind. Chimpanzees are probably able to represent some, but not all of the mental states grasped by adult humans. However, whether and how they understand another's emotional states is unknown, since the level of cognitive and emotional processing in chimpanzee empathy has not been addressed in detail. We propose a model for chimpanzee empathy, using the development of empathy in humans as a comparative viewpoint. Human empathy develops gradually with increasing cognitive complexity. In the first developmental stages the following levels can be distinguished: emotional contagion in neonates, transition from egocentric to veridical empathy during the second year of life, and finally cognitive empathy at 3 to 4 years of age. The current evidence suggests that chimpanzees are capable of emotional contagion, may be capable of veridical empathy, but probably do not achieve cognitive empathy. Thus, we propose that chimpanzee empathy operates on a continuum from egocentric, to

Correspondence should be addressed to Leverhulme Centre for Human Evolutionary Studies, Department of Biological Anthropology, University of Cambridge, Fitzwilliam Street, Cambridge CB2 1QH, UK. E-mail: sek39@cam.ac.uk

Lucie Burgers Foundation for Comparative Behaviour Research, Arnhem, the Netherlands, and the Academy of Finland are thanked for financial support (to SEK).

We thank William McGrew, Lucie Salwiczek, Maaike Kempes, Mieke Ketelaar, Berry Spruijt, and two anonymous reviewers for insightful comments that greatly improved the earlier versions of this manuscript.

http://www.psypress.com/edp   DOI: 10.1080/17405620902986991

quasi-egocentric, to veridical empathy. We evaluate evidence for this hypothesis and discuss possible ways to test it.

Keywords: Chimpanzee; Cognition; Empathy; Theory of Mind.

INTRODUCTION

Empathic concern expressed in prosocial behaviour is considered a crucial feature for the evolution of human co-operation, altruism and morality (de Waal, 2008; Flack & de Waal, 2000). The evolutionary function of empathy is suggested to be in enhancing parental care (Preston & de Waal, 2002a), co-operation and communication (de Vignemont & Singer, 2006), and altruism, morality and ethics (Hoffman, 2000; de Waal, 2008). The importance of parental care, co-operation and communication to a broad array of vertebrate species evokes the intriguing question about the evolutionary history of empathy. We do not, however, elaborate on the evolutionary base of empathy, as it has been discussed extensively elsewhere (e.g., de Vignemont & Singer, 2006; de Waal, 2008; Decety & Jackson, 2004; Eisenberg, 2000; Preston & de Waal, 2002a, 2002b). The aim of our paper is to discuss the empathy of the chimpanzee (*Pan troglodytes*), which, along with the bonobo (*Pan paniscus*), is our nearest living relative, with a focus on the mechanism and the level of cognitive involvement in chimpanzee empathy. Chimpanzees appear empathic in their behaviour towards group mates. They are argued to show empathy in various ways, for example when consoling group members, suggesting that they understand and respond to others' emotions (Boesch & Boesch-Achermann, 2000; de Waal, 2008; O'Connell, 1995). Furthermore, apes are suggested to be the only primates to have a capacity to cognitively empathize with others (de Waal, 2008; de Waal & Aureli, 1996). However, evidence of chimpanzee empathy is limited regarding both its propensity and mechanism.

We hypothesize a level of cognitive complexity in chimpanzee empathy. The hypothesis derives from development of empathy and cognition in humans. Empathy in humans is intrinsically linked to understanding others' mental states and thereby to Theory of Mind (ToM) (e.g., Blair, 2005; Preston & de Waal, 2002a). While chimpanzees' ToM has been a subject of active research (see Call & Tomasello, 2008; Penn & Povinelli, 2008, for recent reviews), their ability to attribute emotions to others has not been studied rigorously. Consequently, the level of cognitive involvement in chimpanzee empathy is yet unknown. We argue that to address the level of empathy in chimpanzees, it is useful to examine chimpanzees' mental state attribution skills and compare those to the skills of human children during the phases of empathy development. We propose a model for the kind of empathy that chimpanzees may exhibit based on this comparison.

Earlier work, especially the influential target article of Stephanie Preston and Frans de Waal (2002a; see also de Waal, 2008), has outlined a scale of cognitive involvement from emotional contagion to cognitive empathy in non-human empathy. Our paper scrutinizes the levels of cognitive processing in more detail. Especially, we call attention to the fine-grained differences in cognitive representation in human empathy development, which allows us to make predictions about cognitive processing in chimpanzee empathy.

In the first part of the paper we discuss the structure of mature human empathy, and thereafter describe the phases of empathy and cognitive development in humans. In the second part we discuss the chimpanzees' cognitive and emotional processing, based on which we propose our hypothesis. Thereafter, we evaluate the evidence of chimpanzee empathy in the light of the hypothesis, and bring forward some directions that may help testing the derived predictions.

Defining empathy

First, we define empathy (cf. definitions by, e.g., Eisenberg & Fabes, 1990; Hoffman, 2000; Preston & de Waal, 2002a, 2002b; Wispé, 1987). Some definitions of empathy view it as a highly cognitive process in which a subject "steps into the other's shoes" and reckons their state with a reference to another's personal history and current context. Other researchers stress the vicarious emotional involvement in other's feelings. Recent research has viewed empathy as a multi-component process, in which the cognitive and affective components are involved and interact (e.g., Blair, 2005; Decety & Jackson, 2004; Lamm, Meltzoff, & Decety, in press; Preston & de Waal, 2002a; Singer, 2006). We employ a definition of empathy that emphasizes the emotional process but also allows a cognitive representation, following Hoffman (2000) and Preston (2007): *Empathy is any process in which the perception of another's state generates a state in the subject that is more appropriate with the other's state or situation than to subject's own prior state or situation.*

I. HUMAN EMPATHY

Empathy in adult humans

When we empathize, we vicariously "feel for the other" and understand how they feel. This requires both emotional resonance of another's emotion and a cognitive representation of their emotional state, comparable to representing non-emotional mental states (Blair, 2005; Hoffmann, 2000). Thus, empathy in adult humans involves Theory of Mind (ToM).

The vicarious feeling for the other is the emotional component of empathy. Subject matches his own emotional state to the other's emotional state, so that the response to other's observed or imagined state stimulates a similar state in a subject. This *emotional contagion* (a.k.a. affective resonance) is automatic, although subjected to cognitive control (Lamm, Porges, Cacioppo, & Decety, 2008; Preston & de Waal, 2002a). Emotional contagion is suggested to be based on perception–action coupling, which also results in synchrony and imitation of facial expressions, postures and movements in interactions (Hatfield, Cacioppo, & Rapson, 1994; Preston, 2007). There is fairly extensive support for emotional contagion underlying empathic processing, also in adults (see Eisenberg, 2000; Singer, 2006, for reviews). For example, similar brain areas activate when we observe emotion in another and when we experience the emotion in ourselves (see below), changes in brain temperature, skin conductance and heart rate are observed, and facial muscles contract similarly to experiencing the emotion first hand (e.g., Bauer, 1998; Decety & Meyer, 2008; Fabes, Eisenberg, & Eisenbud, 1993; Lamm et al., 2008).

The cognitive representation of other's emotion requires us to take the other's perspective and to comprehend that an emotion is theirs. We distinguish our own emotional state from the other's state, and regulate the initial emotional resonance (Decety & Jackson, 2004; Decety & Meyer, 2008). Cognitive representation also enables inclusion of another's personal narrative and the context in the evaluation of the other's state (see Hoffmann, 2000, for a review). The cognitive "stepping into the other's shoes" is similar to representing others' non-emotional mental states. In addition, executive functions, including inhibition and self-control, are necessary to allow the self–other separation and representation of the other's state (e.g., Perner & Lang, 1999); without control the initial emotion would prevail (de Vignemont & Singer, 2006; Decety & Meyer, 2008).

The emotional and cognitive components are both necessary for a fully functioning mature human empathy (Blair, 2005; Preston, 2007; Preston et al., 2007). The dual nature of empathy is confirmed by the partial dissociation of the involved neural substrates. Emotional contagion is hypothesized to be based on the mirror-neuron circuit (Blakemore & Decety, 2001). Mirror neurons, identified in rhesus monkeys' premotor cortex, fire when performing an action and perceiving the similar action being performed (Rizzolatti, Fogassi, & Gallese, 2001). Although in humans the activation has not been identified at the single-neuron level, shared neural activation when experiencing emotions first hand and when observing them in another is consistent with the perception–action coupling by mirror neuron activation (see Jackson, Brunet, Meltzoff, & Decety, 2006, for a review). The brain areas that show activation during emotional processing include limbic areas, cerebellum, amygdala, sensorimotor cortices, anterior insula and anterior cingulate cortex (e.g., Carr, Iacoboni, Dubeau, Mazziotta, & Lenzi, 2003; Jackson et al., 2006; Singer, 2006). In contrast, the cognitive representation of others' emotion activates brain areas involved in self–other distinction and cognitive representations, including temporal lobes, temporo-parietal junction, superior temporal sulcus, medial pre-frontal cortex, right inferior parietal cortex, and anterior cingulate cortex (Brühne & Brühne-Cohrs, 2006; Preston et al., 2007; Singer, 2006). These brain areas also activate during non-emotional ToM tasks (Singer, 2006). However, the dissociation of neural substrates is not complete: the anterior cingulate cortex (ACC) is connected to both emotional and cognitive processing. The ACC has a regulatory role in empathy (Singer, 2006) and in response inhibition (Braver, Barch, Gray, Molfese, & Snyder, 2001), suggesting its importance in modulating the emotional process. In addition, pre-frontal cortex, temporal lobes and temporo-parietal junction are important in executive functions, including cognitive flexibility and inhibition (Decety & Meyer, 2008).

The importance of the regulatory processes in empathy has gained increasing interest, and both top-down and bottom-up processes are suggested to be important (e.g., de Vignemont & Singer, 2006; Decety & Jackson, 2004; Decety & Meyer, 2008; Lamm et al., 2008). Bottom-up regulation refers to the influence of the affective resonance on the cognitive perspective taking, and top-down regulation refers to the executive control of the emotion through selective attention, inhibition, and cognitive appraisal. The latter modulates and controls the primary level process, adds flexibility and allows metacognitive contemplation (Decety & Meyer, 2008). For example, knowledge of the cause of the emotion and moral evaluation of another's behaviour can increase or decrease the empathy (Lamm, Batson, & Decety, 2007; Singer et al., 2006).

Empathy may also lead to prosocial actions towards another. Although empathy is arguably the underlying mechanism of altruism (Batson & Shaw, 1991; de Vignemont & Singer, 2006; de Waal, 2008), prosocial acts are often distinguished from empathy per se (Eisenberg & Fabes, 1990). Whether empathic concern evokes prosocial action, is subjected to regulatory control, influenced by similarity, familiarity, and context (Preston & de Waal, 2002a). Prosocial acts can also stem from cognitive processing without empathy (e.g., helping another because of a principle, not because of emotional motivation), and, conversely, we can also decide not to act prosocially, even if we feel empathy towards the other (de Vignemont & Singer, 2006). Therefore, assessing prosocial acts alone is not sufficient to prove, or give a full account of, a person's empathic tendency.

Empathic dysfunctions

The importance of the emotional and cognitive components is apparent in two well-known psychopathologies that limit empathic abilities, namely psychopathy and autistic spectrum disorders (ASD). Psychopaths appear capable of forming cognitive representations of another's emotional states, but are hindered in their ability to respond emotionally (Blair, 2005; Ritchell et al., 2003). In contrast, people with ASD have a fundamentally impaired ToM acquisition and performance, which suggests that their difficulties with empathizing are due to dysfunctional cognitive processing (Baron-Cohen, Wheelwright, Skinner, Martin, & Clubley, 2001; Brent, Rios, Happé, & Charman, 2004; Brühne & Brühne-Cohrs, 2006; Dziobek et al., 2008). For example, they have difficulties recognizing emotional facial expressions and in general do not exhibit prosocial behaviour unless verbally prompted (see Begeer, Koot, Rieffe, Terwogt, & Stegge, 2008, for a review). The problems may rise from impaired executive functioning rather than cognitive impairment per se (e.g., Hill, 2004). Nevertheless, their emotional processing appears less impaired, although evidence is contradictory. People with ASD show an aberrant mirror-neuron system (see Decety & Meyer, 2008, for a review), and muted (but not absent) facial mimicry and emotional responsiveness to other's emotions (Scambler, Hepburn, Rutheford, Wehner, & Rogers, 2007). They are also reported to lack contagious yawning (Senju et al., 2007), although that may reflect aberrant mentalizing abilities rather than emotional processing (Platek, Critton, Myers, & Gallup, 2003). On the other hand, ASD patients show skin conductance changes and self-reported emotional responses to emotional stimuli similar to matched controls (Blair, 1999; Dziobek et al., 2008). Overall, ASD patients' problems with empathizing seem to stem from multiple dysfunctions, of which emotional processing is perhaps less impaired than cognitive processing.

In sum, mature, fully functioning human empathy requires emotional resonance and cognitive perspective taking. The emotional component of empathy is regulated as we cognitively form a representation of another's emotional state. In addition, we may take prosocial actions towards another based on the empathic processing.

Development of human empathy and cognition

The development of empathic skills in humans proceeds gradually from emotional resonance with no cognitive representation to increasing levels of cognitive complexity (e.g., Hoffman, 2000; Zahn-Waxler, Radke-Yarrow, Wagner, & Chapman, 1992; see Tables 1 & 2). The cognitive processing is dependent on a child's mental representation skills (Decety & Jackson, 2004), so we outline here some of the cognitive milestones that are reached during the first four years of life, in parallel to the emotional development.

Emotional contagion is present in newborn babies, who spontaneously respond to others' emotional behaviour with similar emotional behaviour (e.g., neonatal contagious crying; Hatfield, Cacioppo, & Rapson, 1993;

TABLE 1
The development of human infant mental state attribution in age categories, paralleled with chimpanzee cognitive performance

Human cognitive processing		Age	Chimpanzee cognitive processing
No representational self–other distinction	Neonatal imitation	0–5 mo	Yes
Interactive social orientation	Joint attention, social referencing	9–12 mo	No, yes
Others' visual trajectories, seeing	Gaze follow around barriers	9–12 mo	Yes
Gestural communication	Declarative and imperative pointing	9–12 mo	Yes: gestural communication indicating intentionality, persistence, flexibility
Executive control	Inhibition and working memory in A-not-B task	9–12 mo	Yes: inhibition
Connecting goals and desires		14–24 mo	Yes
Self-awareness	Mirror self-recognition, self-conscious emotions	18–24 mo	Yes
Knowledge, goals, desires, intentionality	Distinguish between accidental and purposeful, understand goals in action	18–24 mo	Yes
Level 1 visual perspectives		18–24 mo	Yes
Belief attribution	False and true beliefs	By 48 mo	No

Note: The citations are to be found within the text.

Martin & Clarke, 1982). The affective response is an agitated response identical to the state of the child in actual discomfort. Neonates also respond to facial expressions and body movements by imitating them (Meltzoff & Moore, 1977; Nagy, Kompagne, Orvos, & Pal, 2007). At this stage, emotional contagion operates with no self–other distinction.

Neonatal imitation and contagious crying decrease by 5 months of age (Martin & Clark, 1982). In 6-month-olds the regulation of emotional resonance is still weak and susceptible to an increased intensity of others' distress, so that a repeated witnessing of others' cry causes an infant to cry as well (Hay, Nash, & Pedersen, 1981). The infant's increasing orientation to its social world is expressed by interactive smiling, joint attention (i.e., interaction with another individual towards an external, shared goal), and social referencing (i.e., seeking emotional cues from another in ambiguous situations) at 9–12 months (Carpenter, Nagell, Tomasello, Butterworth, & Moore, 1999; Mundy & Newell, 2007; see Decety & Jackson, 2004, for a

TABLE 2

The development of human emotional processing, prosocial behaviour and the corresponding empathic level in age categories

Human emotional processing and prosocial behaviour	Empathic level (graded continuum)	Age
Contagious cry	Emotional contagion	Newborn–5 mo
Regulation of emotion improves, confusion of who is in distress	Egocentric empathy	9–12 mo
Regulation of emotion further improves, separation of self and other	Quasi-egocentric empathy	14 mo
Initial other-regard, but response appropriate to own, not other's needs		
Instrumental helping		14–18 mo
Suppression of outward emotions, understand emotion without facial cues, response appropriate to other's needs	Veridical empathy	18–24 mo
Representation of complex emotions, individual variation, hidden emotions, etc.	Cognitive empathy	By 48 mo

Note: The citations are to be found within the text.

review). By the first birthday, children follow others' gaze around barriers, showing some understanding of others' visual trajectory and the act of seeing (Moll & Tomasello, 2004). In addition, they begin gestural communication, most notably pointing around the same time (Carpenter et al., 1999). Executive control in early infancy has received less research attention than that from 3 years onwards. However, in a simple inhibitory control task ("A-not-B"; see discussion for the importance of inhibition, memory and computational systems in the test, e.g., Marcovitch & Zelazo, 2009; Miyake et al., 2000) 10-month-olds make mistakes, while 12-month-olds are more often successful (Marcovitch & Zelazo, 2009).

During the second year of life a child's cognitive processing reaches important milestones. Self-conscious emotions are shown by 18- to 24-month-olds, along with categorization of self in relation to others, and mirror self-recognition (Courage & Howe, 2002; Johnson, 1983; Nielsen, Suddendorf, & Slaughter, 2006), indicating an understanding of self beyond the "ecological" sense of self (i.e., self in the immediate physical environment). At the same age children can attribute knowledge/ignorance and desires to others (see Flavell, 2000, for a review). Furthermore, they understand others as intentional beings, distinguish between accidental and purposeful actions, and represent the goal of other's actions (Carpenter, Akhtar, & Tomasello, 1998; Meltzoff, 1995; Tomasello, Carpenter, Call, Behne, & Moll, 2005). Also, by 2 years of age, a child understands what another sees, i.e., reaches level 1 visual perspective taking (Moll & Tomasello, 2006).

The cognitive development from 6 to 24 months of age allows empathy to go beyond unregulated emotional contagion. Initially, as the self–other distinction is still weak, children express *egocentric empathy*, i.e., a child confuses who is actually in distress and comforting is self-oriented (Zahn-Waxler & Radke-Yarrow, 1990). For example, a child observing a friend crying goes to its own mother to be comforted. This also implies that regulatory control of own emotions is weak. Soon, however, this confusion wanes and a child responds with initial stages of other-regard (Eisenberg, Lennon, & Roth, 1983; Hoffmann, 2000; Zahn-Waxler et al., 1992). Yet, one's own and another's emotional states are not yet fully separated and the child still shows emotional distress and tries to help the other by doing what would comfort itself, hence the term *quasi-egocentric empathy* (Hoffman, 2000). For example, rather than going to its mother to be comforted, a 14-month-old child now brings the crying friend to its own mother (but not to the friend's mother).

By the end of the second year children can consider others as separate entities and reach the *veridical empathy* stage. Personal distress declines due to improved regulatory control and cognitive separation of self and other, and the comforting efforts become varied and more appropriate to the other's needs (Zahn-Waxler & Radke-Yarrow, 1990; Zahn-Waxler et al., 1992), indicating an increasing ability to take the other's affective perspective. Recently, 18- and 24-month-olds were reported to show concern and subsequent prosocial behaviour towards another in a distressful situation without the other expressing emotional cues (Vaish, Carpenter, & Tomasello, 2009). This implies a cognitive representation of the other's emotional state. Furthermore, 2-year-olds can make causal links between desire, goal and consequent emotion, i.e., they understand that what the other wants leads to happiness if satisfied, and sadness if unsatisfied (Wellman, Phillips, & Rodriguez, 2000). This link may already be found earlier, since 14- and 18-month-olds spontaneously help an experimenter reach a goal they cannot reach themselves, i.e., perform instrumental helping (Warneken & Tomasello, 2006; Warneken, Hare, Melis, Hanus, & Tomasello, 2007). Instrumental helping suggests a potential connection of the representation of the other's goal of the action to the desire to reach that goal. An understanding of the other's desire and that reaching the goal results in satisfaction, may prompt prosocial action in the subject (i.e., to help the other reach the goal). At the very least it shows an understanding of another's situation as separate from one's own and of the goal, and the willingness to help (Warneken & Tomasello, 2006). The interconnectedness of desire, perception and emotion into a coherent whole is important, since it suggests that 2-year-olds' attribution of these mental states forms a coherent, co-ordinated psychology (Wellman et al., 2000).

Thus, the second-year-transition from self-oriented egocentric to other-oriented veridical empathy reflects the increased understanding of others' mental states, ability to connect these mental states, and marks the onset of sympathetic concern allowing prosocial actions (de Waal, 2008; Hoffmann, 2000).

During the third to fourth year of life a child reaches a capacity for a full representation of others' mental states as separate from their own, and represents beliefs in addition to goals and perspectives (Flavell, 2000, 2004). Four-year-olds famously pass the False Belief Test (see Wellman, Cross, & Watson, 2001, for a review), implying a desire-belief ToM (Perner & Lang, 1999). Although the appropriate ways to test belief attribution is discussed (e.g., Blijd-Hoogewys, van Geert, Serra, & Minderaa, 2008; Wellman & Liu, 2004), in general evidence supports the view that belief attribution appears later in development than the attribution of perspectives, goals, knowledge and desires (Saxe, Carey, & Kanwisher, 2004; Wellman & Liu, 2004). This difference is supported by a neural anatomy: the activated brain areas in the belief attribution are distinct from goal and perception attribution (Saxe et al., 2004). Furthermore, inhibitory control improves dramatically between 3 and 4 years of age (Carlson, Moses, & Claxton, 2004; Perner & Lang, 1999). Inhibition and planning tasks show a positive correlation with false-belief attribution in pre-schoolers (Carlson & Moses, 2001), supporting the view that executive functioning is important for metacognitive abilities.

The development of a full representation of own and others' mental states and the improved executive control allows a child to represent others' emotional states fully and accurately, and thus reach the *cognitive level* of empathy. Empathic understanding can now be reached by knowledge about the particular event that the other experiences and understanding of the causes and consequences of emotions, even when they are complex. For example, a child understands a friend being disappointed in its own poor performance (Hoffman, 2000). The child also understands that the same situation can cause different emotions in different people, and that people can attempt to control their emotions (Hoffman, 2000), implying an understanding of hidden emotions (but see Vaish et al., 2009, for 18-month-olds understanding emotions without facial cues). Furthermore, the range of emotions that are represented now includes complex emotions of shame and embarrassment (Hoffman, 2000). Prosocial actions become more complex and varying, subjected to modifications according to the others' specific needs.

Human empathy (and cognition) develops to yet more cognitively sophisticated levels. Around 8–10 years of age children can empathize with another's condition even when it overrides the behavioural cues, for example by feeling sorry for a terminally ill, but smiling child (Hoffmann, 2000).

Adult humans can form empathic representations at exceedingly complex levels (e.g., empathize with imagined situations and global problems: Commons & Wolfsont, 2002; Hoffman, 2000). However, as these levels are not likely to be in the reach of non-human primates, we limit our discussion to the levels until cognitive empathy is reached.

II. CHIMPANZEES

To examine the cognitive processing in chimpanzee empathy, we employ research on chimpanzee mental state attribution as an indicator of their empathic potential. We parallel human empathy and cognitive development to chimpanzee cognition, and use the human development as a yard stick against which we estimate the chimpanzee's empathic potential. Our working hypothesis is that chimpanzees attribute emotional states to others in a similar way to their attribution of non-emotional mental states, and that this corresponds to a phase in human empathic (and cognitive) development. This comparison provides a viewpoint from which to formulate testable predictions on chimpanzee empathy. Our hypothesis goes into more detail than the earlier work on chimpanzee empathy. Preston and de Waal (2002a) and de Waal (2008) have formulated a scale of empathy, from emotional contagion (based on perception–action coupling) via sympathetic concern to cognitive empathy. Our proposal emphasizes the variation in the degree of cognitive involvement between emotional contagion and cognitive empathy. This variation is relevant for understanding to what extent a subject can maintain the other's perspective and whether empathic acts are truly self- or other-concerning. Furthermore, the role of inhibitory control facilitating cognitive processing is important to include in the consideration.

Chimpanzee emotional resonance

Although only limited research has been done on chimpanzees' empathic processing, their capacity to emotional contagion and perhaps to some cognitive processing of others' emotional states is supported by experimental research. Chimpanzees respond to emotional video images by a vicarious emotional response, as measured by decreased skin temperature (Parr, 2001) and increased tympanic membrane temperature (Parr & Hopkins, 2001), which are known correlates of emotional arousal in humans (e.g., Bauer, 1998; Wittling, 1995). Newborn chimpanzees also show imitation of facial expressions, similar to newborn human babies (Bard, 2007). Furthermore, chimpanzees exhibit contagious yawning (Anderson, Myowa-Yamakoshi, & Matsuzawa, 2004; Campbell,

Carter, Proctor, & de Waal, 2008). Contagious yawning is connected to empathic tendencies in humans, although the exact mechanism of contagion is unclear and may depend on higher cognitive processes rather than emotional contagion (Senju et al., 2007). The combined, albeit limited, evidence thus supports chimpanzees' ability to emotional resonance.

Chimpanzee mental state attribution

Little is known of chimpanzees' cognitive representation of emotions. A study by Lisa Parr (2001) showed that chimpanzees can match a facial expression to the appropriate non-facial stimulus that has a corresponding emotional connotation, suggesting that they understand the emotional meaning of facial expressions. Interestingly, people with ASD have marked difficulties with recognizing emotional facial expressions (Begeer et al., 2008), suggesting that chimpanzees may exceed (low functioning) individuals with ASD in their cognitive representation of emotional information. However, as direct evidence of the level of cognitive processing in chimpanzee empathy is scarce, we need to examine their cognitive performance in non-emotional paradigms. The debate of chimpanzee cognition is lively and opinions differ greatly (e.g., Call & Tomasello, 2008; de Waal, 2008; Hare, 2007; Penn & Povinelli, 2007). Some argue that evidence for chimpanzees' mentalistic abilities is inconclusive and that it shows only chimpanzees' skills as "behaviour-readers" (Penn & Povinelli, 2007). However, we think that the recent evidence from numerous ToM paradigms shows that chimpanzee cognition allows representations of some mental states of others (see below; see Call & Tomasello, 2008; Moll & Tomasello, 2007, for reviews). We base our discussion on this evidence.

Chimpanzee early social development shows similarities to that of human babies: besides neonatal imitation, 9-month-old chimpanzees follow gaze similarly to 6-month-old human infants (Tomonaga et al., 2004). Chimpanzee infants also exhibit social referencing (Russell, Bard, & Adamson, 1997), but there is no evidence for joint attention (Tomasello & Carpenter, 2005). Adult chimpanzees exhibit mirror self-recognition (Hirata, 2007; Kitchen, Denton, & Brent, 1996), a crucial test of initial stages of self–other distinction. They also exhibit level 1 visual perspective taking, i.e., understanding of what another can and cannot see and what they have seen in the immediate past, and can use this to their own benefit (Bräuer, Call, & Tomasello, 2007; Hare, Call, & Tomasello, 2006; Melis, Call, & Tomasello, 2006; Okamoto-Barth, Call, & Tomasello, 2007). Visual perspective taking, similar to 2-year-old children, implies that chimpanzees can put themselves into "the other's shoes", at least when it comes to visual perception. Chimpanzees also attribute knowledge (and ignorance) to others (see Call & Tomasello, 2008, for a review), as well as goals and intentions in action: they distinguish others' unwillingness versus inability to reach a particular goal (Call, Hare, Carpenter, & Tomasello, 2004) and purposeful versus accidental action (Call & Tomasello, 1998), and copy actions based on their understanding of the model's intention (Buttelmann, Carpenter, Call, & Tomasello, 2007). Furthermore, they understand the need for an attentive audience for successful gestural communication, alternate their gaze between the desired object and the target of communication, and persist and elaborate their signalling in the absence of a positive response (Leavens, Russell, & Hopkins, 2005; Liebal, Pika, Call, & Tomasello, 2004). Finally, chimpanzees provide instrumental help to a conspecific and to a human experimenter in similar paradigms as 18-month-old humans (Warneken et al., 2007), suggesting a possible connection between representations of other's goals and emotions (incl. desire, possibly also satisfaction if goal is reached). The combined evidence thus suggests that chimpanzees attribute goals, knowledge, intentions and perspectives to others, and may form cognitive links between these representations, much like humans before and around their second birthday. However, similarly to children under 4 years of age, chimpanzees seem not to grasp another's prior intentions (i.e., knowing another's goal before the action; Tomasello et al., 2005), or attribute beliefs to others (Kaminski, Call, & Tomasello, 2008). Considering the developmental gap in humans between the attribution of belief and the attribution of goal, desire and perception, supported by neuroanatomical data (see above; Saxe et al., 2004), the current chimpanzee data roughly agrees with this separation. It suggests that chimpanzees may, indeed, have a ToM that is bound to knowledge, perception, desire and goal attribution, but does not reach belief attribution (Call & Tomasello, 2008).

Chimpanzee executive control

Cognitively processed levels of empathy require regulation of the emotional processing. Chimpanzees pass a simple memory and inhibitory control task that children master at 12 months of age (A-not-B; Amici, Aureli, & Call, 2008). Also, recent evidence from several delay-of-gratification tasks suggests that chimpanzees can control their behavioural impulses and act by countering them. Chimpanzees can hold a small food reward for up to 4–8 minutes in order to obtain a much larger one (Dufour, Pele, Sterck, & Thierry, 2007). This exceeds the duration of the 2–4 minute delay shown by 4-year-old children in a similar task (Mischel, Shoda, & Rodriguez, 1989). Chimpanzees also can wait for up to 2 minutes when asked to choose between a small immediate or large future reward in a temporal discounting task (Amici et al., 2008; Rosati, Stevens, Hare, & Hauser, 2007) and perform better at this task than adult humans, although the poor performance of humans is likely to reflect lower motivation to obtain food rather than money (Rosati et al., 2007). Similarly, in a task with a self-imposed delay, chimpanzees can wait for 5–11 minutes to gain a reward (Beran & Evans, 2006). Moreover, chimpanzees ignore a coveted reward to collect a tool that allows access to a yet unobserved but expected reward (Osvath & Osvath, 2008). Altogether, these findings indicate that chimpanzees are capable of suppressing immediate impulses to attain food in order to derive more food in the (near) future. These studies suggest that chimpanzees are able to inhibit emotional responses to some extent.

The proposal of chimpanzee empathy

The chimpanzee cognitive performance presented above can be paralleled to that of a child around 18–24 months of age (cf. Moll & Tomasello, 2007; Suddendorf & Whiten, 2001). Specifically, chimpanzees maintain the self–other distinction, represent some mental states of others (desire, knowledge, perspective, intentions, emotions), but do not understand beliefs and communicative intentions (see Part I and Table 1). Their executive control may allow maintaining the difference between own and others' emotional state to some extent.

We hypothesize that the level of cognitive processing in chimpanzee empathy depends on these cognitive abilities, i.e., chimpanzee empathy exceeds direct, unregulated emotional contagion of young infants, but does not reach the level of cognitive empathy of a 4-year-old human. Thus, it is positioned in the continuum of egocentric, via quasi-egocentric, to veridical empathy. More specifically, 1.5- to 2-year-old children represent others' emotional states (even without emotional cues) and make cognitive connections between representations before they reach a full-blow meta-representational level, which in empathic processing coincides with the veridical stage. Since chimpanzees can function at a similar cognitive level, we hypothesize that chimpanzees may reach the veridical end of the continuum: they represent others' emotional states, possibly link emotions to goals and desires, but can not represent emotional states in more demanding contexts (see below).

We predict that if chimpanzees perform on a veridical empathy level, they control their outward emotional responses. They show physiological markers of arousal, such as skin temperature and conductance changes, but behavioural indicators of arousal are suppressed. Potential prosocial actions are mostly appropriate to others' needs, inasmuch as they can connect the cause of the emotion and the resulting emotional state. However, veridical empathy does not allow accommodating responses to the other's individually varying needs. Therefore, it is possible that at the veridical stage, a chimpanzee can only respond appropriately to another's need if it is similar to its own need in a similar situation. Veridical empathy also does not allow accounting for another's personal history that influences the emotional valence of the situation, understanding conflicting emotions, hidden emotions, or emotions with contradicting behavioural indicators. These abilities require fully cognitive empathy.

If chimpanzee empathy operates more in the ego- or quasi-egocentric end of the continuum, we predict that they respond to others' emotion with limited regulation of emotional contagion and thus with visible arousal. Cognitively there is a confusion of own and others' emotion. On the egocentric level, comforting efforts are self-directed and cannot be behaviourally distinguished from responses to emotional contagion. In quasi-egocentric empathy there is improved regulatory control, and potential prosocial acts are directed to others but with a confusion of own and others' needs; an individual would do something that would comfort itself, regardless of whether it is accurate to the other's needs.

In this hypothesis we make the assumption that chimpanzee empathy is similarly dependent on their representational and executive abilities as it is in humans, and that chimpanzee cognitive abilities are similar enough to human cognitive abilities to allow such paralleling. We acknowledge that chimpanzee cognition is in some respects different from developing human child cognition, especially regarding social cognition (Call & Jensen, 2006; Moll & Tomasello, 2007). However, the similarities of the key components (self–other distinction, attribution of some mental states, and executive control) allow us to argue that these assumptions are plausible.

Problematically, the development from egocentric to cognitive empathy is gradual, which inevitably blurs the precision of exact categories with clearly defined characteristics. Yet, we believe that seeking to characterize chimpanzee empathy within a graded continuum of cognitive complexity is useful and can be done more precisely than has been achieved thus far (cf. de Waal, 2008; O'Connell, 1995; Preston & de Waal, 2002a, 2002b).

Evaluating current evidence for chimpanzee empathic processing

Above we have summarized the available evidence for chimpanzees' emotional contagion and motor mimicry, which indicate that chimpanzees respond to emotional stimuli in an emotional manner. Furthermore, they appear able to represent the emotional facial expression according to its valence. As far as we know, no studies have directly tested egocentric, quasi-egocentric, veridical, or cognitive empathy in chimpanzees. This scant evidence highlights the need for targeted experimental research on affective resonance, its cognitive control and cognitive representation of others' emotions.

However, we can examine cases of prosocial behaviour in chimpanzees. As outlined above, prosocial actions are likely to be rooted in empathic processing (e.g., de Waal, 2008; Eisenberg, 2000) and, thus, prosocial actions are the observable level that can show potential empathic processing. Several anecdotes of seemingly empathic acts are reported from captive and wild chimpanzees. Examples range from helping a thirsty group mate by bringing water, trying to rescue another individual from danger, sometimes even at a risk to own life, and comforting distressed individuals (Boesch & Boesch-Achermann, 2000; de Waal, 2005; Goodall, 1986; O'Connell, 1995). Some of these examples, such as the case of an adult, unrelated, chimpanzee jumping into a water moat to rescue a juvenile that had fallen in and was about to drown (O'Connell, 1995), are dramatic and suggest extensive prosociality, at very least requiring an understanding of the situation and the other's goal, and willingness to help. On the other hand, some other examples, such as tending another's wound (Boesch & Boesch-Achermann, 2000) or reconciling after a conflict (O'Connell, 1995), do not necessarily require any mental state attribution. So, it is not clear how many of these cases require empathy and on which level empathy operates. Indeed, a collection of anecdotes does not constitute strong evidence on the phenomenon or its mechanism (e.g., McGrew, 2004). While they can hint towards the existence of empathic prosociality, they leave us in the dark with regard to the mechanism and frequency of chimpanzee empathy.

Post-conflict behaviour is often brought forward to highlight chimpanzee empathy. However, although plentiful and rigorous data exist for chimpanzees' post-conflict behaviour, its empathic base is questionable. Reconciliation between former opponents after an aggressive encounter has been suggested to reflect empathy (O'Connell, 1995). While reconciliation is likely to have an emotional undertone, as anxiety is proposed to act as a mediating emotion in reconciliation (Aureli & Schaffner, 2002), the emotion (anxiety) stems from the individual's own situation rather than from empathy towards the other's situation. Subject's post-conflict anxiety depends largely on the damage to the relationship with the conflict opponent and the consequent loss of benefits brought by that relationship (Aureli & Schaffner, 2002; Koski, Koops, & Sterck, 2007). Reconciliation is therefore unlikely to rely on empathic processing.

Another post-conflict interaction, consolation, has received attention as unequivocal evidence for chimpanzees' empathic tendency (e.g., de Waal, 2005, 2008; Palagi, Cordoni, & Borgonini Tarli, 2006; Preston & de Waal, 2002b). Consolation, i.e., post-conflict third-party-initiated affiliation towards a former conflict victim (de Waal & van Roosmalen, 1979), is common in chimpanzees (e.g., de Waal & Aureli, 1996; Fraser, Stahl, & Aureli, 2008; Koski & Sterck, 2007; Wittig & Boesch, 2003), and is observed also in bonobos and gorillas (Mallavarapu, Stoinski, Bloomsmith, & Maple,

2006; Palagi, Paoli, & Borgonini Tarli, 2004). It is assumed to reflect bystanders' empathic response to a conflict victim's distress (de Waal & Aureli, 1996). Further, consolation has been interpreted to operate at the cognitive level of empathy, because the affiliators are argued not to exhibit signs of anxiety before giving affiliation to a conflict participant (de Waal, 2008; de Waal & Aureli, 1996). Moreover, the apparent lack of consolation in monkeys (see Watts, Colmenares, & Arnold, 2000, for a review) may follow from their inability to empathize at a cognitive level (de Waal & Aureli, 1996). However, it is unclear whether third-party-initiated affiliation relies on (cognitive) empathy. There are no published data for chimpanzees on the emotional state of the third parties before they make an affiliative contact. It is equally frequently given to conflict opponents who show no stress-related behaviours and to those who do (Koski & Sterck, 2007). In addition, third-party-initiated post-conflict affiliation does exist in some monkeys (stump-tailed macaques: Call, Aureli, & de Waal, 2002; baboons: Wittig, Crockford, Wikberg, Seyfarth, & Cheney, 2007), and indeed several functions for third-party affiliation have been suggested for monkeys, which may apply to ape third-party-initiated affiliation as well (Fraser, Koski, Wittig, & Aureli, in press; Koski & Sterck, 2009). Finally, the evidence for the comforting effects of third-party-initiated affiliation is contradictory (pro: Fraser et al., 2008; contra: Koski & Sterck, 2007). These aspects weaken the argument of empathic consolation in apes and non-empathic affiliation in monkeys. Instead, recent discussion has emphasized multiple functions in third-party-initiated affiliation, one of which concerns comforting the other and thus possibly represents empathic prosociality (Fraser et al., in press; Koski & Sterck, 2009; Wittig, in press). Since both the function and the mechanism of third-party-initiated affiliation are unclear, the assumption of its empathic base is premature and warrants more research.

In experimental research, food-related paradigms have consistently yielded negative evidence for chimpanzee prosociality (Jensen, Hare, Call, & Tomasello, 2006; Silk et al., 2005; Vonk et al., 2008). These paradigms test chimpanzees' willingness to give food to others, regardless of the other's emotional state (i.e., the test situation was not specifically designed to elicit emotions in a subject or partner). Thus, presence of prosociality was tested in a situation not likely to rely on empathizing with another's emotion. It is possible that the negative evidence is indicative of a general absence of prosocial tendency in chimpanzees, or it may follow from their indifference specifically in food-related contexts. Also, it is possible that the absence of an emotional undertone is an important variable. Instrumental helping of chimpanzees shows positive evidence for prosocial behaviour; it involves behaviour for the benefit of another even with a cost to self (Warneken et al., 2007; Warneken & Tomasello, 2006). Interestingly, these paradigms involve an emotional state of the other (i.e., in the test situation a human experimenter or a partner chimpanzee expresses a wish to reach a goal, and the chimpanzee responds to this by helping the other to reach that goal). Therefore, helping might be based on a cognitive connection of the other's emotional state and the goal, leading to prosocial action to aid the other to reach its goal. This would lend indirect, although tentative, support to our hypothesis for chimpanzee veridical empathy. However, helping also can stem from understanding another's goal and motivation to reach that goal, without a representation of the other's emotional state, and as such does not prove chimpanzees' empathic tendency or the cognitive level at which it may operate (Moll & Tomasello, 2007; Warneken & Tomasello, 2007). To test between these two possibilities, an assessment of the emotional state in the subject would be informative.

In conclusion, the available information on chimpanzee prosocial behaviour does not allow us to assess whether our hypothesis that chimpanzees may exhibit veridical empathy fits the data. Testing the level of cognitive processing and physiological indicators of emotional processing is necessary to pinpoint the precise mechanism of chimpanzee empathy.

III. TESTING THE PROPOSAL

We have outlined a hypothesis on the level of cognitive involvement in chimpanzee empathy and below we present some suggestions that could be helpful in testing the phenomenon. Crucially, the different components of empathy, emotional processing, cognitive representations and executive control, need to be addressed.

Regarding the emotional component of empathy, the research of Parr (2001; Parr & Hopkins, 2000) is informative. This involves subjecting chimpanzees to emotionally charged videos or other stimuli and monitoring their physiological and behavioural indicators of the emotional state, i.e., skin and brain temperature. In addition to these measures, heart-rate variation could provide an additional method to assess empathic response. It is commonly used in human empathy research (e.g., Eisenberg & Fabes, 1990; Field, Diego, Hernandez-Reif, & Fernandez, 2007), and has been employed to measure stress levels in monkeys (Aureli, Preston, & de Waal, 1999; Bowers, Crockett, & Bowden, 1998). In addition, cardiac vagal tone correlates with heart-rate variance and is an index of emotion regulation in humans (Calkins, Graziano, & Keane, 2007; Porges, 2007). Cardiac vagal tone is proposed to be a valid index of stress vulnerability also in non-human mammals (Porges, 1995), and may help to pinpoint the degree of emotion regulation in chimpanzee empathy (cf. Eisenberg et al., 1996; Fabes et al., 1993). In addition to the physiological measures, self-directed behaviours can be indicative of internal emotional states, at least in contexts with negative valence (Maestripieri, Schino, Aureli, & Troisi, 1992; Troisi, 2002). For example, Japanese macaque mothers' emotional response to observing their offspring being a victim in a conflict was measured by self-directed behaviours (Schino, Geminiani, Rosati, & Aureli, 2004).

Cognitive representation of another's emotional state can be studied with adaptations of the paradigms used for human children. These commonly rely on showing or telling a story of someone in an emotion-eliciting situation, and afterwards asking how the other felt. Obviously, chimpanzees cannot be tested on paradigms that rely on verbal reports of the projected emotion. Instead, we can measure the subsequent behaviour towards the other after an emotional stimulus; if the subject exhibits an increased tendency to affective behaviour towards the other than after non-emotional stimulus, it may be inferred to have represented—on some level—the situation as emotional. This can be adjusted to include or exclude emotional facial expressions by the other (cf. Vaish et al., 2009) to test subjects' attribution of emotion without expressive cues. In addition, a measure on chimpanzees' behavioural and physiological indicators of emotional arousal in the test situation would help assess its emotional state during the stimulus and subsequent behaviour. The latter would give an indication of the distinction between egocentric and veridical empathy: in egocentric empathy we expect both behavioural and physiological indicators of arousal, in veridical empathy only physiological ones. As stressed above, prosocial acts do not per se prove empathy, but combined with physiological and/or behavioural measures of subjects' emotional state they can give an indication of the empathic processing. Paradigms used for infants, in which the measured response is other- or self-comforting behaviour, might also be informative. The appropriateness of subjects' responses to others' needs indicates whether subjects represent others' emotional states as separate from their own. A potentially informative paradigm could involve another showing emotional arousal and need of help/assistance, and in the test situation the subject has an option to act for itself, for the other, or not at all. Crucially (and different from the previous work on prosociality in food paradigms; Jensen et al., 2006; Silk et al., 2005; Vonk et al., 2008), the context should be emotionally charged for the other, and thus allow the subject to respond empathically. The subject's response accuracy to the other's needs, and the behavioural and physiological indicators of arousal can be measured to indicate both emotional and cognitive processing. Furthermore, acting *for* the other would indicate a connected representation of the other's emotion and goal. The above scenario can also be adapted so that the other fosters a false belief of a situation (and gets consequently "wrongly" aroused by it), to tap into the connection of emotion and belief representations. If the subject knows that the other's expectation does not fit the actual situation, it may attempt to correct the other, aiming to adjust its beliefs to the real situation. However, lacking evidence that chimpanzees pass false-belief tasks (Kaminski et al., 2008), we may first aim to detail chimpanzee empathic processes at less complex levels of empathy. Finally, chimpanzees' executive control in other tasks than those of delayed gratification would be helpful to assess their level of cognitive flexibility and control.

IV. GENERAL DISCUSSION

We have proposed a hypothesis that chimpanzee empathy operates between egocentric and veridical empathy, potentially leaning towards the veridical end of the continuum. Our hypothesis assumes much similarity between human and ape cognitive and emotional processing. Specifically, it assumes that human and chimpanzee cognition contain at least partly the same components and that emotion attribution is similarly connected to cognitive processing in both species. This hypothesis thus argues for conservation of the cognitive capacities in *Pan* and *Homo*. Cognitive correspondence between humans and chimpanzees has been argued by several authors (e.g., de Waal, 2008; Hare, 2007; Suddendorf & Whiten, 2001). However, conservation does not require identical similarity, and humans are superior to other apes especially in social cognition; for example, 2-year-old children outperform chimpanzees in communicative and collaborative tasks, whereas cognitive processing in the physical domain is more similar with chimpanzees (Herrmann, Call, Hernandez-Lloreda, Hare, & Tomasello, 2007). So, humans may be more tuned into others' needs than are chimpanzees (Call & Jensen, 2006). Consequently, it may be that chimpanzees are less empathic and prosocial in general than even young children are.

We also emphasize the mediating role of emotions in cognitive processing in general. Even though empathy comprises the partially dissociated emotional and cognitive components, emotions are not operationally independent from cognition; on the contrary, they interact and influence one another (in empathy as well as in other cognitive tasks). For example, chimpanzees perform better in cognitive tasks that employ paradigms that evoke a sufficient motivation to solve the task (see Call & Tomasello, 2008, for a review). The partially dissociative nature of emotions and cognition in empathy reflects the multi-modality of the process, in which the emotional processing develops earlier than the cognitive processing. Empathy can, and does, operate without fully matured cognitive processing (cf. emotional resonance in ASD, veridical empathic acts), but in functional mature human empathy both components are relevant. The challenge is to understand how these components operate in non-human animals.

In the outlined hypothesis we have assumed roughly equal empathic abilities across sexes and individuals. However, this may not be justified. Sex differences in empathic tendency are well known from humans; females score consistently higher in empathizing measures than do males across cultures (Baron-Cohen, Knickmeyer, & Belmonte, 2005; Costa, Terraciano, & McCrae, 2001; Nettle, 2007). The female bias in empathy has been hypothesized to be rooted in mother–offspring behaviour (Preston & de Waal, 2002a). Recently a male bias in spatial cognition was documented in chimpanzees (Herrmann et al., 2007), which agrees with human (Baron-Cohen et al., 2005) and rat (e.g., Roof, Zhang, Glazier, & Stein, 1993) data. This suggests that a female bias in empathizing may be expected in chimpanzees.

There is also pronounced inter-individual variation beyond sex in human empathic tendency. Empathic tendency is represented in one of the five primary personality constructs, Agreeableness, in the five-factor model personality theory (e.g., Costa & McCrae, 1992). Agreeableness includes descriptors of both emotional and cognitive components of empathy, such as "to have a soft heart", "to feel others' emotions", and "to know how to comfort others" (International Personality Item Pool; Goldberg, 1999). High agreeableness associates with warmth and friendliness (Graziano & Eisenberg, 1997) and with high social-cognitive ToM performance (Nettle & Liddle, 2008). Chimpanzees are argued to show largely similar personality structure to humans, including an agreeableness construct (King & Figueredo, 1997; Weiss, King, & Figueredo, 2000), suggesting that they may exhibit inter-individual variation in empathizing. Unfortunately behavioural validation of chimpanzee personality constructs is mostly lacking (Uher, Asendorpf, & Call, 2007), so the degree of variation in manifest behaviours of the identified personality constructs is unknown. Inter-individual variations in behaviour and their underlying mechanisms, including cognitive and emotional processes, need to be established in chimpanzees. However, we consider it likely that chimpanzee individuals have different empathic tendencies.

CONCLUSION

We have called for attention to chimpanzees' empathic abilities, especially stressing the need for a more detailed assessment on how chimpanzee empathy operates. Based on chimpanzees' general cognitive performance in mental state attribution tasks, we have proposed that chimpanzees may empathize along the continuum of egocentric to veridical empathy. We urge researchers to test this hypothesis. The question of chimpanzee empathy is highly relevant for understanding the evolution of ToM, prosociality, morality and co-operation (cf. Flack & de Waal, 2000). Therefore, addressing the mechanism of prosocial actions has wide implications for assessing the evolution of human social behaviour.

REFERENCES

Amici, F., Aureli, F., & Call, J. (2008). Fission-fusion dynamics, behavioral flexibility, and inhibitory control in primates. *Current Biology, 18*, 1–5.

Anderson, J. R., Myowa-Yamakoshi, M., & Matsuzawa, T. (2004). Contagious yawning in chimpanzees. *Proceedings of the Royal Society B, 271*(Suppl.), S468–S470.

Aureli, F., Preston, S. D., & de Waal, F. B. M. (1999). Heart rate responses to social interactions in free-moving Rhesus macaques (*Macaca mulatta*): A pilot study. *Journal of Comparative Psychology, 113*, 59–65.

Aureli, F., & Schaffner, C. M. (2002). Relationship assessment through emotional mediation. *Behaviour, 139*, 393–420.

Bard, K. A. (2007). Neonatal imitation in chimpanzees (*Pan troglodytes*) tested with two paradigms. *Animal Cognition, 10*, 233–242.

Baron-Cohen, S., Knickmeyer, R. C., & Belmonte, M. K. (2005). Sex differences in the brain: Implications for explaining autism. *Science, 310*, 819–823.

Baron-Cohen, S., Wheelwright, S., Skinner, R., Martin, J, & Clubley, E. (2001). Autism-spectrum quotient (AQ): Evidence from Asperger syndrome/high-functioning autism, males and females, scientists and mathematician. *Journal of Autism and Developmental Disorders, 31*, 5–17.

Batson, D. C., & Shaw, L. L. (1991). Evidence for altruism: Toward a pluralism of prosocial motives. *Psychological Inquiry, 2*, 107–122.

Bauer, R. M. (1998). Physiologic measures of emotion. *Journal of Clinical Neurophysiology, 15*, 388–396.

Begeer, S., Koot, H. M., Rieffe, C., Terwogt, M. M., & Stegge, H. (2008). Emotional competence in children with autism: Diagnostic criteria and empirical evidence. *Developmental Reviews, 28*, 342–369.

Beran, M. L., & Evans, T. A. (2006). Maintenance of delay of gratification by found chimpanzees (*Pan troglodytes*): The effects of delayed reward visibility, experimenter presence, and extended delay intervals. *Behavioral Processes, 73*, 315–342.

Blair, R. J. R. (1999). Psychophysiological responsiveness to the distress of others in children with autism. *Personality and Individual Differences, 26*, 477–485.

Blair, R. J. R. (2005). Responding to the emotions of others: Dissociating forms of empathy through the study of typical and psychiatric populations. *Consciousness and Cognition, 14*, 698–718.

Blakemore, S.-J., & Decety, J. (2001). From the perception of action to understanding of intention. *Nature Reviews Neuroscience, 2*, 561–567.

Blijd-Hoogewys, E. M. A., van Geert, P. L. C., Serra, M., & Minderaa, R. B. (2008). Measuring Theory of Mind in children. Psychometric properties of the ToM storybooks. *Journal of Autism and Developmental Disorders, 38*, 1907–1930.

Boesch, C., & Boesch-Achermann, H. (2000). *The chimpanzees of the Taï Forest: Behavioral ecology and evolution*. Oxford, UK: Oxford University Press.

Bowers, C. L., Crockett, C. M., & Bowden, D. M. (1998). Differences in stress reactivity of laboratory macaques measured by heart period and respiratory sinus arrhythmia. *American Journal of Primatology, 43*, 245–261.

Bräuer, J., Call, J., & Tomasello, M. (2007). Chimpanzees really know what others can see in a competitive situation. *Animal Cognition, 10*, 439–448.

Braver, T. S., Barch, D. M., Gray, J. R., Molfese, D. L., & Snyder, A. (2001). Anterior cingulate cortex and response conflict: Effects of frequency, inhibition and error. *Cerebral Cortex, 11*, 825–836.

Brent, E., Rios, P., Happé, F., & Charman, T. (2004). Performance of children with autism spectrum disorders on advanced theory of mind tasks. *Autism, 8*, 283–299.

Brühne, M., & Brühne-Cohrs, U. (2006). Theory of mind: Evolution, ontogeny, brain mechanisms and psychopathology. *Neuroscience & Biobehavioral Reviews, 30*, 437–455.

Buttelmann, D., Carpenter, M., Call, J., & Tomasello, M. (2007). Enculturated chimpanzees imitate rationally. *Developmental Science, 10*, F31–F38.

Calkins, S. D., Graziano, P. A., & Keane, S. P. (2007). Cardiac vagal regulation differentiates among children at risk for behaviour problems. *Biological Psychology, 74*, 144–153.

Call, J., Aureli, F., & de Waal, F. B. M. (2002). Post-conflict third party affiliation in stumptailed macaques. *Animal Behaviour, 63*, 209–216.

Call, J., Hare, B., Carpenter, M., & Tomasello, M. (2004). "Unwilling" versus "unable": Chimpanzees' understanding of human intentional action. *Developmental Science, 7*, 488–498.

Call, J., & Jensen, K. (2006). Chimpanzees may recognize motives and goals but may not reckon on them. In C. Frith (Ed.), *Empathy and fairness* (pp. 56–70). Chichester, UK: Wiley.

Call, J., & Tomasello, M. (1998). Distinguishing intentional from accidental actions in orang-utan (*Pongo pygmaeus*), chimpanzees (*Pan troglodytes*) and human children (*Homo sapiens*). *Journal of Comparative Psychology, 112*, 192–206.

Call, J., & Tomasello, M. (2008). Does the chimpanzee have a theory of mind? 30 years later. *Trends in Cognitive Sciences, 12*, 187–192.

Campbell, M., Carter, J. D., Proctor, R., & de Waal, F. B. M. (2008). Do chimpanzees yawn contagiously in response to 3D computer animations? *Primate Eye, 96*, 291.

Carlson, S. M., & Moses, L. J. (2001). Individual differences in inhibitory control and children's theory of mind. *Child Development, 72*, 1032–1053.

Carlson, S. M., Moses, L. J., & Claxton, L. J. (2004). Individual differences in executive functioning and theory of mind: An investigation of inhibitory control and planning ability. *Journal of Experimental Child Psychology, 87*, 299–319.

Carpenter, M., Akhtar, N., & Tomasello, M. (1998). Fourteen- through 18-month-old infants differentially imitate intentional and accidental actions. *Infant Behavior and Development, 21*, 315–330.

Carpenter, M., Nagell, K., Tomasello, M., Butterworth, G., & Moore, C. (1999). Social cognition, joint attention, and communicative competence from 9 to 15 months of age. *Monographs of the Society for Research in Child Development, 63*(4).

Carr, L., Iacoboni, M., Dubeau, M.-C., Mazziotta, J. C., & Lenzi, G. L. (2003). Neural mechanism of empathy in humans: A relay from neural systems for imitation to limbic areas. *Proceedings of the National Academy of Sciences, 100*, 5497–5502.

Commons, M. L., & Wolfsont, C. A. (2002). A complete theory of empathy must consider stage changes. *Behavioral and Brain Sciences, 25*, 30–31.

Costa, P. T., Jr., & McCrae, R. R. (1992). Four ways five factors are basic. *Personality and Individual Differences, 13*, 653–665.

Costa, P. T., Terraciano, A., & McCrae, R. R. (2001). Gender differences in personality traits across cultures: Robust and surprising findings. *Journal of Personality and Social Psychology, 81*, 322–331.

Courage, M. L., & Howe, M. L. (2002). From infant to child: The dynamics of cognitive change in the second year of life. *Psychological Bulletin, 128*, 250–277.

de Vignemont, F., & Singer, T. (2006). The empathic brain: How, when and why. *Trends in Cognitive Sciences, 10*, 435–441.

de Waal, F. B. M. (2005). *Our inner ape: A leading primatologist explains why we are who we are.* New York: Penguin Books.

de Waal, F. B. M. (2008). Putting the altruism back into altruism: The evolution of empathy. *Annual Reviews of Psychology, 59,* 279–300.

de Waal, F. B. M., & Aureli, F. (1996): Consolation, reconciliation and a possible difference between macaques and chimpanzees. In A. E. Russon, K. A. Bard, & S. T. Parker (Eds.), *Reaching into thought. The minds of great apes* (pp. 80–110). Cambridge, UK: Cambridge University Press.

de Waal, F. B. M., & van Roosmalen, A. (1979). Reconciliation and consolation among chimpanzees. *Behavioral Ecology and Sociobiology, 5,* 55–66.

Decety, J., & Jackson, P. L. (2004). The functional architecture of human empathy. *Behavioral and Cognitive Neuroscience Reviews, 3,* 71–100.

Decety, J., & Meyer, M. (2008). From emotion resonance to empathic understanding: A social developmental neuroscience account. *Development and Psychopathology, 20,* 1053–1080.

Dufour, V., Pele, M., Sterck, E. H. M., & Thierry, B. (2007). Chimpanzee (*Pan troglodytes*) anticipation of food return: Coping with waiting time in an exchange task. *Journal of Comparative Psychology, 121,* 145–155.

Dziobek, I., Rogers, K., Fleck, S., Bahnemann, M., Heekeren, H. R., Wolf, O. T., et al. (2008). Dissociation of cognitive and emotional empathy in adults with Asperger syndrome using the multifaceted empathy test (MET). *Journal of Autism and Developmental Disorders, 38,* 464–473.

Eisenberg, N. (2000). Emotion, regulation and moral development. *Annual Reviews of Psychology, 51,* 665–697.

Eisenberg, N., & Fabes, R. A. (1990). Empathy: Conceptualization, measurement, and relation to prosocial behavior. *Motivation and Emotion, 14,* 131–149.

Eisenberg, N., Fabes, R. A., Karbon, M., Murphy, B. C., Wosinski, M., Polazzi, L., et al. (1996). The relations of children's dispositional prosocial behaviour to emotionality, regulation, and social functioning. *Child Development, 67,* 974–992.

Eisenberg, N., Lennon, R., & Roth, K. (1983). Prosocial development: A longitudinal study. *Developmental Psychology, 19,* 846–855.

Fabes, R. A., Eisenberg, N., & Eisenbud, L. (1993). Behavioural and physiological correlates of children's reactions to others in distress. *Developmental Psychology, 29,* 655–663.

Field, T., Diego, M., Hernandez-Reif, M., & Fernandez, M. (2007). Depressed mothers' newborns show less discrimination of other newborns' cry sounds. *Infant Behavior and Development, 30,* 431–435.

Flack, J. C., & de Waal, F. B. M. (2000). Any animal whatever. Darwinian building blocks of morality in monkeys and apes. *Journal of Consciousness Studies, 7,* 1–29.

Flavell, J. H. (2000). Development of children's knowledge about the mental world. *International Journal of Behavioral Development, 24,* 15–23.

Flavell, J. H. (2004). Theory-of-mind development: Retrospect and prospect. *Merrill-Palmer Quarterly, 50,* 274–290.

Fraser, O. N., Koski, S. E., Wittig, R. M, & Aureli, F. (in press). Why are bystanders friendly to recipients of aggression? *Communicative and Integrative Biology.*

Fraser, O. N., Stahl, D., & Aureli, F. (2008). Stress reduction through consolation in chimpanzees. *Proceedings of the National Academy of Sciences, 105,* 8557–8562.

Goldberg, L. R. (1999). A broad-bandwidth, public domain personality inventory measuring the lower-level facets of several five-factor models. In I. Merviede, I. Deary, F. de Fruyt, & F. Ostendorf (Eds.), *Personality psychology in Europe* (Vol. 7, pp. 7–28). Tilburg, The Netherlands: Tilburg University Press.

Goodall, J. (1986): *The chimpanzees of Gombe: Patterns of behaviour.* Cambridge, UK: Belknap Press.

Graziano, W. G., & Eisenberg, N. (1997). Agreeableness: A dimension of personality. In R. Hogan, J. Johnson, & S. Briggs (Eds.), *Handbook of personality psychology* (pp. 795–825). San Diego, CA: Academic Press.

Hare, B. (2007). From nonhuman to human mind. What changed and why? *Current Directions in Psychological Science, 16,* 60–64.

Hare, B., Call, J., & Tomasello, M. (2006). Chimpanzees deceive human competitor by hiding. *Cognition, 101,* 495–514.

Hatfield, E., Cacioppo, J., & Rapson, R. L. (1993). Emotional contagion. *Current Directions in Psychological Science, 2,* 96–99.

Hatfield, E., Cacioppo, J., & Rapson, R. L. (1994). *Emotional contagion.* New York: Cambridge Univeristy Press.

Hay, D. F., Nash, A., & Pedersen, J. (1981). Responses of six-month-olds to the distress of their peers. *Child Development, 52,* 1071–1075.

Herrmann, E., Call, J., Hernandez-Lloreda, M. V., Hare, B., & Tomasello, M. (2007). Humans have evolved specialized skills of social cognition: The cultural intelligence hypothesis. *Science, 317,* 1360–1366.

Hill, E. L. (2004). Evaluating the theory of executive dysfunction in autism. *Developmental Review, 24,* 189–233.

Hirata, S. (2007). A note on the response of chimpanzees (*Pan troglodytes*) to live self-images on television monitors. *Behavioral Processes, 75,* 85–90.

Hoffman, M. L. (2000). *Empathy and moral development. Implications for caring and justice.* Cambridge, UK: Cambridge University Press.

Jackson, P. L., Brunet, E., Meltzoff, A. N., & Decety, J. (2006). Empathy examined through the neural mechanisms involved in imagining how I feel versus how you feel pain. *Neuropsychology, 44,* 752–761.

Jensen, K., Hare, B., Call, J., & Tomasello, M. (2006). What's in it for me? Self-regard precludes altruism and spite in chimpanzees. *Proceedings of the Royal Society B, 273,* 1013–1021.

Johnson, D. B. (1983). Self-recognition in infants. *Infant Behavior and Development, 6,* 211–222.

Kaminski, J., Call, J., & Tomasello, M. (2008). Chimpanzees know what others know but not what they believe. *Cognition, 109,* 224–234.

King, J., & Figueredo, A. J. (1997). The five-factor model plus dominance in chimpanzee personality. *Journal of Research in Personality, 31,* 257–271.

Kitchen, A., Denton, D., & Brent, L. (1996). Self-recognition and abstraction in the common chimpanzee studied with distorting mirrors. *Proceedings of the National Academy of Sciences USA, 93,* 7405–7408.

Koski, S. E., Koops, K., & Sterck, E. H. M. (2007). Reconciliation, relationship quality, and postconflict anxiety: Testing the integrated hypothesis in captive chimpanzees. *American Journal of Primatology, 69,* 158–172.

Koski, S. E., & Sterck, E. H. M. (2007). Triadic post-conflict affiliation in captive chimpanzees: Does consolation console? *Animal Behaviour, 73,* 133–142.

Koski, S. E., & Sterck, E. H. M. (2009). Third-party-initiated affiliation in chimpanzees: What's in it for the third party? *American Journal of Primatology, 71,* 409–418.

Lamm, C., Batson, C. D., & Decety, J. (2007). The neural substrate of human empathy: Effects of perspective-taking and cognitive appraisal. *Journal of Cognitive Neuroscience, 19,* 42–58.

Lamm, C., Meltzoff, A. N., & Decety, J. (in press). How do we empathize with someone who is not like us? A functional magnetic resonance imaging study. *Journal of Cognitive Neuroscience.*

Lamm, C., Porges, J. T., Cacioppo, J. T., & Decety, J. (2008). Perspective taking is associated with specific facial responses during empathy for pain. *Brain Research, 1227,* 153–161.

Leavens, D. A., Russell, J. L., & Hopkins, W. D. (2005). Intentionality as measured in the persistence and elaboration of communication by chimpanzees (*Pan troglodytes*). *Child Development*, *76*, 291–306.

Liebal, K., Pika, S., Call, J., & Tomasello, M. (2004). To move or not to move: How apes adjust to the attentional state of others. *Interaction Studies*, *5*, 199–219.

Maestripieri, D., Schino, G., Aureli, F., & Troisi, A. (1992). A modest proposal: Displacement activities as indicators of emotions in nonhuman primates. *Animal Behaviour*, *44*, 967–979.

Mallavarapu, S., Stoinski, T. S., Bloomsmith, M. A., & Maple, T. L. (2006). Postconflict behavior in captive Western Lowland gorillas. *American Journal of Primatology*, *68*, 789–801.

Marcowitch, S., & Zelazo, P. D. (2009). A hierarchical competing systems model of the emergence and early development of executive function. *Developmental Science*, *12*, 1–25.

Martin, G., & Clark, R. (1982). Distress crying in neonates: Species and peer specificity. *Developmental Psychology*, *18*, 3–9.

McGrew, W. C. (2004). *The cultured chimpanzee: Reflections on cultural primatology*. Cambridge, UK: Cambridge University Press.

Melis, A. P., Call, J., & Tomasello, M. (2006). Chimpanzees conceal visual and auditory information from others. *Journal of Comparative Psychology*, *120*, 154–162.

Meltzoff, A. (1995). Understanding the intentions of others: Reenactment of intended acts by 18-month-old children. *Developmental Psychology*, *31*, 1–16.

Meltzoff, A. M., & Moore, M. K. (1977). Newborn infants imitate adult facial gestures. *Science*, *198*, 75–78.

Mischel, W., Shoda, Y., & Rodriguez, M. L. (1989). Delay of gratification in children. *Science*, *244*, 933–938.

Miyake, A., Friedman, N. P., Emerson, M. J., Witzki, A. H., Howerter, A., & Wager, T. D. (2000). The unity and diversity of executive functions and their contributions complex "frontal lobe" tasks: A latent variable analysis. *Cognitive Psychology*, *41*, 49–100.

Moll, H., & Tomasello, M. (2004). 12- and 18-month-old infants follow gaze to spaces around barriers. *Developmental Science*, *7*, F1–F9.

Moll, H., & Tomasello, M. (2006). Level 1 perspective taking at 24-months of age. *British Journal of Developmental Psychology*, *24*, 603–613.

Moll, H., & Tomasello, M. (2007). Co-operation and human cognition: The Vygotskian intelligence hypothesis. *Philosophical Transactions of the Royal Society B*, *362*, 639–648.

Mundy, P., & Newell, L. (2007). Attention, joint attention and social cognition. *Current Directions in Psychological Sciences*, *16*, 269–274.

Nagy, E., Kompagne, H., Orvos, H., & Pal, A. (2007). Gender-related differences in neonatal imitation. *Infant and Child Development*, *16*, 267–276.

Nettle, D. (2007). Empathizing and systemizing: What are they, and what do they contribute to our understanding of psychological sex differences? *British Journal of Psychology*, *98*, 237–255.

Nettle, D., & Liddle, B. (2008). Agreeableness is related to social-cognitive, but not social-perceptual, theory of mind. *European Journal of Personality*, *22*, 323–335.

Nielsen, M., Suddendorf, T., & Slaughter, V. (2006). Mirror self-recognition beyond the face. *Child Development*, *77*, 176–185.

O'Connell, S. M. (1995). Empathy in chimpanzees: Evidence for Theory of Mind? *Primates*, *36*, 397–410.

Okamoto-Barth, S., Call, J., & Tomasello, M. (2007). Great apes' understanding of others individuals' line of sight. *Psychological Science*, *18*, 462–468.

Osvath, M., & Osvath, H. (2008). Chimpanzee (*Pan troglodytes*) and orang-utan (*Pongo abelii*) forethought: Self-control and pre-experience in the face of future tool use. *Animal Cognition*, *11*, 661–674.

Palagi, E., Cordoni, G., & Borgonini Tarli, S. (2006). Possible roles of consolation in captive chimpanzees (*Pan troglodytes*). *American Journal of Physical Anthropology, 129,* 105–111.

Palagi, E., Paoli, T., & Borgonini Tarli, S. (2004). Reconciliation and consolation in captive bonobos (*Pan paniscus*). *American Journal of Primatology, 62,* 15–30.

Parr, L. A. (2001). Cognitive and physiological markers of emotional awareness in chimpanzees (*Pan troglodytes*). *Animal Cognition, 4,* 223–229.

Parr, L. A., & Hopkins, W. D. (2001). Brain temperature asymmetries and emotional perception in chimpanzees, *Pan troglodytes. Physiology & Behavior, 71,* 363–371.

Penn, D. C., & Povinelli, D. J. (2007). On the lack of evidence that non-human animals possess anything remotely resembling "theory of mind". *Philosophical Transactions of the Royal Society B, 362,* 731–744.

Perner, J., & Lang, B. (1999). Development of theory of mind and executive control. *Trends in Cognitive Sciences, 3,* 337–344.

Platek, S. M., Critton, S. R., Myers, T. E., & Gallup, G. G. (2003). Contagious yawning: The role of self-awareness and mental state attribution. *Cognitive Brain Research, 17,* 223–237.

Porges, S. W. (1995). Cardiac vagal tone: A physiological index of stress. *Neuroscience & Biobehavioral Reviews, 19,* 225–233.

Porges, S. W. (2007). The polyvagal theory. *Biological Psychology, 74,* 116–143.

Preston, S. (2007). A perception–action model for empathy. In T. F. D. Farrow & P. Woodruff (Eds.), *Empathy in mental illness* (pp. 428–447). Cambridge, UK: Cambridge University Press.

Preston, S., Bechara, A., Damasio, H., Grabowski, T. J., Stansfield, R. B., Mehta, S., et al. (2007). The neural substrates of empathy. *Social Neuroscience, 2,* 254–275.

Preston, S., & de Waal, F. B. M. (2002a). Empathy: Its ultimate and proximate bases. *Behavioral and Brain Sciences, 25,* 1–72.

Preston, S., & de Waal, F. B. M. (2002b). The communication of emotions and the possibility of empathy in animals. In S. G. Post, L. G. Underwood, J. P. Schloss, & W. B. Harlbut (Eds.), *Altruism and altruistic love: Science, philosophy and religion in dialogue* (pp. 284–308). New York: Oxford University Press.

Ritchell, R. A., Mitchell, D. G., Newman, C., Leonard, A., Baron-Cohen, S., & Blair, R. J. (2003). Theory of mind and psychopathy: Can psychopathic individuals read the "language of the eyes"? *Neuropsychologia, 41,* 523–526.

Rizzolatti, G., Fogassi, L., & Gallese, V. (2001). Neurophysiological mechanisms underlying the understanding and imitation of action. *Nature Reviews Neuroscience, 2,* 266–270.

Roof, R. L., Zhang, Q., Glazier, M. M., & Stein, D. G. (1993). Gender-specific impairment on Morris water maze task after entorhinal cortex lesion. *Behavioural Brain Research, 57,* 47–51.

Rosati, A. G., Stevens, J. R., Hare, B., & Hauser, M. D. (2007). The evolutionary origins of human patience: Temporal preferences in chimpanzees, bonobos, and human adults. *Current Biology, 17,* 1663–1668.

Russell, C. L., Bard, K. A., & Adamson, L. B. (1997). Social referencing by young chimpanzees (*Pan troglodytes*). *Journal of Comparative Psychology, 111,* 185–193.

Saxe, R., Carey, S., & Kanwisher, N. (2004). Understanding other minds: Linking developmental psychology and functional neuroimaging. *Annual Reviews of Psychology, 55,* 87–124.

Scambler, D. J., Hepburn, S., Rutheford, M. D., Wehner, E. A., & Rogers, S. J. (2007). Emotional responsivity in children with autism, children with other developmental disabilities, and children with typical development. *Journal of Autism and Developmental Disorders, 37,* 553–563.

Schino, G., Geminiani, S., Rosati, L., & Aureli, F. (2004). Behavioral and emotional response of Japanese macaque (*Macaca fuscata*) mothers after their offspring receive an aggression. *Journal of Comparative Psychology, 118,* 340–346.

Senju, A., Maeda, M., Kikuchi, Y., Hasegawa, T., Togo, Y., & Osanai, H. (2007). Absence of contagious yawning in children with autism spectrum disorder. *Biology Letters, 3*, 706–708.

Silk, J. B., Brosnan, S. F., Vonk, J., Henrich, J., Povinelli, D. J., Richardson, A. S., et al. (2005). Chimpanzees are indifferent to the welfare of unrelated group members. *Nature, 437*, 1357–1359.

Singer, T. (2006). The neuronal basis and ontogeny of empathy and mind reading: Review of literature and implications for future research. *Neuroscience & Biobehavioral Reviews, 30*, 855–863.

Singer, T., Seymour, B., O'Doherty, J. P., Stephan, K. E., Dolan, R. J., & Frith, C. D. (2006). Empathic neural responses are modulated by the perceived fairness of others. *Nature, 439*, 466–469.

Suddendorf, T., & Whiten, A. (2001). Mental evolution and development: Evidence for secondary representation in children, great apes, and other animals. *Psychological Bulletin, 127*, 629–650.

Tomasello, M., & Carpenter, M. (2005). The emergence of social cognition in three young chimpanzees *Monographs of the Society for Research in Child Development, 70*, 1–132.

Tomasello, M., Carpenter, M., Call, J., Behne, T., & Moll, H. (2005). Understanding and sharing intentions: The origins of cultural cognition. *Behavioral and Brain Sciences, 28*, 675–735.

Tomonaga, M., Tanaka, M., Matsuzawa, T., Myowa-Yamakoshi, M., Kosugi, D., Mizuno, Y., et al. (2004). Development of social cognition in infant chimpanzees (*Pan troglodytes*): Face recognition, smiling, gaze, and the lack of triadic interactions. *Japanese Psychological Research, 46*, 227–235.

Troisi, A. (2002). Displacement activities as a behavioural measure of stress in nonhuman primates and human subjects. *Stress, 5*, 47–54.

Uher, J., Asendorpf, J. B., & Call, J. (2007). Personality in the behaviour of great apes: Temporal stability, cross-situational consistency and coherence in response. *Animal Behaviour, 75*, 99–112.

Vaish, A., Carpenter, M., & Tomasello, M. (2009). Sympathy through affective perspective taking and its relation to prosocial behavior in toddlers. *Developmental Psychology, 45*, 534–543.

Vonk, J., Brosnan, S. F., Silk, J. B., Henrich, J., Richardson, A. S., Lambeth, S. P., et al. (2008). Chimpanzees do not take advantage of very low cost opportunities to deliver food to unrelated group members. *Animal Behaviour, 75*, 1757–1770.

Warneken, F., Hare, B., Melis, A. P., Hanus, D., & Tomasello, M. (2007). Spontaneous altruism by chimpanzees and young children. *PLoS Biology, 5*, 1–7.

Warneken, F., & Tomasello, M. (2006). Altruistic helping in human infants and young chimpanzees. *Child Development, 77*, 640–663.

Warneken, F., & Tomasello, M. (2007). Helping and co-operation at 14 months of age. *Infancy, 11*, 271–294.

Watts, D. P., Colmenares, F., & Arnold, K. (2000). Redirection, consolation and male policing. How targets of aggression interact with bystanders. In F. Aureli & F. B. M. de Waal (Eds.), *Natural conflict resolution* (pp. 281–301). Berkeley, CA: University of California Press.

Weiss, A., King, J. E., & Figueredo, A. J. (2000). The heritability of personality factors in chimpanzees (*Pan troglodytes*). *Behavior Genetics, 30*, 213–221.

Wellman, H. M., Cross, D., & Watson, J. (2001). Meta-analysis of Theory-of-Mind development: The truth about false belief. *Child Development, 72*, 655–684.

Wellman, H. M., & Liu, D. (2004). Scaling of Theory-of-Mind tasks. *Child Development, 75*, 523–541.

Wellman, H. M., Phillips, A. T., & Rodriguez, T. (2000). Young children's understanding of perception, desire, and emotion. *Child Development, 71*, 895–912.

Wispé, L. (1987). History of the concept of empathy. In N. Eisenberg (Ed.), *Empathy and its development* (pp. 17–37). New York: Cambridge University Press.

Wittig, R. M. (in press). Function and cognitive underpinnings of post-conflict affiliation in wild chimpanzees. In E. V. Lonsdorf, S. R. Ross, & T. Matsuzawa (Eds.), *The mind of the chimpanzee: Ecological and experimental perspectives*. Chicago: Chicago University Press.

Wittig, R. M., & Boesch, C. (2003). The choice of post-conflict interactions in wild chimpanzees (*Pan troglodytes*). *Behavior, 140*, 1257–1559.

Wittig, R. M., Crockford, C., Wikberg, E., Seyfarth, R. M., & Cheney, D. L. (2007). Kin-mediated reconciliation substitutes for direct reconciliation in female baboons. *Proceedings of the Royal Society B, 274*, 1109–1115.

Wittling, W. (1995). Brain asymmetry in the control of autonomic physiologic activity. In R. J. Davidson & K. Hughdahl (Eds.), *Brain asymmetry* (pp. 305–357). Cambridge, MA: MIT Press.

Zahn-Waxler, C., & Radke-Yarrow, M. (1990). The origins of empathic concern. *Motivation and Emotion, 14*, 107–130.

Zahn-Waxler, C., Radke-Yarrow, M., Wagner, E., & Chapman, M. (1992). Development of concern for others. *Developmental Psychology, 28*, 126–136.

EUROPEAN JOURNAL OF DEVELOPMENTAL PSYCHOLOGY
2010, 7 (1), 67–84

Ψ Psychology Press
Taylor & Francis Group

Do children start out thinking they don't know their own mind? An odyssey in overthrowing the mother of all knowledge

Peter Mitchell
University of Nottingham, Nottingham, UK

Mark Bennett
University of Dundee, Dundee, UK

Ulrich Teucher
University of Saskatchewan, Saskatoon, Saskatchewan, Canada

In this article we review research into children's developing understanding that they are the principal authority on knowing about themselves. Past research has suggested that when asked how much they know about their own mind and how much their mother knows, typically developing children below about 7 years respond as if they believe they are not best qualified to answer. Older children, in contrast, come to recognize the value of their privileged subjective access to their inner states and hence identify themselves as the authority on knowing themselves. Recent research that involves interviews with parents identifies a surprising degree of congruence in typically developing 10-year-olds' ratings of how well they know themselves and parents' ratings of how well they think their children know themselves. Younger, children, paradoxically, seemed to exaggerate how well they knew themselves.

Keywords: Culture; Self-knowledge; Theory of Mind.

Children as young as 3 to 4 years old correctly identify themselves as the authority on a matter of fact about the physical world, even in the face of a

Correspondence should be addressed to Peter Mitchell, School of Psychology, University of Nottingham, University Park, Nottingham NG7 2RD, UK.
E-mail: peter.mitchell@nottingham.ac.uk

Some of the research reported in this article was supported by the Economic and Social Research Council, UK (grant number, RES-000–23–0386), and by the Daiwa Anglo-Japanese Foundation. Some of the work was based on a PhD by Sarah Burton at the University of Nottingham, UK.

http://www.psypress.com/edp   DOI: 10.1080/17405620802607986

contradicting statement from an adult (e.g., Robinson, Champion & Mitchell, 1999; Robinson & Whitcombe, 2003). Intriguingly, however, when asked about their own physiological and psychological states (such as being tired, or emotions as in feeling happy), children reputedly defer to a relevant adult, like their parent or a teacher (Rosenberg, 1979). In other words, children seem to think that they do not know themselves as well as a significant adult might know them. Some of the states are actually states of mind as in emotions (happy, sad) or even representational states, like thoughts. Some of these states could be inferred by an onlooker from clues in behaviour and might thus be considered *exterior* states, as explained later; but some states would not always be obvious to onlookers and thus qualify as *interior* states Consequently, if children defer to adults on who knows most about their (the children's) interior states, it might seem that they think they do not know their own mind—at least not as well as another person might know.

This is a rather puzzling possibility considering that most people, at least in Western society, seem to think that by and large they have privileged access to their own inner states. Indeed, they suppose that not knowing one's own mind could even be a sign of insanity. The feeling of knowing oneself is echoed in the philosophical literature: "... the conception of agents as responsible for their own actions presumes that they know, in a way that others do not, what their intentions are in so acting. These views assume, as commonsense does, that there is an asymmetry between self-knowledge and knowledge of others in that the former, unlike the latter, is at least sometimes authoritative" (McDonald, 2002, pp. 467–468). Moreover, "... for the most part we know ourselves best—better than we know others and better than they know us" (Wright, 1998, p. 13). This is because, according to Wright, selves have the best evidence about selves, both quantitatively and qualitatively. We have opportunity to observe ourselves more than we have opportunity to observe any other person; and we know ourselves differently than we know other people. Our knowledge of ourselves is not inferred from aspects of behaviour or from assumptions or preconceptions, but from first-person access. Accordingly, we experience our own pain, sensations, beliefs, dreams and so on in a way that another person does not and cannot (Fricker, 1998). So, most of the time we think we know about ourselves a good deal more than we think other people know about us; but this feeling might not be experienced by children. Accordingly, do children start out thinking they don't know their own mind, and then shift to perceiving themselves as an authority on self? Our review sets the scene by considering what we already know about children's early understanding of inner states.

A SKETCH OF CHILDREN'S EARLY
UNDERSTANDING OF THE MIND

Considering that the topic falls broadly in the territory of developmental folk psychology, we should begin by enquiring at what age children show signs of knowing anything about the mind—even about the very existence of mind. Onishi and Bailargeon (2005) demonstrated very early sensitivity to other people's perspectives in a preferential looking task. In the task, infants watched an actor hide a toy in one of two locations. Subsequently a change occurred which meant the actor held a true or false belief about the location, and the critical question is whether infants would expect the actor to search for the toy based on her belief about the location. If the infants expect the actor to search based on her belief they should look longer when that expectation was violated, irrespective of whether the actor holds a true or false belief. Onishi and Bailargeon found that infants looked longer when the search was not based on the belief the actor had of the toy's location, indicating that this behaviour violated the expectation they had. This could only happen if the infants somehow represented the belief held by the actor.

When participating in Onishi and Bailargeon's task, infants demonstrated a working understanding of another person's mind, a prerequisite for adapting to perspectives held by other people. But the questions posed earlier in this article about development in understanding that you are the authority in knowing about yourself relate not so much to working understanding but to reflective understanding. Just because people demonstrate through their behaviour (including gaze direction) that they have adjusted to another person's perspective, it does not necessarily follow that they display insights when asked questions that pertain to mental life. The research of Wellman and colleagues (e.g., see Wellman, 1990, for a review) speaks to this matter. He discovered that children as young as 3 years have reflective insights about thoughts and how they contrast with real things. For example, children understand that, in one's thoughts, one can change the shape of an imaginary balloon, but that this could not be done with a real balloon, particularly if it was out of reach. Conversely, children know that one cannot give the thought of a cookie to another person to satisfy one's hunger and neither could you save it to eat tomorrow.

Beyond about 4 years of age children begin to understand not only that thought has special properties but also, importantly, that thought can be discrepant with reality. In other words, they begin to understand that sometimes people (including themselves) harbour false beliefs (e.g., Wellman, Cross, & Watson, 2001). Beyond this, there remain many subtle features of mental life that children do not seem to grasp until at least 6 years of age. For example, young children have difficulty discriminating between real and apparent emotion (Harris & Gross, 1988) and they seem not to understand that information could be interpreted differently by different people, depending on the contrasting informational history of these individuals (e.g., Apperly & Robinson, 1998; Chandler & Boyes, 1982; Taylor, 1988). Moreover, children have persistent difficulty with a test of false belief when the object of belief is animate (Rai & Mitchell, 2004), when the belief is patently false but the precise content is unknown (Hulme, Mitchell, & Wood, 2003) or when the protagonist is trying to avoid the object of the belief (Friedman & Leslie, 2004). Indeed, even adults have difficulty contrasting their own with another person's belief when the other person might (but might not) hold a true belief (Mitchell, Robinson, Isaacs, & Nye, 1996). In other words, if in doubt, assume people hold the same belief as yourself! This is not just common sense but a bias in reasoning: Adult participants' judgements vary depending on what they themselves believe even when the target person's information remains constant.

Perhaps most important to the current research, there is a pervasive difficulty among young children in understanding the characteristics of other people's ability to make inferences. In assessing what another person knows about you, effectively you need to assess their ability to make inferences about your inner states on the basis of external clues (e.g., cringing when eating disgusting food). Sodian and Wimmer (1987; Rai & Mitchell, 2006) discovered that children aged about 5 or 6 years wrongly deny that another person could make inferences when there is no direct visual access to information; in this circumstance, the other person could work out the correct answer by other means than using direct visual access. Conversely, children of similar age seem to overestimate what another person can infer from directly seeing only a small part of an illustration (Taylor, 1988). Similarly, they tend to overestimate one's ability to correctly interpret an underspecified referential description (e.g., Robinson & Whittaker, 1987).

ASSESSING BELIEFS ABOUT THE PHYSICAL WORLD AND ABOUT PSYCHOLOGICAL PHENOMENA

Most research into a developing theory of mind (ToM) examines children's assessments of what others know about the physical world. That research suggests that despite lingering biases and processing errors, children are largely proficient in judging who is the authority on a matter of fact by the age of 3 or 4 years (Robinson & Whitcombe, 2003). Nevertheless, there is continuing difficulty well into middle childhood and maybe beyond with understanding that (1) contrasting preferences are a subjective rather than objective matter (Rowley & Robinson, 2007) and (2) that subjective opinions cannot be wrong (Banerjee et al., 2007). Indeed, broader capacities in reflective thinking on the characteristics of knowledge could develop well into adulthood (Kuhn, 2000).

There is scant research, though, on children's assessment of who knows what about personal or psychological phenomena. Intuitively, perhaps it seems to border on the preposterous to suggest that those in middle childhood (7 to 11 years of age) think that they are not the principal authority when it comes to knowing themselves. This is precisely what Rosenberg (1979) argued. He invited participants to imagine a situation where he asked them and their mother what kind of person they were deep down, and they said one thing while the mother said something different. He enquired, "Who would be right, you or your mother?" Surprisingly, a majority in middle childhood deferred to their mother. Only the participants in adolescence and adulthood demonstrably preferred to cite themselves. Bar-Tal, Raviv, Raviv, and Brosch (1991) obtained converging evidence: Viewing parents as the authority on knowing about them (the children) remains stable in children between 4 and 9 years of age. Between 9 and 18 years, however, the perception of parents as epistemic authorities is gradually replaced by an increasing reliance on friends, siblings and the self.

Rosenberg (1979) suggested that children are not attuned to the subjectivity of self-knowledge, to the importance of their privileged access to their own inner states, and instead have blind faith in adults' omniscience. Only during adolescence do we see a transition to a state of recognition that we are the authority on knowledge about ourselves. Effectively, Rosenberg was arguing two things: (1) we start out thinking we don't know our own minds; and (2) the developmental transition in recognizing that we are the authority on aspects of ourselves is peculiarly tardy.

In the light of research into children's understanding of the mind, Rosenberg's conclusions appear controversial: How can we reconcile the finding that by middle childhood, participants have sophisticated understanding in many respects with the apparently contrasting suggestion that they think they don't know their own mind? After all, research amply demonstrates that they understand that beliefs (including their own) can be false, that a happy facial expression can belie inner feelings of sadness, that two people can interpret the same piece of information differently, that other people can figure something out by making an inference, and so on. Specifically, if children from the age of 7 years can identify when another person has sufficient or insufficient information for working something out (e.g., Rai & Mitchell, 2006; Taylor, 1988), then why can they not identify what things another person can or cannot work out about themselves? Is it conceivable that Rosenberg's task underestimated children? Would it be possible to pose questions that give children a chance of demonstrating what they do understand instead of leading them to answer in a way that suggests they lack understanding?

INTERIOR AND EXTERIOR SELF-KNOWLEDGE

To investigate such questions, Burton and Mitchell (2003) distinguished between two categories of self-knowledge. Following Schoeneman (1981), *interior* self-knowledge was defined as pertaining to matters a person needs to tell about him- or herself that people would otherwise have difficulty knowing, such as what your secrets are; in contrast, *exterior* self-knowledge was defined as those things about a person that others could know on the basis of evidence, such as how helpful you are. An empirical/pragmatic procedure served to create examples for each type of self-knowledge. A group of undergraduate students generated examples for each category, and subsequently a different group of undergraduates rated the previous group's examples using a Likert scale. The result was six examples each of interior and exterior self-knowledge, as shown in Table 1. Note that the subject of the question could either be the participant herself or hypothetical children Tommy and Beth. Judicious counterbalancing between participant and proxies prevented any confound between the subject and the content of the question. Similarly, the adult in the question could be a parent or teacher, though children also had the option of identifying their friend as the person who knew best. The purpose of varying *subject* and *adult* in the questions was to investigate the generality of children's judgements. If they identified adults as the authority on knowledge would this be confined to circumstances relating to the participants themselves or would they also judge that, for example, Tommy's mother knows best (i.e., better than Tommy) what games he likes?

TABLE 1

Examples of interior and exterior self-knowledge used by Burton and Mitchell (2003)

Interior	Exterior
Things a person would have to tell about themselves in order for other people to know	*Things about a person that other people could know on the basis of evidence*
Who knows best what your secrets are?	Who knows best how good you are at sums?
Who knows best what games Tommy likes?	Who knows best how well Beth can sit still?
Who knows best what you want to be when you grow up?	Who knows best how fast you can run?
When Beth cries, who knows best what is wrong?	Who knows best how hard Tommy works?
Who knows best what your favourite food is?	Who knows best how good you are at tidying your room?
Who knows best when Tommy is feeling hungry?	Who knows best how helpful Beth is?

Interestingly, the pattern of children's judgements was the same whether the subject of the question was themselves or a proxy. In other words, participants were just as likely to cite an adult as knowing best whether the question was about themselves or Tommy, and so the data presented in Figure 1 are collapsed over this variable. The top half of the Figure shows the number of times children judged that the subject (themselves, Tommy, Beth) knows best, out of the six questions of self-knowledge. The bottom half is a mirror of this pattern, showing the number of times the children judged that an adult knows best (Mother, Teacher). The left-hand side of the graph shows the data for six interior questions and the right half shows the data for six exterior questions. The Figure shows that children aged 7 years cited the subject most of the time when answering interior questions. Moreover, even though 6-year-old children did not predominantly cite the subject, they did nevertheless cite the subject more frequently when the question was about interior than exterior self-knowledge (as did older children, of course). Hence, instead of relying exclusively on trends in children's citation of an adult, this research offered a finer investigation into children's tendency to discriminate between different types of self-knowledge. In principle, it seems appropriate to cite the subject more often when the question is about interior than exterior self-knowledge, and this is something young participants demonstrated from the age of 6 years. Evidently, children have surprisingly sophisticated understanding of self-knowledge because they seem to under-stand that other people might not know some things about a person unless she or he told them, while people might be able to work some things out about a person on the basis of evidence.

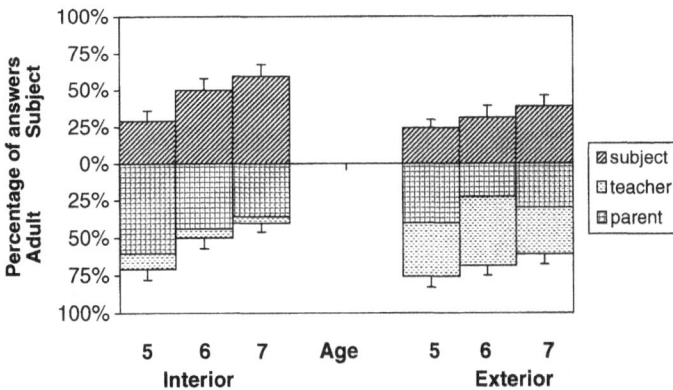

Figure 1. Children's judgements that the subject knows best (Self, Tommy, Beth) and that an adult knows best divided by age group and category (interior, exterior), from Burton and Mitchell (2003). The error bars represent the standard error of the mean.

Despite signs of children's insights, it is notable that 5-year-olds neither discriminated between interior and exterior self-knowledge nor did they tend to cite the subject as an authority on self-knowledge. This is surprising considering that children of this age traditionally perform well in a test of false belief, a test that is regarded by many (e.g., Perner, 1991) as the definitive test of ToM. Also, there is a distinct trend, suggesting that with increasing age, children are more likely to cite the subject. Even if Rosenberg had been wrong about the age at which children begin to recognize themselves as the authority on self-knowledge, at least it seems he was right about the direction of the trend, suggesting that young children do indeed start out thinking that they are not the principal authority in knowing about their own mind.

Recently, Bennett, Downie, and Murray (2007) have queried whether these findings reflect a presupposition contained within the question, "Who knows best ...?" The question seems to imply that other parties at least know something about the self's states and seeks a judgement about *whose* knowledge is superior. Bennett et al. conjectured that where shared knowledge is implied, young children may default to judging that parents' knowledge is superior. To examine this possibility 5-, 7- and 9-year-old children were asked two types of question about their self-knowledge: The standard, "Who knows best ...?" and a form in which child and mother contradict each other on a specific item of the child's self-knowledge (e.g., "Suppose you say you're feeling happy and your mum says you're not feeling happy, who would be right?" Strikingly, however, Bennett et al.'s findings confirmed the robustness of the developmental trend identified by Burton and Mitchell: Over both types of question, older children were significantly more likely to cite the self than were younger children, so that by 9 years they were fairly consistently citing the self, whereas younger children cited their mother. Nevertheless, from about 5 years of age, children begin to judge that mother is even more likely to know best when the state has been disclosed to her than when it has not been disclosed, revealing the beginnings of a grasp of epistemic authority pertaining to self in early childhood (Bennett, Mitchell, & Murray, in press).

In summary, recent research has told us several things that we did not already know. Even the youngest children do not cite themselves or their own mother when asked, "Who knows best when Tommy is feeling hungry?" Hence, children cited a *relevant* adult, suggesting that they thought an adult who is close to the subject might know best (i.e., better than the subject) about aspects of the subject's self-knowledge. If children had been seriously confused by the questions, then a systematic pattern of responding like this would not have emerged. Second, it is notable that by 6 years of age children were beginning to discriminate between interior and exterior self-knowledge and that by 7 years children cited the subject a majority of the time. Third, children assess mother's knowledge about themselves by taking into consideration her informational access from about 5 years of age. Rosenberg would never have anticipated this level of performance and insight in young children. Still, the majority response of the youngest children was to cite an adult and so there is a developmental trend towards citing the subject with increasing age, as Rosenberg had suggested.

Some things remain that we do not yet know about this intriguing aspect of development. In particular, is it correct to suppose that children's estimation of their self-knowledge increases with age? This seems the obvious explanation but there is another possibility that needs to be explored. Perhaps children at various ages estimate their self-knowledge similarly and what actually changes, what actually explains the developmental trend we observed, might be related to their changing estimation of their mother's knowledge. So, it might be that young children think their mother knows a great deal about them while older children think their mother knows less about them. In short, when young children assert that their mother knows best what their favourite food is, we cannot tell from extant data whether they think their mother knows a great deal about their favourite food or conversely whether they think that they themselves do not know much about what their favourite food is. To find out, a new study asked children to quantify how well they know, for example, when they are thinking and to quantify how well their mother knows when they (i.e., the children) are thinking (Mitchell, Teucher, Bennett, Ziegler, & Wyton, in press-a).

QUANTIFYING THE RESPONSES

Children answered seven self-knowledge questions, similar to those developed by Burton and Mitchell (2003). The focal questions asked about feeling sick, hungry, happy, angry, about when they were thinking, and what kind of person they were (self). One of the main challenges was to devise a way of allowing children to quantify how well they knew an aspect of themselves. In particular, a metaphor was needed for quantifying self-knowledge. To this end, children were introduced to 10 counters and asked to stack them in a Perspex tube to indicate how well they knew.

One of two patterns was expected of children's ratings: (1) Young children assign a low value to Self and a modest value to Mother; older children assign a high value to Self and a modest value to Mother. (2) Young children assign a modest value to Self and a high value to Mother; older children assign a modest value to Self and a low value to Mother. Actually, though, participants assigned merely a higher value to Self than to Mother and while this was true for all five age groups tested (5-, 7-, 9-, 11- and 13-year-olds), the contrast was sharper for the older participants. Surprisingly, the difference between the values assigned to Self and assigned to Mother did not change drastically from age 5 to age 13, although there was an increasing trend to assign relatively more knowledge to Self than to Mother or Teacher.

The gentle age-trend averaged over questions belies notable differences that emerged when looking at responses to each question individually. The 5- and 7-year-olds strongly contrasted how much they knew about when they were thinking with how little their mother knew. Interestingly, the contrast was less for 11- and 13-year-olds perhaps suggesting a level of adolescent doubt about how much one can access one's own mental states (cf. Kuhn, 2000). In response to many of the other questions, older participants generally tended to assign higher levels of knowledge to themselves than to an adult, compared with younger participants. An exception was feeling sick. Perhaps participants suppose that the internal signs of sickness are rather ambiguous. For example, a pain in the stomach could either be a sign of mild indigestion or it could be a sign of serious food poisoning. Perhaps participants thought that the external signs, such as pallor, sweating or a rash, would be at least as easy to interpret as internal signs. Alternatively, perhaps participants assume that being able to diagnose sickness requires special knowledge of the kind possessed by a medical professional. They might have assumed that an adult is more likely to have acquired some of that knowledge than they themselves (or any child, for that matter).

Generally, the findings from children's quantification are not fully consistent with the findings from their judgement on "who knows best". It seems that young children are inclined to judge that their mother knows best what their secrets are and yet credit a higher quantity of knowledge to themselves than to their mother when invited to stack counters. Why? There are many differences between question forms and modes of responding. Asking, "Who knows best . . .?" might alert children to the old cliché that "Mother always knows best", and this might bias their judgement. However, Burton and Mitchell (2003) included a condition in which children were asked, "Who knows most . . .?" and the pattern of results was essentially the same. Moreover, even when the mother's judgement is explicitly pitted against that of the child, children persist in deferring to their mother (Bennett et al., 2007). Still, when children have a stark choice between themselves and their mother, perhaps they choose their mother because of a discrepancy in the power relationship rather than because they think their mother knows their mind better than they do themselves.

This discussion brings into focus the fact that in Burton and Mitchell's (2003; and Bennett et al.'s, 2007, in press) studies, children were faced with a choice of contrasting alternatives (e.g., Self or Mother), whereas when stacking counters the values they assigned to self could be made independently of the value they assigned to Mother. Taking this into consideration, it would be interesting to ask children to divide 10 counters between themselves and their mother. In this circumstance, would they assign a greater proportion to their mother, commensurate with their judgement that Mother knows best? Alternatively, would they assign more counters to themselves, as when making mutually exclusive judgements for Self and Mother? If the former, making a relative (even if quantified) judgement would be sufficient to reveal the tendency to over-attribute knowledge to Mother; if the latter, then asking children to quantify (either in a relative or mutually exclusive way) would be sufficient to reveal that children recognize themselves as the authority on their own knowledge.

What have we learned from these studies? Younger children tend to judge that significant adults know best with respect to knowledge about themselves and they also assign a large amount of knowledge to significant adults when asked to quantify. In fairness, they often assign even more knowledge to themselves, but that does not negate the finding that they credit adults with a lot of knowledge. Nevertheless, we see the dawning of sophisticated understanding when 6-year-old children distinguish between interior and exterior self-knowledge, and we see something similar when children aged 5 years assign different relative quantities to Self and Adult, depending on the topic in question and on their sensitivity to whether or not relevant information has been disclosed to the adult. But why do younger children assign a large quantity of knowledge to relevant adults?

OVERTHROWING THE MOTHER OF ALL KNOWLEDGE

At least two possible explanations deserve consideration. Perhaps most obvious is that young children do not fully appreciate their privileged access to their own mental states and therefore feel that they know about their own psychology only about as much as anybody else knows, or perhaps even less than some especially wise people, like their mother or their teacher. In this case, young children can be said to *underestimate* their knowledge of themselves. Another possibility, though, is that they actually have an accurate estimate of knowledge about themselves and what their mother knows about them. Perhaps they truly do not have precise insights into their own states. So, when the child announces that she is not tired but her mother contradicts this assertion, perhaps the mother really is right.

It is difficult to investigate the relation between children's actual states and their estimate of how much they know. A way of gaining circumstantial evidence involves asking children's parents how much children know about their own states. If parents' and children's judgements converge, this might seem too much of a coincidence to have happened by chance, suggesting instead that parents' and children's estimates are roughly correct. Indeed, perhaps parents with younger children will assign relatively low quantities of self-knowledge to their children while parents with older children assign higher quantities.

Mitchell et al. (in press-a) duly interviewed mothers and the data proved to be both surprising and highly illuminating. There was a systematic discrepancy in the ratings of mothers and their children in that mothers effectively judged that they knew more than their children about their children's inner states. This tendency was most marked for the youngest children; older children's judgements were largely in agreement with their mothers' estimates. Although this is only circumstantial evidence in that we do not know objectively about the accuracy of children's judgements, the finding suggested that younger children might actually be *overestimating* how much they know about themselves. If that interpretation is correct, it is extremely surprising for it directly opposes the received wisdom of Rosenberg's work, spanning four decades, which famously implies that young children underestimate how well they know themselves.

In short, when young children are reticent in crediting themselves with more knowledge than their mother about themselves, perhaps they are to be applauded; indeed, perhaps young children ought to be more cautious in how much knowledge they credit to themselves. As they get older, they gradually assign more knowledge to themselves and this developmental change seems to coincide with a corresponding change in their mother, who recognizes her child's increasing understanding of itself.

Why do children change (albeit gradually) as they grow older, whereupon they raise estimations of how much they know about themselves relative to how much they estimate that their mother knows? What aspects of experience stimulate a growing scepticism about Mother knowing best? In a quest to supply an answer it is worth exploring cognitive as well as the social psychological issues.

(1) Cognitive models

A cognitive explanation says that participants develop ability in metacognition that allows them to note that sometimes their mother gives incorrect diagnoses and that these coincide with occasions when, for example, the child deliberately controls facial expressions. The child can then begin to appreciate that Mother's diagnoses of psychological states are merely interpretations and that these are subject to error, as when the child emits misleading cues.

With a view to investigating the cognitive/metacognitive explanation, Burton and Mitchell (2003) included a test of children's understanding of the (limited) value of partial information (Taylor, 1988). In the task, children are invited to estimate another person's interpretation of a scene when their view is restricted to a small portion of the information. Because the view is severely restricted, adults judge (quite correctly) either that the other person will not know what is in the scene or that the other will misinterpret the information. In contrast, children below about 7 years tend to overestimate another's ability to correctly interpret the information. Effectively, they overestimate another person's ability to make correct inferences. If young children generally overestimate people's ability to interpret clues, then this could extend to, and indeed explain, their tendency to over attribute knowledge to their parent on matters of the child's self-knowledge. That is, children might overestimate their parent's ability to infer the child's inner states from the external behavioural clues. However, there was no sign of any correlation between children's judgements of self-knowledge and their overestimation of another person's knowledge in a partial information task. As yet, then, there is no evidence in support of the metacognitive explanation. Why?

One possibility is that development in identifying the self as the authority on self-knowledge is not explicable at the cognitive level. Another possibility is that it is explicable on this level, but the extant evidence is unsuitable for demonstrating thus. It could be unsuitable either because the measure of general inferential ability is less than ideal (Taylor's task), or because the measure of children's recognition of themselves as the authority on self-knowledge is less than ideal (judging who knows best) or both. Evidence collected subsequent to Burton and Mitchell's (2003) study already speaks to the possibility of their measure not being ideal, in the sense that children, even the youngest tested, assign a surprisingly large amount of knowledge to themselves when stacking counters. Perhaps a correlation would emerge between Taylor's measure and the counter-stacking procedure, and this possibility is yet to be tested empirically.

(2) Cultural models: Another version of individualism–collectivism?

A social psychological explanation says that children's developing view of themselves as having privileged access to their own subjective states is determined by their culture. In many developed countries typical of the West, people have an individualistic orientation, where Self is tacitly regarded as a stable and enduring entity that transcends specific situations. So, although behaviour will be strongly influenced by customs and laws, people assume nevertheless that an important explanation for many aspects of behaviour relates to a constellation of personality traits. A sign to this effect manifests in the "fundamental attribution error", which is that when explaining another person's action, participants typically overestimate the role of traits, and underestimate the impact of the situation. Hence, we are attuned to an underlying Self, and it follows that we suppose that we ourselves have privileged access considering that we can know ourselves subjectively via introspection, whereas others could only infer what we are like from clues in our external behaviour. A consequence, according to Nisbett (2003), is that the individual is upheld as paramount.

In sharp contrast, the typical psyche in some collectivist cultures that are common in the East is said to be rather different. There, the self as an enduring and stable entity is not strongly recognized. Instead, people are effectively regarded as being different in different contexts, according to the roles they play. To illustrate, Nisbett reports that Americans and Japanese give very different answers when asked, "Tell me about yourself". Americans tend to talk about inner and enduring traits that transcend context and time period, while Japanese give a myriad of answers, supplying different detail for different contexts. For example, "I am serious at work, but fun-loving at home, etc." Consequently, the focus in a collectivist culture, like Japan, rests not upon the individual but on contexts and especially the relationships between people, where the group rather than the individual is paramount. According to Nisbett, the: "Goal for self in relation to society is not so much to establish superiority or uniqueness, but to achieve harmony within a network of supportive social relationships and to play one's part in achieving collective ends" (2003, p. 55).

Contrasting individualistic and collectivisitic culture proves to be enlightening with respect to our inquiry into children's growing tendency to identify themselves as the principal authority on their own psyche: Presumably, the prevailing cultural attitude in places where data has been collected so far (Britain or, in Rosenberg's case, the USA) is that the individual (Self) is sharply in focus. In this environment, children become attuned to the ways they are different from others; and they are best placed to analyse their own unique characteristics, thanks to their privileged access via introspection. But in collectivistic cultures, the individual is less sharply in focus and so the prevailing view might be that one could know what a person is like from knowing their role and the context. Unique characteristics might not be so readily considered and therefore having privileged access to these via introspection might not be regarded as having great value in determining what you are like. Indeed, if members of a collectivistic society uphold the group as paramount, perhaps they would be attuned to a collective or shared psyche and regard their self as subordinate to that. If so, perhaps they suppose that others know as much about them as they do themselves.

If these speculations are well founded, then there might be a different developmental trend between individualistic Westerners and collectivistic Easterners. While individualistic participants gradually shift to assigning more self-knowledge to themselves than to other people, perhaps this shift does not occur in collectivistic participants. If so, then seemingly culture has an important influence on children's developing understanding of the mind, a possibility that has recently been highlighted by Mitchell, Souglidou, Mills, and Ziegler (2007). More generally, Nisbett (2003) persuasively argued that these culturally shaped attitudes toward the self have a wider impact on diverse aspects of cognitive functioning, ranging from problem solving to perception.

To investigate possible developmental differences between collectivistic and individualistic participants, Mitchell, Teucher, Kikuno, and Bennett (in press-b) conducted a study in which Japanese and British children were asked to quantify how much they know and how much relevant adults know about their inner states. Children in the two cultures generally used the rating scales in a similar way, but there were nevertheless marked differences in developmental trends, which were most salient in children aged around 7 years (the youngest children tested in the study). Generally, the Japanese children were much more likely to assign relatively larger amounts of knowledge about themselves to their parent than children tested in the UK. While the children in both cultures tended to assign similar levels of knowledge to their parent, the British children tended to assign more knowledge to themselves than to their parents; the Japanese children, in contrast, assigned similar amounts of knowledge to themselves as to their parent. Nevertheless, Japanese and British children aged around 9 and 11 years judged similarly to each other in assigning more knowledge to themselves than to their parents.

We have already suggested reasons why Japanese children might be inclined to assign as much knowledge to a parent as to themselves, but why is this cultural difference apparent only in younger children? One possibility is that British children aged 7 years are not entirely adept at appreciating that their parent can infer things about the children when the parent does not have direct access to the child's inner states. This explanation accords with the cognitive model of development proposed above. While Japanese children aged 7 years might also have difficulty grasping how people can know things via inference, belonging to a collectivistic culture could compensate by helping them to understand that their mind is shared with others and therefore accessible to others.

SUGGESTIONS FOR FUTURE RESEARCH

Undoubtedly, the extent to which we credit others with a large amount of knowledge about ourselves will depend on the kind of self-knowledge in question. We already know that from about 6 years children distinguish between interior and exterior self-knowledge (Burton & Mitchell, 2003); but when do they begin to make distinctions between other kinds of self-knowledge and how does this relate to the broader picture of developing an understanding of the mind?

It is puzzling, given the prodigious body of research on children's "theories of mind", that very little is known about possible developmental changes in children's conception of the relation between psychological states and behaviour. In his work on social perspective-taking, Selman (1980; Selman, Lavin, & Brion-Meisels, 1982) found that young children "believe that a person's overt actions will eventually belie his/her inner attitude—that is, if one is a careful observer of another's outside, then one can begin to make a good guess about how that person feels inside" (1983, p. 71). In short, "the child responds as if he/she believes that the inner can be ascertained from the outer" (1983, p. 74). However, to the best of our knowledge, little if any research has followed up such claims. As we have indicated above, we believe that attention to this issue could valuably extend accounts of children's developing folk psychology.

Another consideration that might be addressed by future research relates to judgements about *states* (e.g., feeling hungry) and *traits* (e.g., being shy). While children may correctly cite themselves as knowing a relatively large amount about their psychological *states*, they may lean towards crediting their parent with having a relatively large amount of knowledge in connection with their traits. States are usually ephemeral and rather different from a normal mode of functioning, such that the state being experienced is rather salient to the child. In contrast, the child's traits are relatively stable and therefore perhaps difficult to detect through introspection; instead, children might come to recognize that they have a certain trait on being told as much by others. This might give the impression that significant others know more about this aspect of their self than they do themselves.

Another avenue for further investigation concerns atypical development. To this end, we have recently interviewed adults and adolescents diagnosed with autism to enquire how well they think they know themselves (Mitchell & O'Keefe, 2008). Interestingly, these participants differed from comparison individuals in that they did not credit themselves with having more knowledge about themselves than they assigned to their mother. Effectively, they judged as if they did not recognize that they had first-person privileged and subjective access to their own mind. This gives rise to a paradox, which is that (1) we can plausibly assume that individuals with autism lack understanding of the mind (including their own mind) and (2) individuals with autism seem to recognize that they do not have much insight into (their own) mind. And yet how could they appreciate that they lacked insight into the mind unless they had a certain level of mentalistic appreciation in the first place—hence, the paradox. Perhaps carers of individuals with autism communicate, intentionally or otherwise, that they (the individuals with autism) do not have much insight into the mind. If individuals with autism recognize their own limitations in mentalizing, then this could be beneficial if it motivates them to work at acquiring a better understanding of mental life.

CONCLUSION

Investigations into children's evaluation of how much they know about themselves and how much they think others know throw up a plethora of interesting findings that raise a variety of theoretical questions relevant to central aspects of the human psyche. Surprisingly, it seems we start out thinking that we might not be best qualified to know our mind. Developmental changes in coming to identify ourselves as the authority on self-knowledge seem long drawn out, and these changes appear to be susceptible to cultural influences. Recently, it was established that children begin to appreciate this from about the age of 5 or 6 years. The extent to which we perceive ourselves to be an authority on self-knowledge seems to depend on the kind of self-knowledge at stake. We need to obtain more detail on the various facets of self-knowledge about which children do and do not perceive themselves as the authority. We hope that this review serves to highlight central issues in the early development of folk psychology and that other researchers will be similarly inspired to address the fundamental aspects of reflections on self-knowledge outlined here.

REFERENCES

Apperly, I., & Robinson, E. J. (1998). Children's mental representation of referential relations. *Cognition, 67*, 287–309.

Banerjee, R., Yuill, N., Larson, C., Easton, K., Robinson, E., & Rowley, M. (2007). Children's differentiation between beliefs about matters of fact and matters of opinion. *Developmental Psychology, 43*, 1084–1096.

Bar-Tal, D., Raviv, A., Raviv, A., & Brosch, M. E. (1991). Perception of epistemic authority and attribution for its choice as a function of knowledge area and age. *European Journal of Social Psychology, 21*, 477–492.

Bennett, M., Downie, A., & Murray, P. (2007). Children's judgments about their own self-knowledge: An investigation of the effect of question form. *European Journal of Developmental Psychology, 4*, 241–250.

Bennett, M., Mitchell, P., & Murray, P. (in press). Children's judgments about their own self-knowledge: The role of disclosure to other. *British Journal of Developmental Psychology.*

Burton, S., & Mitchell, P. (2003). Judging who knows best about yourself: Developmental change in citing the self across middle childhood. *Child Development, 74*, 426–444.

Chandler, M., & Boyes, M. (1982). Social-cognitive development. In B. Wolman (Ed.), *Handbook of developmental psychology* (pp. 387–402). Englewood Cliffs, NJ: Prentice-Hall.

Fricker, E. (1998). Self-knowledge: Special access versus artefact of grammar—A dichotomy rejected. In C. Wright, B. C. Smith, & C. MacDonald (Eds.), *Knowing our own minds* (pp. 155–206). Oxford, UK: Clarendon Press.

Friedman, O., & Leslie, A. M. (2004). Mechanisms of belief-desire reasoning: Inhibition and bias. *Psychological Science, 15*, 547–552.

Harris, P. L., & Gross, D. (1988). Children's understanding of real and apparent emotion. In J. W. Astington, P. L. Harris, & D. R. Olson (Eds.), *Developing theories of mind* (pp. 295–314). Cambridge, UK: Cambridge University Press.

Hulme, S., Mitchell, P., & Wood, D. (2003). Six-year-olds' difficulties handling intentional contexts. *Cognition, 87*, 73–99.

Kuhn, D. (2000). Theory of mind, metacognition and reasoning: A life-span perspective. In P. Mitchell & K. J. Riggs (Eds.), *Children's reasoning and the mind* (pp. 301–326). Hove, UK: Psychology Press.

McDonald, C. (2002). Theories of mind and the commonsense view. *Mind and Language, 17*, 467–488.

Mitchell, P., & O'Keefe, K. (2008). Do individuals with autism spectrum disorder think they know their own minds? *Journal of Autism and Developmental Disorders, 38*, 1591–1597.

Mitchell, P., Robinson, E. J., Isaacs, J. E., & Nye, R. M. (1996). Contamination in reasoning about false belief: An instance of realist bias in adults but not children. *Cognition, 59*, 1–21.

Mitchell, P., Souglidou, M., Mills, L., & Ziegler, F. (2007). Seeing is believing: How participants in different subcultures make judgments of people's credulity. *European Journal of Social Psychology, 37*, 573–585.

Mitchell, P., Teucher, U., Bennett, M., Ziegler, F., & Wyton, R. (in press-a). Do children start out thinking they don't know their own minds? *Mind and Language*.

Mitchell, P., Teucher, U., Kikuno, H., & Bennett, M. (in press-b). Developing a sense of knowing your own mind: How children in different cultures quantify knowledge about themselves. *International Journal of Behavioral Development*.

Nisbett, R. E. (2003). *The geography of thought: How Asians and Westerners think differently ... and why*. New York: Free Press.

Onishi, K. H., & Bailargeon, R. (2005). Do 15-month-old infants understand false beliefs? *Science, 308*(5719), 255–258.

Perner, J. (1991). *Understanding the representational mind*. London: MIT Press.

Rai, R., & Mitchell, P. (2004). Five-year-olds' difficulty with false belief when the sought entity is a person. *Journal of Experimental Child Psychology, 89*, 112–126.

Rai, R., & Mitchell, P. (2006). Children's ability to impute inferentially-based knowledge. *Child Development, 77*, 1081–1093.

Robinson, E. J., Champion, H., & Mitchell, P. (1999). Children's ability to infer utterance veracity from speaker informedness. *Developmental Psychology, 35*, 535–546.

Robinson, E., & Whitcombe, E. L. (2003). Children's suggestibility in relation to their understanding about sources of knowledge. *Child Development, 74*(1), 48–62.

Robinson, E. J., & Whittaker, S. J. (1987). Children's conceptions of relations between meanings, messages and reality. *British Journal of Developmental Psychology, 5*, 81–90.

Rosenberg, M. (1979). *Conceiving the self*. New York: Basic Books.

Rowley, M., & Robinson, E. J. (2007). Understanding the truth about subjectivity. *Social Development, 16*, 741–757.

Schoeneman, T. J. (1981). Reports of the sources of self-knowledge. *Journal of Personality, 49*, 284–294.

Selman, R. L. (1980). *The growth of interpersonal understanding*. New York: Academic Press.

Selman, R. L., Lavin, D. R., & Brion-Meisels, S. (1982). Troubled children's use of self-reflection. In F. C. Serafica (Ed.), *Social-cognitive development in context* (pp. 62–99). London: Guilford Press.

Sodian, B., & Wimmer, H. (1987). Children's understanding of inference as a source of knowledge. *Child Development, 58*, 424–433.

Taylor, M. (1988). Conceptual perspective taking: Children's ability to distinguish what they know from what they see. *Child Development, 59*, 703–718.

Wellman, H. M. (1990). *The child's theory of mind*. Cambridge, MA: MIT Press.

Wellman, H. M., Cross, D., & Watson, J. (2001). Meta-analysis of theory of mind development: The truth about false belief. *Child Development, 72*, 655–684.

Wright, C. (1998). Self-knowledge: The Wittgensteinian legacy. In C. Wright, B. C. Smith, & C. MacDonald (Eds.), *Knowing our own minds* (pp. 13–45). Oxford, UK: Clarendon Press.

EUROPEAN JOURNAL OF DEVELOPMENTAL PSYCHOLOGY
2010, 7 (1), 85–103

Ψ Psychology Press
Taylor & Francis Group

Dynamics of the Theory of Mind construct: A developmental perspective

Mieke P. Ketelaars, Marjolijn van Weerdenburg and
Ludo Verhoeven

*Radboud University Nijmegen, Behavioural Science Institute, Nijmegen, The
Netherlands*

Juliane M. Cuperus and Kino Jansonius

Sint Marie, Eindhoven, The Netherlands

Theory of Mind (ToM) encompasses a wide variety of abilities, which develop during childhood. However, to date most ToM research has focused on the single concept of false-belief understanding, and examined ToM only in young children. Furthermore, there is a lack of implementation of a longitudinal design, which examines the dynamics of the ToM construct over several years. Our longitudinal study measured the abilities of a group of 5-year-old children $(n = 77)$ in mainstream education during three consecutive years, on aspects of ToM related to emotion understanding and false-belief understanding. The results provide support for significant improvements in emotion understanding and false-belief understanding between the ages of 5 and 7. Whereas emotion attribution was already largely developed at age 5, more intricate aspects of emotion understanding, such as understanding display rules and understanding mixed emotions showed significant developments. Over the course of the years, children also showed an increasing awareness of false-belief understanding. In addition to the developmental growth, the different ToM aspects were found to be relatively stable over time. Correlations as well as predictive relations between emotion understanding and false-belief understanding could be identified. Finally, there was evidence for the role of language ability in the development of the ToM aspects under consideration. The results support the notion that ToM abilities measured at age 5 are not just a snapshot but provide a longer-term outlook as well.

Keywords: Development; Emotion understanding; False-belief understanding.

Correspondence should be addressed to Mieke Ketelaars, Radboud University Nijmegen, PO Box 9104, NL-6500 HE Nijmegen, The Netherlands. E-mail: M.Ketelaars@pwo.ru.nl

http://www.psypress.com/edp   DOI: 10.1080/17405620903482081

The ability to understand other people's mental states, known as Theory of Mind (ToM), is an important marker in child development, and has been studied extensively (e.g., Baron-Cohen, 2001; Bartsch, 1998; Cutting & Dunn, 1999; Flavell, Flavell, & Green, 1990; Hughes et al., 2000; Moses & Flavell, 1990; Perner & Lang, 1999; Repacholi & Slaughter, 2003; Wellman & Liu, 2004). Whereas early studies on ToM often applied a single-task paradigm limited to false-belief understanding (see Wellman, Cross, & Watson, 2001; Wellman & Liu, 2004, for an overview), more recently researchers have started to embrace the wide variety of abilities that are connected to ToM (e.g., Cutting & Dunn, 1999; Wellman & Liu, 2004), which also includes several aspects of emotion understanding. This has led to the view that early ToM abilities may function as stepping stones for later abilities. However, although there has been an increase in awareness of developmental issues, studies adopting a longitudinal design are still scarce (but see Flynn, 2006, for an example). Those that do apply a longitudinal design often investigate only limited aspects of ToM. For instance, Amsterlaw and Wellman (2006) investigated the gradual development of false-belief understanding, as did Flynn (2006). Brown and Dunn (1996), and Pons and Harris (2005) studied the development of several aspects of emotion understanding. Yet we know little of the interactions involved in the development of different aspects of ToM. This study attempts to answer some issues related to this gap using a large sample of children who have been studied longitudinally over a period of two years. Before going into the design and results of the present study, a short overview will be given of the key ToM concepts of emotion understanding and false-belief understanding, and their developmental trajectories.

According to Buitelaar, Van der Wees, Swaab-Barneveld, and Van der Gaag (1999): "emotion understanding includes the ability to discriminate the various expressions of emotions in facial, gestural, and verbal display and, in doing so, to be sensitive to dimensions of intensity, complexity and contextual colouring" (p. 869). Basic levels of emotion understanding consist of visual recognition of emotions and their causes. As Brown and Dunn (1996) demonstrated, children as young as three years have been reported to understand causal attributions of emotions. The more intricate aspects of emotion understanding do not develop until the early and middle school years (Brown & Dunn, 1996).

One of the more advanced levels of emotion understanding consists of the ability to understand that different (conflicting) emotions can occur together (Brown & Dunn, 1996). Understanding these so-called mixed emotions is manifested for example when children realize they can be both afraid and excited on a ride in a roller-coaster (Kestenbaum & Gelman, 1995). It has been stated that children under the age of 7 appear to experience problems understanding mixed feelings, although they do seem to be able to express their own ambivalent feelings from an early age (Kestenbaum & Gelman, 1995).

A second advanced level of emotion understanding consists of the ability to understand and apply display rules that govern emotions (Underwood, Coie, & Herbsman, 1992). At a young age, children begin to understand that there are social norms that apply in the expression of emotion (Banerjee, 1997). For example, they conceal their real emotion upon receiving a present they do not really like. Consistent with the developmental pathway of mixed emotions, Banerjee (1997) found the application of display rules to develop before the understanding of these rules. Moreover, it seems that this ability gradually develops during childhood: in a study by Saarni (1979) only 10-year-old children were able to offer a justification when asked about display rules, but 6- and 8-year-olds did understand rules governing emotions when prompted specifically. Banerjee (1997), however, found that children as young as 3 years were able to understand the intricacies involved in display rules.

Emotion understanding seems to evolve gradually and in several steps. In a longitudinal design Pons and Harris (2005) found that emotion understanding, as measured with a variety of tasks, followed a predictable course of change in children aged 7 to 11 through three stages. At the first stage children understand external cues of emotions, e.g., facial expressions, whereas at the second stage they also understand mental aspects of emotions, e.g., the role of beliefs and desires on emotions. The final stage consists of more reflective aspects of emotion, e.g., mixed emotions. Pons and Harris also found a certain stability of emotion understanding, i.e., children with low emotion understanding showed similar low performance one year later. In an older study by Hughes and Dunn (1998), longitudinal correlations in emotion understanding were also visible in a younger sample of 4- and 5-year-old children over a period of one year.

The second key concept of ToM consists of false-belief understanding. False-belief understanding is defined as the ability to understand that others can have an inaccurate understanding (a false belief) of reality. As stated, false-belief understanding is often considered to be the litmus test of ToM (Wellman et al., 2001). In a comprehensive meta-analysis on the emergence of first-order false-belief understanding, Wellman et al. (2001) found evidence for a "conceptual shift" between the ages of 2½ and 5 years. A second developmental shift occurs at around the age of 6 or 7, when children are also able to succeed on second-order false-belief tasks, i.e., beliefs about beliefs (Perner & Wimmer, 1985). Nevertheless, as shown by Mutter, Alcorn, and Welsh (2006), first-order false-belief understanding is by no means fully developed by the age of 5, and great individual variance exists in the age at which children are able to successfully pass tests of false belief. As with emotion understanding, false-belief understanding develops gradually, with clear precursors such as understanding diverse beliefs and desires (Wellman & Liu, 2004). Although false-belief understanding is often considered a hallmark in the cognitive development of ToM, the longitudinal stability of false-belief understanding has not been established unequivocally. For instance, Hughes and Dunn (1998) could not establish a significant correlation in ToM performance of 4-year-olds and their performance one year later, although they did find several significant correlations over a period of half a year. Similarly, in another study by Hughes (1998), no significant correlation was found over a period of one year.

Emotion understanding and false-belief understanding are related in nature, since they both hinge on an understanding of subjective mental states rather than reality and thus require reasoning about beliefs and desires (Bloom, 2003). Despite this relation, research in these areas has been developing quite independently (Cutting & Dunn, 1999). Buitelaar et al. (1999) found a moderate correlation between false-belief understanding and emotion understanding. However, their research was based solely on emotion recognition using visual expressions. Converging evidence comes from a study by Cutting and Dunn (1999), who showed that both aspects should be considered distinct abilities, though they are significantly related (with correlations between .39 and .44). Their conclusion was based on the fact that neither variable contributed unique variance once family background, age, and language were taken into account. De Rosnay, Pons, Harris, and Morrell (2004) also found a significant correlation between emotion attribution and false-belief understanding. It should be noted that they assessed the ability to make (false) belief-based emotion attributions.

In conclusion, longitudinal research into ToM viewed as a dynamic construct involving a variety of skills is scarce. Although a start has been made in studying ToM in a longitudinal setting, the main bulk of literature has focused on cross-sectional data. In addition, the studies that have used a longitudinal design have focused mainly on young children. This is not without reason, since major steps in the development of ToM take place during these early years. However, ToM is by no means fully developed by this time. It would, therefore, be worthwhile to investigate the developmental trajectories of ToM beyond the early preschool years. This study attempted to address some issues regarding these later developments. More specifically, this study had the following goals:

1. To examine the developmental progression of ToM.
2. To gain more insight into the dimensions of ToM and their stability over time.
3. To explore the dynamics of ToM abilities as a function of children's age.
4. To explore the dynamics of ToM abilities as a function of children's language ability.

Additionally, we considered the influence of gender and socioeconomic status (SES) of the parents in relation to the developmental progression of ToM.

METHOD

Participants

The sample included 77 children (54 boys, 23 girls) who were part of a larger study. All children spoke Dutch as a first language and did not show any learning problems or behavioural problems according to their teachers. Their mean age at Time 1 was 5;6 years, at Time 2 their mean age was 6;5 years and at Time 3 their mean age was 7;5 years. Additional information on the participants is provided in Table 1. Teachers were also asked to classify the highest level of completed education of the parents on a 4-point scale. A score of 1 was given when parents finished only elementary education. A score of 2 was given when parents had a degree in lower general secondary education, whereas a score of 3 was given when parents had a degree in higher general secondary education. A score of 4 was given when parents attained a college or university degree. No parents were classified into the lowest educational level.

Measures

For the measurement of ToM abilities a booklet was created by the authors. The booklet contained pictures that were accompanied by stories. All items in the tasks consisted of similar procedures using verbal stories and visual aid (see Figure 1 for a sample of a story illustration). The faces of the story characters were depicted in a neutral fashion. During the stories, several questions were asked regarding emotion understanding (emotion attribution, mixed emotions, display rules) and false-belief understanding (change of location, conceptual perspective taking). The following paragraphs provide information on the tasks and the scoring of the different ToM tasks.

TABLE 1
Participants information

	Time 1	Time 2	Time 3
Number of participants	77	76	74
Boys/girls	54/23	54/22	52/22
Age in years (*SD* in months)	5;6 (3.5)	6;5 (3.3)	7;5 (3.8)
Range of age (in months)	59–73	72–86	83–99

Figure 1. Story illustration sample.

Emotion attribution. The children were presented with four emotion-attribution tasks. In these tasks, children heard an emotion-evoking story (e.g., finding out someone is cheating while playing hide and seek). Having heard the story, children were asked to make an emotion attribution: "*How would [story character] feel? Would he/she feel happy, sad, angry or scared?*" Children received a score of 2 for an item when the answer was considered correct. A score of 1 was granted when a child substituted an emotion with a correctly poled emotion (either negative or positive) that was considered partly correct but simplified (i.e., substituting the emotion attribution scared for the emotion sad and angry when someone has run away from home). Since one of the items was considered too easy, with a success rate of 97% at Time 1, it was decided to eliminate this item from the analyses. The score for this task is the mean score achieved on the three items.

Mixed emotions. The children were presented with two mixed-emotion tasks. In these tasks children heard a story that would provoke two conflicting emotions in the story character (e.g., two friends are playing soccer in a match. One of them scores, while the other one does not although he really wanted to.) Having heard the story, children were asked an emotion-attribution question and a justification question: "*Would [story character] feel happy, sad or both happy and sad at the same time? Why?*" The justification question had to be answered correctly to get credited a score of 2. In all other cases a score of 0 was assigned. The score for this task is the mean score achieved on the two items.

Display rules.   The children were presented with two display-rules tasks. In these tasks children heard an emotion-evoking story in which the hiding of the emotion would be provoked (e.g., being scared to go off a high slide in the swimming pool, but having a friend nearby who does want to go off the slide). Having heard the story, children were asked whether the protagonist would display the emotion or not. Subsequently they were asked to justify their answer: "*Would [story character] show that he/she is scared? Why?*" A probe question was asked if a child did not answer correctly. The probe question was asked to inform the child that a choice existed: "*In this story [story character] can either choose to show her feelings or hide them. What would you do? Why?*" Answers were only considered correct and granted a score of 2 when either one of the questions was answered correctly in combination with an accurate justification. In all other cases a score of 0 was assigned. The score for this task is the mean score achieved on the two items.

False-belief understanding.   The children were presented with three change-of-location, first-order false-belief tasks (e.g., a boy hiding from his mother after playing in the living room—subsequently the mother tries to find her son). Change of location could include a person as in the example, but also an object. After hearing the story, children were asked about the false belief of one of the story characters: "*Where would [story character] look for [the object]?*" To obtain a score of 1 on the first-order false-belief questions, a memory question pertaining to the actual location of the object had to be answered correctly as well as the false-belief question. The score for this task is the mean score achieved on the three items.

Conceptual perspective taking.   The children were presented with two conceptual-perspective-taking tasks. Adapted from Lalonde and Chandler (2002), children were shown a picture and asked what was on it. Subsequently, part of the picture was covered, in such a way that only a small part (which could not be identified as the whole picture) was still visible. Children were asked to infer about the belief of a classmate: "*If a classmate walked into the room and saw this picture, what would he/she think was on it?*" Only answers not pertaining to the true nature of the picture were considered correct and granted a score of 1. Following the scoring procedure of Lalonde and Chandler, answers that referred partly to the true nature of the picture were granted a score of 1. The score for this task is the mean score achieved on the two items.

Phi correlations for each of the items within a subtask were computed. All items within a subtask correlated significantly ($p < .05$), except for the phi correlation between two emotion understanding items ($p = .07$) and the phi correlation between two false-belief understanding items.

Receptive vocabulary.   For measuring receptive vocabulary, a subtest of the Dutch Language Test for Children (Verhoeven & Vermeer, 2001) was administered. The TAK is a standardized test for 4- to 10-year-old children. In the receptive vocabulary subtest, the child is presented with a word and is asked to select the picture illustrating that word out of four pictures. The maximum number of items is 96, and the task is discontinued after five consecutive errors.

Procedure

At all points in time, the children were tested at their schools in two sessions of approximately 50 minutes each. Upon entering the room the children were first familiarized with the situation and with the experimenter. Since the ToM items were asked over the course of several stories, the tasks were completed in a fixed order. The measurements at Time 1, Time 2, and Time 3 were separated by a time interval of approximately one year.

RESULTS

Developmental progression of ToM

To assess the developmental progression of ToM abilities, means and standard deviations were computed for all ToM tasks at Time 1, Time 2, and Time 3. Next, repeated-measures analyses of variance (ANOVAs) with planned repeated contrasts were performed to assess whether there was significant growth in ToM abilities from Time 1 to Time 2, and from Time 2 to Time 3. As can be gathered from Table 2, the repeated-measurement ANOVAs showed a time effect for four of the five ToM tasks.

The repeated-measures ANOVA on the emotion-attribution scores was the only task that did not reveal a significant time effect. No increase in scores was visible between either time point. All other increases were significant with the following exceptions: the display rules score did not

TABLE 2
Means and standard deviations of ToM scores at Time 1, Time 2, and Time 3 and the
results of the repeated-measures ANOVA

Task	Time 1		Time 2		Time 2		F	df	p	η_p^2
	M	SD	M	SD	M	SD				
Emotion attribution	1.54	0.35	1.55	0.37	1.56	0.35	0.13	2,142	.88	.00
Mixed emotions	0.46	0.65	0.86	0.81	1.21	0.84	22.37	2,142	.00	.24
Display rules	0.16	0.43	0.63	0.66	0.74	0.73	10.51	2,84	.00	.20
False belief	0.61	0.35	0.72	0.28	0.81	0.26	14.11	2,142	.00	.17
Conceptual perspective taking	0.95	0.84	1.52	0.71	1.69	0.58	24.11	2,118	.00	.29

Note: Range of Emotion attribution scores $= 0–2$; Range of Mixed emotions score $= 0–2$; Range of Display rules score $= 0–2$; Range of False belief score $= 0–1$; Range of Conceptual perspective score $= 0–2$.

increase from Time 2 to Time 3, and neither did the conceptual perspective-taking score.

Of the five ToM tasks standardized z-scores were computed with $M = 0$ and $SD = 1$ using the entire 3-year set of measurements. Figure 2 graphically depicts the development of the different ToM abilities over time, using the z-scores to allow for comparisons between the tasks.

Although we found evidence for developmental growth on several measures, we wanted to roughly assess the year that children started to grasp the notion of the tasks. For this, one-sample t-tests were performed. An arbitrary crossover performance level of 50% correct answers was chosen to indicate an awareness of the measured ability. A one-sample t-test on the mixed-emotions task showed that the scores at Time 1 fell significantly below the 50% performance level ($p < .001$), indicating a disposition expecting the sensation of one emotion rather than two. At Time 2 the mean score on the mixed-emotion task did not differ from our reference performance level ($p = .27$). Similarly, the mean performance on the conceptual-perspective-taking task at Time 1 did not differ from our reference performance level ($p = .55$). Finally, the mean performance on the display-rules task did not reach our reference performance level at any time point ($p < .01$ for Time 1 and Time 2, $p < .05$ for Time 3), indicating that the understanding of display rules is still largely unknown territory for our 7-year-olds.

Effect of socioeconomic status and gender

To explore the influence of parental educational level (both paternal and maternal) on ToM performance Pearson's correlations were computed. The

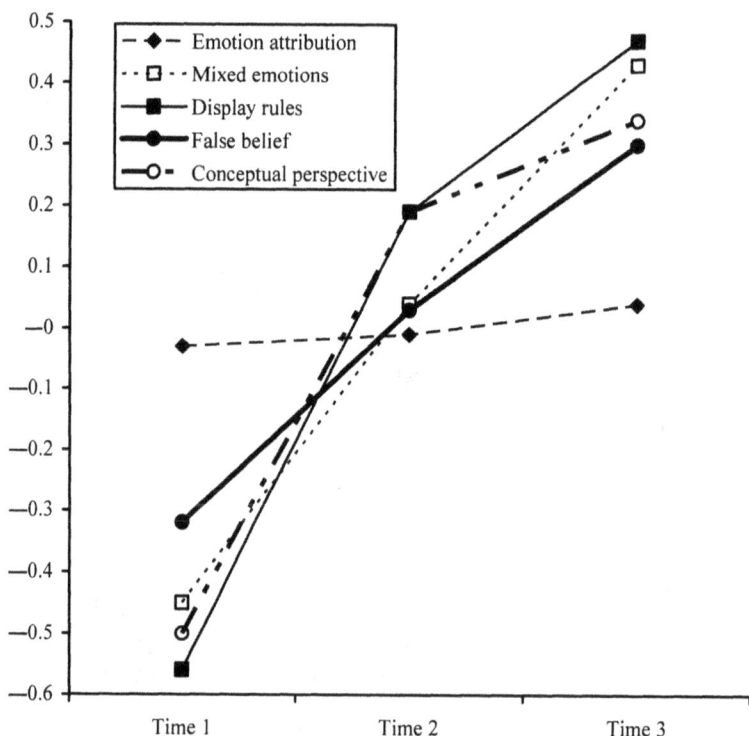

Figure 2. Developmental progression of ToM abilities over Time 1, Time 2, and Time 3.

paternal educational level correlated with ToM performance to a limited extent. It was only correlated to the first-order false-belief score at Time 3 ($r = .30$, $p < .05$). Maternal educational level, however, persistently correlated with several ToM aspects. At Time 1, it was positively correlated with the false-belief score ($r = .32$, $p = .01$). The correlation with false-belief understanding persisted at Time 2 ($r = .22$, $p = .08$, marginally significant) and Time 3 ($r = .35$, $p < .01$). Moreover, maternal educational level was also persistently correlated with the understanding of mixed emotions ($r = .29$, $p < .05$; $r = .27$, $p < .05$; and $r = .29$, $p < .02$, for the three consecutive time points). In addition there was a significant negative correlation at Time 3 with the emotion-attribution task ($r = -.29$, $p < .05$). This result can possibly be explained by the fact that the relatively easy emotion-attribution task put some children on the wrong track: they came up with more intricate emotions, and thus failed the task. To explore possible gender differences in ToM understanding, we conducted t-tests. No significant differences were found for gender.

Dimensions of ToM

To verify that our ToM items could indeed be subdivided into several aspects of ToM abilities, we performed a principal component analysis with varimax rotation at all time points (see Table 3). Since even our 7-year-olds did not show an active awareness on our display-rules task at any time point, it was decided to eliminate this task from the analysis. The factor analysis provided four factors which explained 59% of the variance. The first factor was related to both conceptual perspective-taking items and explained roughly 22% of the variance. The second factor was related to the first-order false-belief items and explained roughly 14% of the variance. The third factor consisted of the mixed-emotion items, explaining 13% of the variance. The final factor consisted of the emotion-attribution items and explained an additional 10% of the variance. As such, the results of the factor analysis supported our division into four sets of ToM-related tasks.

Stability in change of ToM over time

Using structural equation modelling (SEM) in AMOS 6.0 (Arbuckle, 2005), longitudinal stability of the various ToM abilities was investigated for each of the measured ToM abilities using quasi-simplex models. The goodness-of-fit statistics of the four models are shown in Table 4 (Models A–D). Goodness of fit of the models was assessed by several indices: the standard χ^2 test and alternative goodness-of-fit indices such as the *Adjusted Goodness of Fit Index* (AGFI), the *Comparative Fit Index* (CFI), the *Normed Fit Index* (NFI), the *Root Mean Square Error of Approximation* (RMSEA) and the *Standardized Root Mean Square Residual* (SRMR). The AGFI, CFI, and

TABLE 3
Varimax rotated four-factor solution for the ToM items on all time points combined

	Factor 1	*Factor 2*	*Factor 3*	*Factor 4*
Conceptual perspective 1	.83			
Conceptual perspective 2	.89			
Emotion attribution 1				.66
Emotion attribution 2				.58
Emotion attribution 3				.62
False belief 1		.61		
False belief 2		.75		
False belief 3		.63		
Mixed emotions 1			.71	
Mixed emotions 2			.86	

Note: Eigenvalues > 1.0; Values > .30 are reported.

TABLE 4
Goodness of fit statistics for structural models at three time points

Model	χ^2	df	p	AGFI	CFI	NFI	RMSEA	SRMR
A: Quasi-simplex emotion attribution	7.02	1	.01	.67	.00	.17	.28	.12
B: Quasi-simplex mixed emotions	2.36	1	.12	.88	.92	.88	.13	.06
C: Quasi-simplex false belief	4.36	1	.04	.79	.90	.88	.21	.08
D: Quasi-simplex conceptual perspective	2.68	1	.10	.87	.90	.88	.15	.07
E: Final integrated model	28.07	24	.26	.87	.96	.78	.05	.09

NFI should ideally be higher than .80 (Hu & Bentler, 1999). The RMSEA should be lower than .05 to reflect a good fit, while values of .08 indicate a reasonable fit (Browne & Cudeck, 1993). The SRMR finally should ideally be below .08 to reflect a good fit (Hu & Bentler, 1999), while values below .10 are considered acceptable.

As the different goodness-of-fit indices suggest, the fit of most quasi-simplex models was acceptable, with the exception of the emotion-attribution measure. This exception can be explained by the presence of a ceiling effect: due to the high scores of children at Time 1, any skill improvements of these children at later times are not registered, while decreases in skill levels are. Due to this anomalous effect, we investigated the stability of emotion attribution using an alternative technique. We analysed the percentages of children who regressed, performed at a similar level, and showed improved performance. Of all children who did not achieve the maximum score at Time 1 ($n = 66$), 82% performed at a similar level or improved at Time 2. The results from Time 2 to Time 3 were similar.

Dynamics of ToM over time

After establishing the stability of three of the four factors, SEM analyses were conducted to investigate the dynamic relations between the different ToM abilities. Since the emotion-attribution tasks did not show an acceptable stability over time, this measure was not included. Applying an iterative process on the three quasi-simplex models, significant relationships were added to the model, to find an integrated model with the best fit. The fit indices of this integrated model (Model E) are presented in Table 4. As can be gathered from the indices, this integrated model shows a good fit. Figure 3 provides a graphical presentation of the integrated model. Only significant relations are shown in Figure 3, with the exception of the relationship between the understanding of mixed emotions at Time 1 and

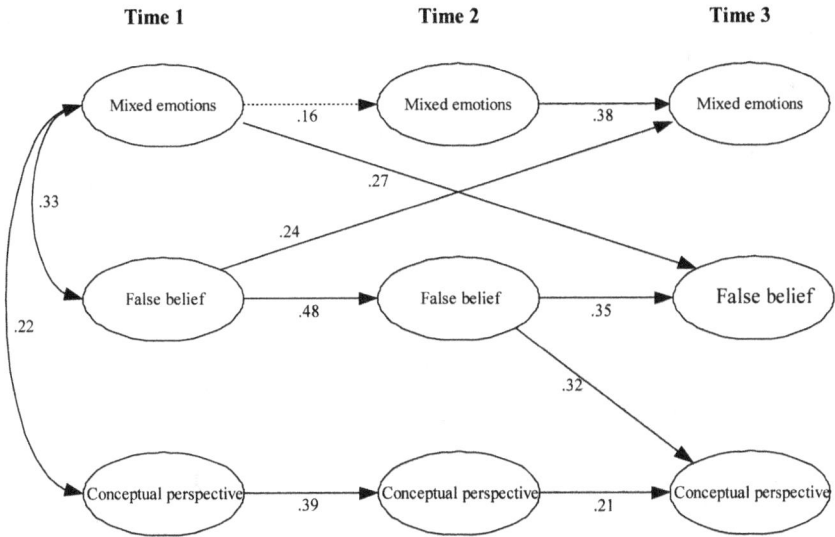

Figure 3. Final SEM model of relationships between ToM measures at Time 1, Time 2 and Time 3.

Time 2 (standardized regression coefficient = .16, $p = .15$). The figure shows that there are several relations between ToM abilities over time. At Time 1, there is a significant relation between the mixed-emotions score and the false-belief score. Additionally mixed-emotions understanding is also related to conceptual perspective taking. Longitudinally, several relations proved significant. For example, understanding mixed emotions at Time 1 predicts a modest but significant part of the performance of false-belief understanding at Time 3. Likewise, performance of understanding mixed emotions at Time 3 is predicted by false-belief understanding at Time 1. Furthermore, false-belief understanding at Time 2 predicts performance on the conceptual perspective taking task at Time 3.

To find out whether language would play a mediating role in ToM understanding, a last SEM model was computed applying an iterative process, including receptive vocabulary at Time 1 as a predictor for all time points. Scores on the receptive vocabulary task at Time 1 ranged from 30 to 89 ($M = 64.90$, $SD = 10.78$). The model showed a good fit according to the different fit indices, $\chi^2(28) = 26.77$, $p = .53$, AGFI = .88, CFI = 1.00, NFI = .85, RMSEA = .00, and SRMR = .06. Receptive vocabulary was found to predict significant variance of ToM performance. We found significant correlations between receptive vocabulary and the three ToM measures at Time 1 ($r = .28$ for mixed emotions, $r = .25$ for false-belief understanding, and $r = .26$ for conceptual perspective taking, all $ps < .05$).

Additionally, receptive vocabulary predicted a considerable part of variance of mixed-emotions understanding at Time 2 (standard regression coefficient = .52) and conceptual perspective taking (standard regression coefficient = .23). Finally, the predictive power of receptive vocabulary on mixed-emotions understanding persisted at Time 3 (standard regression coefficient = .25). All existing relations of the basic integrated model held when receptive vocabulary was entered into the model.

DISCUSSION

This longitudinal study attempted to address some issues on the developmental trajectories of several ToM abilities. These issues concern the development of ToM, its underlying dimensions and the dynamics of ToM abilities as a function of age.

With respect to our first goal, i.e., the development of ToM aspects of emotion understanding and false-belief understanding, we found evidence of developmental growth on two of the three measured aspects of emotion understanding and on both measured aspects of false-belief understanding. The greatest improvements in performance were found between the ages of 5 and 6 years. Skills related to emotion attribution did not improve during this period, which could be the result of a high level of emotion-attribution understanding at an earlier age. We found clear evidence for an emerging understanding of mixed emotions between 5 and 7 years. Whereas the performance of the 5-year-olds did not reveal a significant appreciation of mixed emotions, some 6-year-olds did reveal an appreciation of mixed emotions, and at age 7 the children understood mixed emotions more often than not. Similarly to the mixed-emotion understanding at age 5, we found no evidence for an active understanding of display rules at age 5. Although there was a significant improvement in performance on the display rules task from age 5 to 6, children still showed a predisposition to incorrectly predict that protagonists would show rather than hide emotions. Concerning the development of false-belief understanding, developmental growth was also established. Although literature often states that children reach this hallmark at around the age of 4 (Wellman et al., 2001, for a review), it does seem to be the case that false-belief understanding is still under development in the age range under consideration. In addition to a standard measure of false-belief understanding (i.e., change of location), we also used an alternative task following Lalonde and Chandler (2002). Whereas the "standard" false-belief tasks clearly have a right and a wrong answer, the conceptual-perspective-taking task demands a certain degree of creativity, since there is no such thing as the right answer. Though linguistically easier, the task might be more difficult on a conceptual level, a hypothesis that is corroborated by the fact that both our study and the study done by Lalonde and Chandler (2002) show relatively low scores on the conceptual-perspective-taking task at age 5. However, the children in our study showed a rapid improvement on this task. Overall, the results concerning developmental change in emotion understanding and false-belief understanding are largely consistent with the literature (Brown & Dunn, 1996; Kestenbaum & Gelman, 1995; Mutter et al., 2006; Saarni, 1979), and provide evidence of a growing awareness of more complex aspects of ToM, such as understanding mixed emotions and display rules.

As expected, performance on ToM tasks was related to socioeconomic status (SES). Maternal educational level was found to be significantly correlated to several ToM abilities, a finding that replicates results from other studies (e.g., Cutting & Dunn, 1999). This effect of maternal educational level was visible in all years. With regard to gender, our study did not show a significant difference between boys and girls.

Our second goal pertained to the underlying dimensions of ToM and their stability over the years. Taking into account the development of the ToM abilities, we found a robust stability across several tasks. As such, early emotion understanding and false-belief understanding seem to be predictive of later emotion understanding and false-belief understanding. As an exception to this established stability, we did not find evidence for stability of emotion attribution over the years. However, this might be related to the high initial level over emotion attribution, which led to a ceiling effect on our task.

The third goal of this study pertained to the dynamics of ToM. Some studies have indicated a lack of coherence within ToM batteries (Carlson, Mandell, & Williams, 2004). In our study we found some evidence for interrelations between emotion understanding and false-belief under-standing. At Time 1 we found several correlations between emotion understanding and false-belief understanding. Surprisingly, our first-order false-belief task did not show any relation with the conceptual-perspective-taking task, which is theoretically related to false-belief understanding. The absence of a correlation between both tasks might have been the result of the fact that performance on the conceptual-perspective-taking task was still at a low level at the first year. However, this was not true for the scores at Time 2. We did find evidence for a relation from Time 2 to Time 3.

Another interesting finding related to the coherence of ToM abilities, is the result that understanding of mixed emotions at age 5 predicted false-belief understanding at age 7. Alternatively, false-belief understanding at age 5 served as a predictor of awareness of mixed emotions at age 7. Awareness of mixed emotions requires an understanding of two (conflicting) beliefs, which is similar to the understanding of false-belief understanding.

Finally, to find out whether language ability was related to emotion understanding and false-belief understanding, we added a measure of receptive vocabulary to our model. Language ability was found to correlate with ToM performance and also to predict a considerable amount of variance in ToM performance in following years. Several studies such as the study by Astington and Jenkins (1999) have established strong predictive relations between language skills and ToM over time. Whereas some relation between language and ToM is to be expected, due to the linguistic nature of ToM tasks, one can also argue for a more fundamental relationship (Astington & Jenkins, 1999). Although our results corroborate the relationship between language and ToM, it is not possible to answer questions pertaining to the nature of the relationship.

The results of this study shed more light on the developmental trajectories and interrelations in the realm of ToM skills. However, some limitations are worth mentioning. First, the ToM skills we measured consisted of a limited set of items. As a consequence, floor and ceiling effects were easily attained. In addition, it would have been preferred to counterbalance the order of presentation across the children. To investigate the age of acquisition of more difficult ToM skills such as display-rules understanding, a broader age range would need to be studied. Furthermore, it would seem useful to apply a microgenetic approach. Such an approach has recently been adopted in ToM studies (e.g., Amsterlaw & Wellman, 2006; Flynn, 2006) and provides us with the opportunity to pinpoint the exact moment of onset of a certain skill. Finally, it would be interesting to explicitly study the relation between the ability to understand about emotions and beliefs and the ability to apply these skills. Regarding future research, it would be interesting to investigate the relation between ToM abilities and cognitive skills such as executive functioning and language over time. Although some developments have been made in this area (Astington & Jenkins, 1999; Carlson et al., 2004; Flynn, 2007), much research has focused on young children only. Investigating the ongoing relationship in older children employing a longer longitudinal study would help to expand our understanding of these relations.

In summary, the results of this study replicate, extend and integrate earlier findings on the development of ToM abilities. In the age range from 5 to 7, children display a significant improvement in both emotion under-standing and false-belief understanding. The differences in performance seem to be relatively stable and several interrelations are visible. On the whole, the results seem to suggest that ToM consists of separate but connected skills. These skills show similar developmental trajectories, although some develop at a later age than others. Wellman and Liu (2004) mention Flavell's concepts (1972) of modification or mediation to explain the interconnected developmental trajectories of ToM skills. Rather than simple addition or substitution of skills, earlier skills represent initial insights that broaden over time to later insights. The fact that our tasks did not show complete interrelations also suggests that ToM should be treated as consisting of multiple skills, and that measuring ToM skills by a single concept does not paint a representative picture of the complete ToM skills of an individual.

In addition to the predictive relations within the realm of ToM skills, we found linguistic ability to function as an important predictor. Since all ToM tasks were assessed using verbal tasks, linguistic ability would function to some extent as a prerequisite for successful performance. Lacking further information, it could be argued that the interrelationships between ToM skills within and even between assessment times could all be explained by a common dependence on language skills. However, even after controlling for language skills, these relations remained. This suggests that although language is a prerequisite for ToM performance, it is not enough to account for the variability of ToM performance found in our population and that there are more factors at play.

Since ToM abilities are considered essential for understanding and applying socially appropriate behaviour (Astington & Jenkins, 1995; Beer, Heerey, Keltner, Scabini, & Knight, 2003), timely assessment of ToM problems may help to prevent consequent social repercussions. The stability of performance found in the present study, combined with the measured predictive relations between the abilities over time, provide an indication that measured ToM performance at age 5 is not just a snapshot but can provide information on the long-term outlook as well.

REFERENCES

Amsterlaw, J., & Wellman, H. M. (2006). Theories of mind in transition: A microgenetic study of the development of false belief understanding. *Journal of Cognition and Development, 7*, 139–172.

Arbuckle, J. L. (2005). *AMOS 6.0* [computer software]. Spring House, PA: Amos Development Corporation.

Astington, J. W., & Jenkins, J. M. (1995). Theory of mind development and social understanding. *Cognition and Emotion, 9*, 151–165.

Astington, J. W., & Jenkins, J. M. (1999). A longitudinal study of the relation between language and Theory-of-Mind development. *Developmental Psychology, 35*, 1311–1320.

Banerjee, M. (1997). Hidden emotions: Preschoolers' knowledge of appearance–reality and emotion display rules. *Social Cognition, 15*, 107–132.

Baron-Cohen, S. (2001). Theory of mind in normal development and autism. *Prisme, 34*, 174–183.

Bartsch, K. (1998). False belief prediction and explanation: Which develops first and why it matters. *International Journal of Behavioral Development, 22*, 423–428.

Beer, J. S., Heerey, E. A., Keltner, D., Scabini, D., & Knight, R. T. (2003). The regulatory function of self-conscious emotion: Insights from patients with orbitofrontal damage. *Journal of Personality and Social Psychology, 85*, 594–604.

Bloom, M. (2003). Theory of Mind and emotion. *Perspectives in Psychology, 6*, 1–8.

Brown, J. R., & Dunn, J. (1996). Continuities in emotion understanding from three to six years. *Child Development, 67*, 789–802.

Browne, M. W., & Cudeck, R. (1993). Alternative ways of assessing model fit. In K. A. Bollen & J. S. Long (Eds.), *Testing structural equation models* (pp. 136–162). Newbury Park, CA: Sage.

Buitelaar, J. K., Van der Wees, M., Swaab-Barneeld, M., & Van der Gaag, R. J. (1999). Verbal memory and performance IQ predict theory of mind and emotion recognition ability in children with autistic spectrum disorders and in psychiatric control children. *Journal of Child Psychology and Psychiatry, 40*, 869–881.

Carlson, S. M., Mandell, D. J., & Williams, L. (2004). Executive function and theory of mind: Stability and prediction from ages 2 to 3. *Developmental Psychology, 40*, 1105–1122.

Cutting, A. L., & Dunn, J. (1999). Theory of mind, emotion understanding, language, and family background: Individual differences and interrelations. *Child Development, 70*, 853–865.

De Rosnay, M., Pons, F., Harris, F., & Morrell, J. M. B. (2004). A lag between understanding false belief and emotion attribution in young children: Relationships with linguistic ability and mothers' mental-state language. *British Journal of Developmental Psychology, 22*, 197–218.

Flavell, J. H. (1972). An analysis of cognitive-developmental sequences. *Genetic Psychology Monographs, 86*, 279–350.

Flavell, J. H., Flavell, E. R., & Green, F. L. (1990). Young children's understanding of fact beliefs versus value beliefs. *Child Development, 61*, 915–928.

Flynn, E. (2006). A microgenetic investigation of stability and continuity in theory of mind development. *British Journal of Developmental Psychology, 24*, 631–654.

Flynn, E. (2007). The role of inhibitory control in false belief understanding. *Infant and Child Development, 16*, 53–69.

Hu, L., & Bentler, P. (1999). Cutoff criteria for fit indexes in covariance structure analysis: Conventional criteria versus new alternatives. *Structural Equation Modeling, 6*, 1–55.

Hughes, C. (1998). Finding your marbles: Does preschoolers strategic behavior predict later understanding of mind? *Developmental Psychology, 34*, 1326–1339.

Hughes, C., Adlam, A., Happé, F. G. E., Jackson, J., Taylor, A., & Caspi, A. (2000). Good test–retest reliability for standard and advanced false-belief tasks across a wide range of abilities. *Journal of Child Psychology and Psychiatry, 41*, 483–490.

Hughes, C., & Dunn, J. (1998). Understanding mind and emotion: Longitudinal associations with mental-state talk between young friends. *Developmental Psychology, 34*, 1026–1037.

Kestenbaum, R., & Gelman, S. A. (1995). Preschool children's identification and understanding of mixed emotions. *Cognitive Development, 10*, 443–458.

Lalonde, C. E., & Chandler, M. J. (2002). Children's understanding of interpretation. *New Ideas in Psychology, 20*, 163–190.

Moses, L. J., & Flavell, J. H. (1990). Inferring false beliefs from actions and reactions. *Child Development, 61*, 929–945.

Mutter, B., Alcorn, M. B., & Welsh, M. (2006). Theory of mind and executive function: Working-memory capacity and inhibitory control as predictors of false-belief task performance. *Perceptual and Motor Skills, 102*, 819–835.

Perner, J., & Lang, B. (1999). Development of theory of mind and executive control. *TRENDS in Cognitive Sciences, 3*, 337–344.

Perner, J., & Wimmer, H. (1985). "John thinks that Mary thinks that." attribution of second-order beliefs by 5- to 10-year-old children. *Journal of Experimental Child Psychology, 39*, 437–471.

Pons, F., & Harris, F. (2005). Longitudinal change and longitudinal stability of individual differences in children's emotion understanding. *Cognition and Emotion, 19*, 1158–1174.

Repacholi, B., & Slaughter, V. (Eds.). (2003). *Individual differences in theory of mind: Implications of typical and atypical development.* New York: Psychology Press.

Saarni, C. (1979). Children's understanding of display rules for expressive behavior. *Developmental Psychology, 15*, 424–429.

Underwood, M. K., Coie, J. D., & Herbsman, C. R. (1992). Display rules for anger and aggression in school-age children. *Child Development, 63*, 366–380.

Verhoeven, L., & Vermeer, A. (2001). *Taaltest Alle Kinderen (TAK)* [Language Test for all Children]. Arnhem, The Netherlands: CITO.

Wellman, H. M., Cross, D., & Watson, D. (2001). Meta-analysis of theory-of-mind development: The truth about false belief. *Child Development, 72*, 655–684.

Wellman, H. M., & Liu, D. (2004). Scaling of theory-of-mind tasks. *Child Development, 75*, 523–541.

EUROPEAN JOURNAL OF DEVELOPMENTAL PSYCHOLOGY
2010, 7 (1), 104–122

Ψ Psychology Press
Taylor & Francis Group

Using Theory of Mind to represent and take part in social interactions: Comparing individuals with high-functioning autism and typically developing controls

Sander Begeer

VU University Amsterdam, Amsterdam, The Netherlands

Bertram F. Malle

Brown University, Providence, RI, USA

Mante S. Nieuwland

*Tufts University, Medford, and MGH/MIT/HMS Athinoula A. Martinos
Center for Biomedical Imaging, Charlestown, MA, USA*

Boaz Keysar

University of Chicago, Chicago, IL, USA

The literature suggests that individuals with autism spectrum disorders (ASD) are deficient in their Theory of Mind (ToM) abilities. They sometimes do not seem to appreciate that behaviour is motivated by underlying mental states. If this is true, then individuals with ASD should also be deficient when they use their ToM to represent and take part in dyadic interactions. In the current study we compared the performance of normally intelligent adolescents and adults with ASD to typically developing controls. In one task they heard a narrative about an interaction and then retold it. In a second task they played a communication game that required them to take into account another person's perspective. We found that when they described people's behaviour the ASD individuals used fewer mental terms in their story narration, suggesting a lower tendency to represent interactions in mentalistic terms. Surprisingly, ASD individuals and control participants showed the same level of performance in the communication game that required them to distinguish between their beliefs and the other's beliefs. Given that ASD individuals show no deficiency in using their ToM in real interaction, it is unlikely that they have a systematically deficient ToM.

Keywords: Autism; Egocentrism; Mental mindedness; Perspective taking; Theory of Mind.

Correspondence should be addressed to Sander Begeer, VU University Amsterdam, Developmental Psychology, Van der Boechorststraat 1, NL-1081 BT Amsterdam, The Netherlands. E-mail: s.begeer@psy.vu.nl

http://www.psypress.com/edp   DOI: 10.1080/17405620903024263

Autism spectrum disorders (ASD) are defined by behavioural and developmental impairments in social and communicative domains and by repetitive behaviour (American Psychiatric Association, 1994). Among the most striking features ascribed to individuals with ASD are claimed to be their poor "Theory of Mind" abilities (Volkmar, Lord, Bailey, Schultz, & Klin, 2004). Theory of Mind (ToM) refers to the ability to ascribe mental states to others or oneself and to explain and predict behaviour in terms of underlying mental states (Baron-Cohen, Tager-Flusberg, & Cohen, 2000). Even though the latter part of this definition entails verbal and conceptual abilities, the term "Theory of Mind" originates from a study of chimpanzee behaviour (Premack & Woodruff, 1978) and in principle allows for tacit interpretation skills that do not require sophisticated concepts or verbal abilities. However, most studies on ToM have operationalized this construct by evaluating conceptual knowledge of mental constructs in young, typically developing children (Wellman, Cross, & Watson, 2001) or in children with autism spectrum disorders (Baron-Cohen, Leslie, & Frith, 1985; Yirmiya, Erel, Shaked, & Solomonica-Levi, 1998).

Yet the main function of a ToM is to master social situations. It is thus surprising that the way people apply their ToM skills to social interactions has been largely ignored in developmental psychology (Frith, Happé, & Siddons, 1994; Keysar, Lin, & Barr, 2003; Klin, Jones, Schultz, & Volkmar, 2003). Social psychology has contributed significantly to this research under slightly different headings—empathy, perspective taking, and attribution of mental states (e.g., Ames, 2004; Epley, Keysar, Van Boven, & Gilovich, 2004; Malle & Hodges, 2005; Malle, Knobe, O'Laughlin, Pearce, & Nelson, 2000). The goal of the current study was to investigate the use of perspective taking and mental-state inference in representing and taking part in dyadic interactions and to compare the performance of adolescents and adults with ASD to the performance of typically developing controls.

Research on the development of ToM has focused on young children and has assumed a quite idealized, and in some respect erroneous, ToM ability in adults. Recent findings in social psychology reveal a more complex picture of adults. One line of research has demonstrated that adults have a sophisticated concept of intentional action. They attend in detail to the mental states involved in it, and they use these concepts widely when they describe and explain behaviour. Yet, even though people attempt to infer the thoughts and feelings of another person, their accuracy is far from perfect (e.g., Ickes, 1993; Klein & Hedges, 2001). In particular, people often have difficulties appreciating that others may be ignorant about some fact or have a false belief about it (Apperly, Riggs, Simpson, Chiavarino, & Samson, 2006). Consequently, at times they behave egocentrically, assuming that the other individual has access to their private knowledge (Keysar et al., 2003; Nickerson, 1999).

Limitations of the adult ToM can be identified if an adult-appropriate task is used that leaves room for error. In the widely used standard false-belief task, which is assumed to demonstrate a fully-fledged ToM from six years of age onward (Wellman et al., 2001; Wimmer & Perner, 1983), the subject knows the actual hiding location of an object and also knows that another person falsely believes it is hidden in a different place. When asked to predict where that person will look for the object, young children tend to confound their knowledge with the knowledge of the other person and predict that the other will look where the object really is, not where that person (falsely) believes it is. This failure to attribute false beliefs disappears after age four. Yet, by slightly modifying this task, Birch and Bloom (2007) showed a lingering confounding of self- and other-knowledge even with adults. Instead of asking for a categorical prediction about where the person will look for the object, the researchers asked for a probability estimate. Indeed, adults estimate the probability that the other will look at the true location to be higher when they themselves know the location than when they don't, again confounding somewhat their own knowledge with the knowledge ascribed to the other. In evaluating ToM in individuals with autism, then, it is crucial to measure ToM performance in tasks that are sensitive both to the ability and its limitation. We will describe two such tasks that are new to the literature on autism and ToM and examine the relative performance of individuals with ASD and neurotypical controls.

Do individuals with ASD show limited ToM abilities? The literature does not provide a clear-cut answer to this question (e.g., Gernsbacher & Frymiare, 2005). The results vary with age, IQ, and the nature of the task (Begeer, Koot, Rieffe, Meerum Terwogt, & Stegge, 2008; Rajendran & Mitchell, 2007). One of the most common ways to evaluate ToM skills has been to use conceptual tasks such as the false-belief task. This approach has provided evidence for impaired ToM abilities in school-aged children with ASD (Yirmiya et al., 1998). However, adolescents and adults with ASD, in particular those with normal IQ (high-functioning ASD) often pass conceptual ToM tasks at various levels of complexity (Bowler, 1992; Dahlgren & Trillingsgaard, 1996). Moreover, their performance on such tasks does not predict social behaviour in everyday settings (Fombonne, Siddons, Achard, & Frith, 1994; Frith et al., 1994; Peterson, Slaughter, & Paynter, 2007; Travis, Sigman, & Ruskin, 2001).

Though adolescents with high-functioning ASD often perform adequately on standard conceptual ToM tasks, they seem to perform worse on more advanced measures of ToM. These can include advanced "static" tests such as paper-and-pencil tasks that focus on the conceptual understanding of relatively complex interactions, requiring inferences of second-order mental states and the understanding of irony or emotional display rules. These tests have uncovered robust differences between children with high-functioning ASD and controls (Happé, 1994; Jolliffe & Baron-Cohen, 1999; Kaland et al., 2002). However, adults with high-functioning ASD show no impairments on these tasks, and, just like controls, are able to acknowledge both the existence and the importance of mental states (Roeyers, Buysse, Ponnet, & Pichal, 2001). Such adequate performance of high-functioning ASD adults is often attributed to cognitive compensation, the ability to use general cognitive and language skills to circumvent the conceptual ToM problem and still find a solution to the task (Bowler, 1992; Frith et al., 1994; Tager-Flusberg, 1993).

More dynamic, behavioural tests did indicate ToM limitations in high-functioning adults with ASD, even in those who pass static tests (Dziobek et al., 2006; Golan, Baron-Cohen, Hill, & Golan, 2006; Jolliffe & Baron-Cohen, 1999; Kleinman, Marciano, & Ault, 2001). For example, movie clips of acted or naturally occurring social interactions consistently elicit less-adequate explanations and less empathic accuracy in adults with high-functioning ASD than in controls (Heavey, Phillips, Baron-Cohen, & Rutter, 2000; Ickes, 1993; Roeyers et al., 2001).

Though there is evidence for ToM impairments in ASD individuals, none of the evidence emerged from situations in which these individuals were engaged in actual interaction. Conversely, some evidence suggests that even children with high-functioning ASD might perform unimpaired in some settings of actual interactions. In a study by Begeer, Rieffe, Meerum Terwogt, and Stockmann (2003) children with high-functioning ASD showed clear impairments in correcting another person's false beliefs during natural interactions, but their performance improved when they were motivated to respond adequately. Moreover, a study by Ponnet, Buysse, Roeyers, and de Corte (2005) suggests that adults with high-functioning ASD can spontaneously ascribe thoughts and feelings to a person with whom they just interacted at similar rates as controls. Thus, more research is clearly needed to examine the scope and limits of adequate ToM performance of high-functioning ASD individuals in contexts of social interaction.

In the current study we compared high-functioning ASD adolescents and adults with typically developing controls on two new tasks. The *narrative task* requires participants to read a story describing an ambiguous social interaction and to later retell the story. The *interaction task* requires participants to engage with another person in a highly structured communication game. Thus, both tasks require the handling of a social interaction, but a represented one in the narrative task and an experienced one in the interaction task. Both require linguistic processes, but of production in the narrative task and of comprehension in the interaction task. Most important, both require mental state inferences, but one in service of meaningful representation and the other in service of successful mastery of an interaction goal.

STUDY 1: NARRATIVE TASK

Typically developing adults routinely use mental-state terms in their narrative representation of social interactions (Barker & Givón, 2005), but there are no data on adults with high-functioning ASD on this ability. There is some indication that they use fewer mental-state formulations than control participants when interpreting ambiguous geometric shapes that enact a social plot in a cartoon animation (Klin, 2000; Klin et al., 2003). In the current study, a simpler method was employed, taking advantage of the ubiquitous situation of hearing or reading about an interaction and having to describe it to another person. All participants read a short story about an ambiguous interaction between two people (Malle & Holland Rogers, 2008). The story described the story characters' behaviours but made no explicit reference to their mental states, such as beliefs, desires, or emotions. After some delay, participants were asked to retell the story. If people spontaneously make sense of ambiguous social interactions by inferring underlying mental states, these inferences should emerge in the retelling as mental state words such as "wanted", "thought", "was confused" and "trusted", even though none of those words were part of the original story. Consistent with Klin et al.'s results, we expected that the ASD group would include fewer references to mental states in their retelling narratives than control participants.

Method

Participants.   Participants were 68 adolescents and adults (53 males, 15 females), including 34 participants with an autism spectrum disorder and 34 typically developing control participants, who were matched on chronological age and cognitive abilities. The ASD participants were recruited from two psychiatric institutions in the Netherlands. Their diagnostic classification was based on assessments by a psychiatrist and multiple informants (psychologists and educationalists). All participants fulfilled established diagnostic criteria according to the DSM-IV-TR (American Psychiatric Association, 2000). For part of the ASD sample, additional diagnostic information was obtained from the Children's Social Behaviour Questionnaire (CSBQ; Luteijn, Minderaa, & Jackson, 2002) and from the self-reported and parental-reported Autism Spectrum Quotient (Baron-Cohen, Hoekstra, Knickmeyer, & Wheelwright, 2006; Baron-Cohen, Wheelwright, Skinner, Martin, & Clubley, 2001). These measures confirmed the clinical diagnoses (see Table 1).

The control group was recruited from schools, colleges and universities around Amsterdam, the Netherlands. IQ scores for all participants were

TABLE 1
Details of the two participant groups

	ASD (n = 34)	Control (n = 34)	Group comparison
Age (years;months)	16;7 (4;2)	16;8 (3;8)	p = .94
Gender (Male/Female)	26/8	27/7	p = .77
FSIQ[a]	108.5 (21.1)	105.8 (18.3)	p = .62
CSBQ (parent)[a]	41.8 (17.6)	6.4 (8.5)	p < .000
	(n = 16)	(n = 19)	
AQ (parent)[a]	35.3 (3.0)	21.9 (3.8)	p < .000
	(n = 6)	(n = 6)	
AQ (self-report)[a]	33.0 (3.9)	23.5 (2.6)	p < .000
	(n = 9)	(n = 9)	

Notes: ASD = Autism Spectrum Disorder, FSIQ = full-scale IQ; CSBQ = Children's Social Behaviour Questionnaire; AQ = Autism Quotient Questionnaire. [a]Means (SD).

obtained by a short version of the Wechsler Intelligence Scale for Children-III (Wechsler et al., 1991) or the Wechsler Adult Intelligence Scale (Wechsler, 1997). Four subtests (Vocabulary, Arithmetic, Block Design, and Picture Arrangement) were administered to assess intelligence. These subtests are known to correlate highly with Full-scale IQ in the general populations (Donders, 2001).

Material. In this task, participants read a short story about an interaction between a man and a woman in a domestic context (Malle & Holland Rogers, 2008; see appendix). The story included no terms that explicitly referred to mental states such as beliefs, desires, emotions or intentions. However, the text provided clues about the story character's mental states—for example, by referring to their physical state (a trembling hand) or their behaviour (suddenly leaving the room). After an average of 20 minutes (during which the interaction task, described in Study 2, was administered), participants were asked "Could you retell the story?" and "Could you tell me what the story was about?"

Procedure. The participant first read the narrative task story on a computer screen and then completed the interaction task. The confederate was then asked to wait in another room while the participant answered the two questions about the story they had read, and finally they completed the IQ test and were debriefed.

Dependent variables. Participant's retelling of the story was transcribed and scored for the use of mental-state terms. Mental-state terms included all references to beliefs, ideas, or thoughts (e.g., "he thinks", "she knows"), references to desires, hoping, longing or preferences (e.g., "she needed", "he didn't want") as well as references to emotional states (e.g., "he was angry", "he was feeling sad"). These results held up in separate analyses of specific mental-state categories, beliefs, desires and emotions (ds ranging from 0.40 to 0.68). Overall agreement between two independent raters of mental-state references was .78. Disagreements were resolved through discussion.

Results

Differences between the number of mental-state references in the narrative of individuals with ASD or typical development were analysed with an ANCOVA, controlling for participants' age and full-scale IQ. The ASD group reported fewer mental-state references ($M = 1.06$, $SD = 1.32$) than the control group ($M = 2.38$, $SD = 1.99$); $F(1, 64) = 13.60$, $p < .001$, $d = 0.89$. When the number of mental-state references was divided by the overall number of words used in each recounted story, the ASD participants still reported a lower proportion of mental-state references ($M = 0.02$, $SD = 0.02$) than controls ($M = 0.04$, $SD = 0.04$); $F(1, 64) = 4.36$, $p < .05$, $d = 0.51$.

STUDY 2: INTERACTION TASK

This task was designed to engage participants in an interaction that could be successfully mastered when taking into account the perceptions and beliefs of their interaction partner. Each participant played a communication game in which another person (the "director") instructed the participant ("the addressee") to move objects in a grid (Epley, Morewedge, & Keysar, 2004; Keysar et al., 2003; Wu & Keysar, 2007). The two individuals shared knowledge about the location of mutually visible objects, while other objects were visible only to the addressee but not the director. For example, as shown in Figure 1, when the director says to move "the big spoon" the intended target must be the mutually visible spoon. However, if the addressee fails to take the director's perspective, he or she may consider the occluded spoon as the referent. This confusion may delay the identification of the actual target spoon and possibly even cause the addressee to mistakenly move the occluded spoon that the director could not have referred to, which would be an egocentric error. This task requires the spontaneous and repeated use of ToM to interpret the other person's behaviour in an unfolding social interaction. If ASD individuals are deficient in their use of ToM, then they should make more egocentric errors and show a longer latency to move the target objects than control participants.

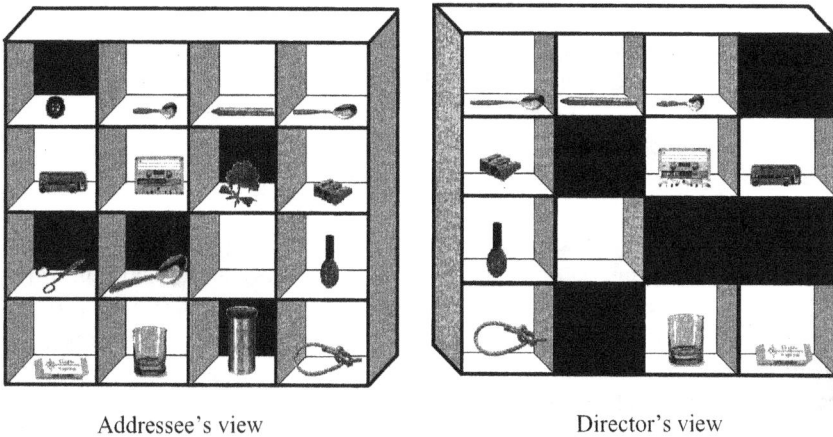

Addressee's view   Director's view

Figure 1. Array of objects presented from the addressee's and the director's perspective. One of the critical instructions for the director in this trial was to "move the big spoon to the empty slot". Moving the mutually visible spoon in the top corner slot would suggest adequate perspective taking. In contrast, moving the occluded spoon would suggest an egocentric interpretation. To view this figure in colour, please visit the online version of this Journal.

Method

Participants.   The participants were the same as in Study 1.

Material.   Participants were seated on opposite sides of a grid that consisted of 16 (4 × 4) open slots. One person was always a female confederate who served the role of director, instructing participants to move objects around in the grid. Five of the slots were occluded from the director's view but were clearly visible to the participant (see Figure 1). One mutually visible slot was empty. All other slots were filled with different objects. The task consisted of five blocks in which the participant moved a total of 64 target objects, four blocks with 12 objects and one block with 16 objects. Out of these 64 objects, 18 were designated "critical": They involved a competitor object that was, from the participant's perspective, a potential referent of the director's instruction (e.g., "Take the big spoon"), but because the object was occluded from the director's view, it could not have been the intended referent. These trials thus contained ambiguous directions, which were contrasted with neutral (non-ambiguous) trials to form a within-subject factor of target type.

The target object and competitor object were always arranged in diagonally opposite quarters of the grid, making the object of attention and reaching easy to discern on video. The instructions in critical trials contained either size ambiguity (e.g., "Move the big spoon") or semantic ambiguity (e.g., the instruction "Move the tape" when a cassette tape was mutually visible but a roll of Sellotape was visible only to the addressee). The position of the critical trials varied in a predetermined random fashion.

Participants were filmed with a digital video camera positioned in the centre of the second row from the top, focused on their face. The camera was approximately 50 cm from their head. A second camera located behind the participants recorded their reaching.

Procedure. The participant and the confederate learned that they would be playing a communication game, which involved one of them telling the other which objects to move around in the grid. To make sure the addressee understood the director's perspective, both participants practiced the roles of director and addressee. The role of the director was then (purportedly randomly) assigned to the confederate, and the role of addressee was assigned to the participant. The director received a drawing that showed the grid from her perspective and specified the order in which the objects should be moved. After each block of moving objects the experimenter returned the objects to their original position in the grid. In the meantime, to make sure that participants believed that the director could not see the objects in the occluded slots, the director was asked to turn around while the grid was being filled with objects.

Dependent variables. Two raters who were unaware of the hypothesis and of participants' diagnosis coded the videotapes for egocentric errors and the latency to move the target object. Egocentric errors were scored when the participant moved the occluded object (e.g., the hidden spoon) and placed it in the empty slot. Inter-rater reliability was 1.00. The latency to move the target object was defined as the temporal window from the director's mention of the object to be moved (e.g., "Move the big *spoon*") to the addressee's putting down the object in another slot.

Results

To examine egocentric errors, we conducted a 2 (Target Type: ambiguous vs. neutral) × 2 (Group: ASD vs. typically developing controls) ANCOVA, controlling for participants' age and full-scale IQ. In general, participants made more egocentric errors in ambiguous trials ($M = 39\%$) than in neutral trials ($M = 0\%$); $F(1, 64) = 33.16$, $p < .001$, $d = 1.76$. ASD individuals showed a nominally *smaller* error rate ($M = 34\%$) than the control group ($M = 43\%$), but this difference was not significant; $F(1, 64) = 2.52$, *ns*. The same pattern emerged for the percentage of people in each group who were able to avoid all egocentric errors: ASD ($M = 21\%$) vs. control group ($M = 9\%$); $F(1, 64) = 1.65$, *ns*. So the tendency to avoid making egocentric errors clearly showed no advantage for control over ASD individuals.

The number of egocentric errors of the ASD group in the ambiguous condition was substantially correlated with chronological age, $r(34) = -.47$, $p < .01$, and full-scale IQ, $r(34) = -.51$, $p < .01$. The corresponding correlations in the control group were small and non-significant, chronological age: $r(34) = -.12$, ns; full-scale IQ: $r(34) = -.20$, ns. However, the difference between the correlations in the ASD and control groups did not reach traditional significance levels (for age with egocentric errors: $z = 1.53$, $p = .14$, for IQ and egocentric errors: $z = 1.41$, $p = .17$, respectively).

Participants' latencies of moving objects were longer in ambiguous trials ($M = 3.20$ s, $SD = 0.91$) than in neutral trials ($M = 2.69$ s, $SD = 0.65$), indicating that the presence of a competitor delayed the selection of the target. Importantly, this delay was not significantly larger for the ASD group ($M = 0.60$ s, $SD = 0.58$) than for the control group ($M = 0.42$ s, $SD = 0.51$). Thus, a 2 (Group: ASD vs. control) × 2 (Trial Type: ambiguous vs. neutral) repeated-measures ANCOVA (controlling for participants' age and full-scale IQ) showed a significant main effect of Trial Type; $F(1, 64) = 5.67$, $p < .05$, $d = 0.58$, but no effect of Group ($F < 1$) or interaction; $F(1, 64) = 1.87$, ns.

The latencies in the ambiguous condition of both the ASD and control groups were significantly correlated with chronological age, $r(34) = -.55$, $p < .01$ and $r(34) = -.59$, $p < .01$, respectively, and full-scale IQ, $r(34) = -.35$, $p < .05$ and $r(34) = -.20$, $p < .05$, respectively, suggesting that all participants were able to respond more quickly with increasing chronological and mental age.

In sum, all participants, whether ASD or control group members, produced some errors of perspective taking, but ASD individuals produced no more than did control participants. Response latencies, too, showed no group differences (see Table 2).

Correspondence between narrative and interaction tasks. Separate analyses of the HFASD and control groups indicated no correlations between mental-state references in the narrative task and either egocentric errors

TABLE 2

Mean (*SD*) proportion of reaching errors and reaction times following neutral or ambiguous instructions on the perspective taking task

	Reaching errors		Reaction time (s)	
	Ambiguous	*Neutral*	*Ambiguous*	*Neutral*
ASD (*n* = 34)	0.34 (0.23)	0	3.29 (0.99)	2.68 (0.70)
Control (*n* = 34)	0.43 (0.21)	0	3.12 (0.82)	2.70 (0.60)

(HFASD: $r = .05$; control: $r = .22$) or delays (HFASD: $r = .12$; control: $r = .10$) in the interaction task.

GENERAL DISCUSSION

This study compared adolescents and adults with ASD and typically developing control participants on two tasks. One task required participants to represent and narrate a social interaction scene, the other required them to take the perspective of the other in a structured social interaction. The narration task showed the documented difference in the use of mental-state terms, such that ASD individuals used fewer terms of belief, desire, and emotion when retelling a short story than did control participants. By contrast, ASD individuals and controls were identical in their ability to take another person's knowledge into account when interpreting what she/he said. This demonstrates that ASD individuals can be just as effective as controls in using their ToM when it really matters: When they try to understand others' behaviour. These results, therefore, argue against the suggestion that ASD individuals have a deficient ToM.

The most sceptical interpretation of our findings would point out that they are null results that contrast with the vast literature that suggests ToM impairments in autism (e.g., Baron-Cohen, 1995; Yirmiya et al., 1998). But Rajendran and Mitchell (2007) argued against a dismissal of tests that don't show differences between ASD and neurotypical individuals. Such a dismissal stems from "the assumption that individuals with autism do have an impaired ToM, implying that tests which do not reveal impairments must be insensitive or unsuitable" (p. 229). However, performance on the interaction task is sensitive to a variety of factors. It varies with mood as people perform more egocentrically when they are happy than when they are sad (Converse, Lin, Keysar, & Epley, 2008); it varies with culture as Westerners show more egocentrism than East Asians (Wu & Keysar, 2007) and it varies with levels of friendship, as friends show more egocentrism than strangers (Savitsky, Keysar, Epley, Carter, & Swanson, 2009). So the task captures something psychologically real and systematic, and it demands the very perspective taking processes that are assumed to be lacking in autistic individuals.

Most importantly, one of the most trusted methods used to argue that ASD individuals lack ToM is the false-belief task (Baron-Cohen, Leslie, & Frith, 1985). The present interaction task and the false-belief task employ the same underlying logic. They both dissociate the knowledge of self and that of the other and assess the ability of the self to take the perspective of the other. Therefore, if the false-belief task is supposed to reflect ToM ability, then the interaction task must reflect it as well. Furthermore, our task requires participants to use their ToM to interpret actions in real time, thus requiring spontaneous, non-reflective use of this ability. The interaction task is thus directly related to one of the main functions of ToM to begin with—to interpret the behaviour of others. Therefore, the fact that the task does not display differences between ASD and control individuals must be explained rather than dismissed.

One explanation of the lack of differences in the interaction task is that when individuals with ASD need to process the other person's beliefs and knowledge in a real social interaction, they can do so just as well as typically developing individuals. Therefore, they appear to have an intact ToM when it counts—when they have to interpret the behaviour of real others in a real setting. This may be too strong a conclusion, however, because the interaction task represents only one particular kind of interaction—a structured referential communication—and does not always generalize to other social interactions. Even so, our results are consistent with other findings that have shown that structured social interactions elicit adequate use of ToM skills, as evidenced by similar responses to others' mental or emotional states and similar empathic accuracy in children and adults with ASD and matched controls (Begeer, Rieffe, Meerum Terwogt, Stegge, & Koot, 2007; Begeer et al., 2003; Begeer, Rieffe, Meerum Terwogt, & Stockmann, 2006; Ponnet et al., 2005).

What is it about structured interactions that allows successful social behaviour in ASD individuals? Structured interactions remove two challenges that normally hamper ASD individuals' social behaviour in unstructured, freely unfolding social interactions. First, ASD individuals are easily over aroused, which often results in attempts to regulate their arousal with stereotypic and withdrawal behaviour (Belmonte & Yurgelun-Todd, 2003; Liss, Saulnier, Kinsbourne, & Kinsbourne, 2006; Raymaekers, van der Meere, & Roeyers, 2004). Such behaviours make interactions awkward and difficult to conduct. Second, children with ASD often process information in a piecemeal rather than holistic way, thus failing to integrate information on a global, abstract level. Information that emerges during unstructured social interactions often requires such global processing to understand the meaning of the interaction (Frith, 2003; Happé, 1993). Both over arousal and piecemeal processing may be neutralized in structured social interaction. Such interactions are rule driven and therefore predefine the meaning of most steps in the interaction, so global processing is no longer essential for appropriate responses (see also Gallagher, 2004).

The availability of a well-defined structure also opens the possibility that ASD individuals may not have solved the critical trials in the interaction task by using a ToM. Rather, they might have adopted the general rule never to pay attention to the "objects with a black background" because the director could not refer to them. Whether such a rule requires a prior mental state ascription that the director doesn't *see* them or doesn't *know* about them, is an interesting further question. One finding in our study is consistent with the idea that ASD individuals might have solved the task by way of such a "smart rule". In the ASD group, we found a correlation between reaching errors, age, and IQ. The older and more intelligent the ASD participants were, the more effective they were in the interaction task. Thus, they might have relied more on their experience and general cognitive abilities than on actual inferences about mental states. Similar correlations, in particular between IQ and social competence, have been shown in earlier studies on ASD (Bolte & Poustka, 2003; Buitelaar, van der, Swaab-Barneveld, & van der Gaag, 1999; Kamio, Wolf, & Fein, 2006; Klin et al., 2007; Steele, Joseph, & Tager-Flusberg, 2003; Yirmiya, Sigman, Kasari, & Mundy, 1992). The absence of such correlations among typically developing individuals are often explained by assuming that these individuals rely on a more intuitive, automatic perspective-taking ability that requires less conscious cognitive reflection (Klin et al., 2003). However, the interaction task does not by itself reveal what cognitive processes individuals used to solve the task. Furthermore, using a smart rule is still likely triggered by considering what the other person knows. Moreover, it may often be adaptive to use rules in social interactions and we should be careful not to argue that typically developing individuals wholly refrain from using rules in their ToM behaviour. These issues are important considerations in future research.

In contrast to the structured interaction task, the situation described in the narrative task was unstructured and ambiguous. To the extent that the meaning of this interaction was difficult to comprehend for individuals with ASD, they may have tried to restate verbatim what was said in the story, resulting in fewer mental-state references. However, gist recall beyond the given text does not necessarily include mental-state references, so a difference in memory functions can not fully explain the current findings. Still, it could be that in response to unstructured social interactions, individuals with autism do not recruit mental-state inferences but that in response to structured interactions they do recruit mental-state inferences.

Second, the ability to take another's perspective during actual interactions may be triggered in a different way than the ability to attribute mental states to story characters that one is not engaging with (Slaughter, Peterson, & Mackintosh, 2007; Taumoepeau & Ruffman, 2008). The absence of a direct engagement may hamper the motivation to ascribe mental states to story characters in ASD individuals, who strongly depend on explicit cues (Begeer et al., 2007). The frequency of mental-state referencing in children with ASD was recently even found to be independent from the actual tendency to engage in conversations about mental states in real-life interactions (Muller & Schuler, 2006). Furthermore, a perspective-taking error in social interaction could elicit direct feedback from interaction partners. This may provide a beneficial context for individuals with ASD who have shown improved performances under explicit and goal-directed conditions (Begeer et al., 2006, 2007; Rajendran & Mitchell, 2007).

Two further limitations of our study must be acknowledged. First, the limited availability of information from standardized diagnostic measures could reduce the validity of participants' diagnoses. However, when the analyses were run for only those participants for whom this information was available all the effects of interest remained, even though the number of participants was reduced to 22 ASD and 22 control individuals. Second, age and IQ were correlated in both ASD and control individuals in our sample. While this has no impact on our main question, it did not allow us to disentangle the separate contributions of IQ and experience on ToM performance.

The vast majority of the substantial body of ToM publications (750 papers in the period 1985–2000 alone) used variants of false-belief tasks (Hughes et al., 2000). It is high time that research turned to an analysis of the multiple components and dimensions that constitute ToM skills (Malle, 2008). Our studies take a small step in this direction by examining dimensions such as represented versus experienced social interaction; structured versus ambiguous social tasks; and linguistic production versus comprehension. We found that comprehension in experienced structured interactions may not pose a problem for ASD individuals' ToM performance. Systematic variation of these and other components in future research may reveal the specific kind of ToM deficits that ASD individuals display. A careful examination of age groups between childhood and adulthood is another imperative for future research. To that end, more information is needed on neurotypical adult ToM skills along multiple dimensions and across multiple tasks to provide the baseline for studying these dimensions in adults with ASD. Knowledge at this level of specific components may then suggest specific training approaches to alleviate particular difficulties that ASD individuals encounter.

REFERENCES

American Psychiatric Association. (1994). *Diagnostic and statistical manual of mental disorders (DSM-VI)*. Washington, DC: American Psychiatric Association.

American Psychiatric Association. (2000). *Diagnostic and statistical manual of mental disorders, text revision (DSM-VI-TR)*. Washington, DC: American Psychiatric Association.

Ames, D. R. (2004). Inside the mind reader's tool kit: Projection and stereotyping in mental state inference. *Journal of Personality and Social Psychology, 87*, 340–353.

Apperly, I. A., Riggs, K. J., Simpson, A., Chiavarino, C., & Samson, D. (2006). Is belief reasoning automatic? *Psychological Science, 17*, 841–844.

Barker, M., & Givón, T. (2005). Representation of the interlocutor's mind during conversation. In B. F. Malle & S. D. Hodges (Eds.), *Other minds: How humans bridge the divide between self and others* (pp. 223–238). New York: Guilford Press.

Baron-Cohen, S. (1995). *Mindblindness: An essay on autism and theory of mind.* Cambridge, MA: MIT Press.

Baron-Cohen, S., Hoekstra, R. A., Knickmeyer, R., & Wheelwright, S. (2006). The Autism-Spectrum Quotient (AQ) – Adolescent version. *Journal of Autism and Developmental Disorders, 36,* 343–350.

Baron-Cohen, S., Leslie, A. M., & Frith, U. (1985). Does the autistic child have a theory of mind. *Cognition, 21,* 37–46.

Baron-Cohen, S., Tager-Flusberg, H., & Cohen, D. J. (2000). *Understanding other minds: Perspectives from developmental cognitive neuroscience.* Oxford, UK: Oxford University Press.

Baron-Cohen, S., Wheelwright, S., Skinner, R., Martin, J., & Clubley, E. (2001). The Autism-Spectrum Quotient (AQ): Evidence from Asperger syndrome/high-functioning autism, males and females, scientists and mathematicians. *Journal of Autism and Developmental Disorders, 31,* 5–17.

Begeer, S., Koot, H. M., Rieffe, C., Meerum Terwogt, M., & Stegge, H. (2008). Emotional competence in children with autism: Diagnostic criteria and empirical evidence. *Developmental Review, 28,* 342–369.

Begeer, S., Rieffe, C., Meerum Terwogt, M., Stegge, H., & Koot, H. M. (2007). Do children with autism acknowledge the influence of mood on behaviour? *Autism, 11,* 503–521.

Begeer, S., Rieffe, C., Meerum Terwogt, M., & Stockmann, L. (2003). Theory of mind-based action in children from the autism spectrum. *Journal of Autism and Developmental Disorders, 33,* 479–487.

Begeer, S., Rieffe, C., Meerum Terwogt, M., & Stockmann, L. (2006). Attention to facial emotion expressions in children with autism. *Autism, 10,* 37–51.

Belmonte, M. K., & Yurgelun-Todd, D. A. (2003). Functional anatomy of impaired selective attention and compensatory processing in autism. *Cognitive Brain Research, 17,* 651–664.

Birch, S. A. J., & Bloom, P. (2007). The curse of knowledge in reasoning about false beliefs. *Psychological Science, 18,* 382–386.

Bolte, S., & Poustka, F. (2003). The recognition of facial affect in autistic and schizophrenic subjects and their first-degree relatives. *Psychological Medicine, 33,* 907–915.

Bowler, D. M. (1992). "Theory of mind" in Asperger's syndrome. *Journal of Child Psychology and Psychiatry, 33,* 877–893.

Buitelaar, J. K., van der, W. M., Swaab-Barneveld, H., & van der Gaag, R. J. (1999). Verbal memory and performance IQ predict theory of mind and emotion recognition ability in children with autistic spectrum disorders and in psychiatric control children. *Journal of Child Psychology and Psychiatry, 40,* 869–881.

Converse, A. B., Lin, S., Keysar, B., & Epley, N. (2008). In the mood to get over yourself: Mood affects theory-of-mind use. *Emotion, 8,* 725–730.

Dahlgren, S. O., & Trillingsgaard, A. (1996). Theory of mind in non-retarded children with autism and Asperger's syndrome. A research note. *Journal of Child Psychology and Psychiatry, 37,* 759–763.

Donders, J. (2001). Using a short form of the WISC-III: Sinful or smart? *Child Neuropsychology, 7,* 99–103.

Dziobek, I., Fleck, S., Kalbe, E., Rogers, K., Hassenstab, J., Brand, M., et al. (2006). Introducing MASC: A movie for the assessment of social cognition. *Journal of Autism and Developmental Disorders, 36,* 623–636.

Epley, N., Keysar, B., Van Boven, L., & Gilovich, T. (2004). Perspective taking as egocentric anchoring and adjustment. *Journal of Personality and Social Psychology, 87,* 327–339.

Epley, N., Morewedge, C. K., & Keysar, B. (2004). Perspective taking in children and adults: Equivalent egocentrism but differential correction. *Journal of Experimental Social Psychology, 40*, 760–768.

Fombonne, E., Siddons, F., Achard, S., & Frith, U. (1994). Adaptive behaviour and theory of mind in autism. *European Child and Adolescent Psychiatry, 3*, 176–186.

Frith, U. (2003). *Autism: Explaining the enigma.* Oxford, UK: Blackwell Publishers.

Frith, U., Happé, F., & Siddons, F. (1994). Autism and theory of mind in everyday life. *Social Development, 3*, 108–124.

Gallagher, S. (2004). Understanding interpersonal problems in autism: Interaction theory as an alternative to theory of mind. *Philosophy, Psychiatry, & Psychology, 11*, 199–217.

Gernsbacher, M. A., & Frymiare, J. (2005). Does the autistic brain lack core modules? *Journal of Developmental and Learning Disorders, 9*, 3–16.

Golan, O., Baron-Cohen, S., Hill, J. J., & Golan, Y. (2006). The "Reading the Mind in Films" Task: Complex emotion recognition in adults with and without autism spectrum conditions. *Social Neuroscience, 1*, 111–123.

Happé, F. G. E. (1993). Parts and wholes, meaning and minds: Central coherence and its relation to theory of mind. In S. Baron-Cohen, H. Tager-Flusberg, & D. Cohen (Eds.), *Understanding other minds: Perspectives from developmental cognitive neuroscience* (pp. 203–222). Oxford, UK: Oxford University Press.

Happé, F. G. E. (1994). An advanced test of theory of mind: Understanding of story characters' thoughts and feelings by able autistic, mentally handicapped, and normal-children and adults. *Journal of Autism and Developmental Disorders, 24*, 129–154.

Heavey, L., Phillips, W., Baron-Cohen, S., & Rutter, M. (2000). The Awkward Moments Test: A naturalistic measure of social understanding in autism. *Journal of Autism and Developmental Disorders, 30*, 225–236.

Hughes, C., Adlam, A., Happé, F., Jackson, J., Taylor, A., & Caspi, A. (2000). Good test–retest reliability for standard and advanced false-belief tasks across a wide range of abilities. *Journal of Child Psychology and Psychiatry, 41*, 483–490.

Ickes, W. (1993). Empathic accuracy. *Journal of Personality, 61*, 587–610.

Jolliffe, T., & Baron-Cohen, S. (1999). The Strange Stories Test: A replication with high-functioning adults with autism or Asperger syndrome. *Journal of Autism and Developmental Disorders, 29*, 395–406.

Kaland, N., Moller-Nielsen, A., Callesen, K., Mortensen, E. L., Gottlieb, D., & Smith, L. (2002). A new "advanced" test of theory of mind: Evidence from children and adolescents with Asperger syndrome. *Journal of Child Psychology and Psychiatry, 43*, 517–528.

Kamio, Y., Wolf, J., & Fein, D. (2006). Automatic processing of emotional faces in high-functioning pervasive developmental disorders: An affective priming study. *Journal of Autism and Developmental Disorders, 36*, 155–167.

Keysar, B., Lin, S., & Barr, D. J. (2003). Limits on theory of mind use in adults. *Cognition, 89*, 25–41.

Klein, K. J. K., & Hedges, S. D. (2001). Gender differences, motivation, and empathic accuracy: When it pays to understand. *Personality and Social Psychology Bulletin, 27*, 720–730.

Kleinman, J., Marciano, P. L., & Ault, R. L. (2001). Advanced theory of mind in high-functioning adults with autism. *Journal of Autism and Developmental Disorders, 31*, 29–36.

Klin, A. (2000). Attributing social meaning to ambiguous visual stimuli in higher-functioning autism and Asperger syndrome: The Social Attribution Task. *Journal of Child Psychology and Psychiatry, 41*, 831–846.

Klin, A., Jones, W., Schultz, R., & Volkmar, F. (2003). The enactive mind, or from actions to cognition: Lessons from autism. *Philosophical Transactions of the Royal Society London: Series B. Biological Sciences, 358*, 345–360.

Klin, A., Saulnier, C. A., Sparrow, S. S., Cicchetti, D. V., Volkmar, F. R., & Lord, C. (2007). Social and communication abilities and disabilities in higher functioning individuals with autism spectrum disorders: The Vineland and the ADOS. *Journal of Autism and Developmental Disorders, 37,* 748–759.

Liss, M., Saulnier, C., Kinsbourne, D. F., & Kinsbourne, M. (2006). Sensory and attention abnormalities in autistic spectrum disorders. *Autism, 10,* 155–172.

Luteijn, E. F., Minderaa, R., & Jackson, S. (2002). *Vragenlijst voor Inventarisatie van Sociaal gedrag bij Kinderen (VISK), handleiding* [The Children's Social Behavior Questionnaire (CSBQ), Manual]. Lisse, The Netherlands: Swets & Zeitlinger.

Malle, B. F. (2008). The fundamental tools, and possibly universals, of social cognition. In R. Sorrentino & S. Yamaguchi (Eds.), *Handbook of motivation and cognition across cultures* (pp. 267–296). New York: Elsevier/Academic Press.

Malle, B. F., & Hodges, S. D. (2005). *Other minds: How humans bridge the divide between self and others.* New York: Guilford Press.

Malle, B. F., & Holland Rogers, B. (2008). *Short assessment for mental state inferences in the narrative representation of social interaction (SAMSI).* Retrieved August 12, 2008, from http://uoregon.edu/~bfmalle/SAMSI.htm

Malle, B. F., Knobe, J., O'Laughlin, M. J., Pearce, G. E., & Nelson, S. E. (2000). Conceptual structure and social functions of behaviour explanations: Beyond person–situation attributions. *Journal of Personality and Social Psychology, 79,* 309–326.

Muller, E., & Schuler, A. (2006). Verbal marking of affect by children with Asperger syndrome and high-functioning autism during spontaneous interactions with family members. *Journal of Autism and Developmental Disorders, 36,* 1089–1100.

Nickerson, R. S. (1999). How we know—and sometimes misjudge—what others know: Imputing one's own knowledge to others. *Psychological Bulletin, 125,* 737–759.

Peterson, C. C., Slaughter, V. P., & Paynter, J. (2007). Social maturity and theory of mind in typically developing children and those on the autism spectrum. *Journal of Child Psychology and Psychiatry, 48,* 1243–1250.

Ponnet, K., Buysse, A., Roeyers, H., & De Corte, K. (2005). Empathic accuracy in adults with a pervasive developmental disorder during an unstructured conversation with a typically developing stranger. *Journal of Autism and Developmental Disorders, 35,* 585–600.

Premack, D., & Woodruff, G. (1978). Does the chimpanzee have a theory of mind? *Behavioral and Brain Sciences, 1,* 515–526.

Rajendran, G., & Mitchell, P. (2007). Cognitive theories of autism. *Developmental Review, 27,* 224–260.

Raymaekers, R., Van der Meere, J., & Roeyers, H. (2004). Event-rate manipulation and its effect on arousal modulation and response inhibition in adults with high functioning autism. *Journal of Clinical and Experimental Neuropsychology, 26,* 74–82.

Roeyers, H., Buysse, A., Ponnet, K., & Pichal, B. (2001). Advancing advanced mind-reading tests: Empathic accuracy in adults with a pervasive developmental disorder. *Journal of Child Psychology and Psychiatry, 42,* 271–278.

Savitsky, K., Keysar, B., Epley, N., Carter, T., & Swanson, A. (2009, February). *The perils of (perceived) self–other similarity: Egocentrism among friends and strangers.* Paper presented at the annual conference of the Society for Personality and Social Psychology, Tampa, FL.

Slaughter, V., Peterson, C. C., & Mackintosh, E. (2007). Mind what mother says: Narrative input and theory of mind in typical children and those on the autism spectrum. *Child Development, 78,* 839–858.

Steele, S., Joseph, R. M., & Tager-Flusberg, H. (2003). Brief report: Developmental change in theory of mind abilities in children with autism. *Journal of Autism and Developmental Disorders, 33,* 461–467.

Tager-Flusberg, H. (1993). Language and understanding minds in children with autism. In S. Baron-Cohen, H. Tager-Flusberg, & D. Cohen (Eds.), *Understanding other minds: Perspectives from developmental cognitive neuroscience* (pp. 124–150). Oxford, UK: Oxford University Press.

Taumoepeau, M., & Ruffman, T. (2008). Stepping stones to others' minds: Maternal talk relates to child mental state language and emotion understanding at 15, 24, and 33 months. *Child Development, 79,* 284–302.

Travis, L., Sigman, M., & Ruskin, E. (2001). Links between social understanding and social behaviour in verbally able children with autism. *Journal of Autism and Developmental Disorders, 31,* 119–130.

Volkmar, F. R., Lord, C., Bailey, A., Schultz, R. T., & Klin, A. (2004). Autism and pervasive developmental disorders. *Journal of Child Psychology and Psychiatry, 45,* 135–170.

Wechsler, D. A. (1991). *Wechsler Intelligence Scale for Children–Third Edition (WISC-III).* San Antonio, TX: Psychological Corporation.

Wechsler, D. A. (1997). *Wechsler Adult Intelligence Scale–Third Edition (WAIS-III).* San Antonio, TX: Psychological Corporation.

Wellman, H. M., Cross, D., & Watson, J. (2001). Meta-analysis of theory-of-mind development: The truth about false belief. *Child Development, 72,* 655–684.

Wimmer, H., & Perner, J. (1983). Beliefs about beliefs: Representation and constraining function of wrong beliefs in young children's understanding of deception. *Cognition, 13,* 103–128.

Wu, S. L., & Keysar, B. (2007). The effect of culture on perspective taking. *Psychological Science, 18,* 600–606.

Yirmiya, N., Erel, O., Shaked, M., & Solomonica-Levi, D. (1998). Meta-analyses comparing theory of mind abilities of individuals with autism, individuals with mental retardation, and normally developing individuals. *Psychological Bulletin, 124,* 283–307.

Yirmiya, N., Sigman, M. D., Kasari, C., & Mundy, P. (1992). Empathy and cognition in high-functioning children with autism. *Child Development, 63,* 150–160.

APPENDIX

The mental state story

Justine came into the dining room, cupping her hand beneath a spoon that dripped yellow sauce. "Aren't those flowers great? Four dollars for the bouquet, how about that? Did you wind the clock?"

Howard did not look up from the newspaper. "Later," he said.

"Please?"

He looked up. "Watch the spoon. You're going to stain the carpet."

"It chimed seven. This clock is really slow."

"You just dribbled."

She looked down. "I caught it." She showed him her cupped hand. "See? Dinner is going to be great. Now would you wind the clock?"

He took in a deep breath, then exhaled loudly. "All right." He closed the paper. The headline read, "DEATH TOLL RISES".

After she had gone back into the kitchen, he read the lead story again. Then he stood and went to the mantle where the clock sat among ballerina figurines. He opened the clock's crystal. As he fitted the key into the clock, his hand trembled. He hesitated. He took another deep breath, let it out slowly, and dropped the key into his pocket without winding the clock.

Howard looked toward the kitchen, bit his lip, then took the clock down from the mantle. Inside the door was taped a business card from the jeweller who had replaced a broken spring. Howard pulled the card free, then jammed it against the flywheel. The clock stopped ticking. Then he wound it.

He returned to the table just as Justine carried in their salad bowls. "Did you wind it?" she asked.

"Didn't I say I would?"

She put the bowls down and turned back toward the kitchen. "I'm fussing, I know. The house just isn't right without that clock chiming the quarter hours."

Howard folded his newspaper, and after she had again left the room he said, "I agree."

She came back in with their dinner plates. "How was your day? Mine was marvellous. Business was slow all over the store, but I had three big ring-ups. Bianca said it's all about attitude."

He cut his meat.

"So how was your day?"

"My day." He shook his head.

"Not so good? Tomorrow will be better."

"I'm not counting on it."

"Well your job has always given you a great deal of..."

"It's not my job," he said. He nodded at the paper.

She followed his gaze towards the headline. "You can't let that get you down."

"Can't I?"

She twisted her napkin in her hands. "It doesn't have to touch us."

"It's better if it does touch us. It's touching everyone."

If the clock had been running, it would have struck the quarter-hour by now.

He said, "There are times when it is obscene to be cheery. Obscene!"

Justine's face was white. She threw her wadded napkin onto the plate. She knocked her chair over in her hurry to stand and leave.

Howard's hands trembled again as he speared a bite.

EUROPEAN JOURNAL OF DEVELOPMENTAL PSYCHOLOGY
2010, 7 (1), 123–134

Ψ Psychology Press
Taylor & Francis Group

How impaired is mind-reading in high-functioning adolescents and adults with autism?

Herbert Roeyers and Ellen Demurie

Ghent University, Ghent, Belgium

Difficulties in understanding the mental states of others are considered to be a core cognitive feature of autism spectrum disorders (ASD). Traditional false-belief tasks were not suitable to measure mind-reading in adolescents and adults with ASD and were replaced by so-called more "advanced" tasks. A first series of tasks included the presentation of static stimuli in the visual or auditory modality. More recently, more dynamic, naturalistic tasks were developed. The most ecologically valid task to measure mind-reading is probably the empathic accuracy paradigm. Research with advanced mind-reading tests has demonstrated that high-functioning adults with ASD should not be underestimated since they may have good and in some cases very good mind-reading skills. Impairments are most obvious when an unstructured, dynamic and naturalistic task is being used.

Keywords: Autism; Empathic accuracy; Mind-reading; Theory of Mind.

One of the most striking characteristics of people with autism is their strange way of making contact with other people (Kanner, 1943). The social and communicative abnormalities that are characteristic of the disorder according to the DSM-IV-TR criteria (American Psychiatric Association, 2000) have often been linked to an impaired theory of mind (ToM; Baron-Cohen, Jolliffe, Mortimore, & Robertson, 1997a). ToM can be described as the ability to attribute mental states, such as intentions, beliefs and desires, to oneself and to others (Baron-Cohen, Leslie, & Frith, 1985). Difficulties in understanding the mental states of others are considered to be a core cognitive feature of autism spectrum disorders (ASD; Baron-Cohen, 2001a).

Correspondence should be addressed to Herbert Roeyers, Department of Experimental Clinical and Health Psychology, Ghent University, Henri Dunantlaan 2, B-9000 Gent, Belgium. E-mail: Herbert.Roeyers@Ugent.be

This paper was supported by a grant of the Fund for Scientific Research-Flanders (Belgium) awarded to the second author.

http://www.psypress.com/edp   DOI: 10.1080/17405620903425924

In its narrow use, the term theory of mind refers only to the ability to impute cognitive or volitional states to others (Premack & Woodruff, 1978). In its broader use, however, the term also refers to mind-reading, that covers more direct on-line processing of mental-state information including both verbal and nonverbal cues, thoughts and feelings.

Mind-reading deficits in autism spectrum conditions appear to occur early in lifetime, with joint attention deficits as one of the precursors, and seem to be universal (Baron-Cohen, 2001b). Frith, Happé, and Siddons (1994) found that a subgroup of children with autism who passed standard ToM tasks gave evidence of mentalizing in their everyday-life behaviour, as measured with the Vineland Scales of Adaptive Behaviour (Sparrow, Balla, & Cicchetti, 1984). It should be noted, however, that children with autism who pass ToM tasks were rated by their teachers to be even worse than younger typically developing ToM-failers in applying mind-reading in everyday social interaction and conversation (Peterson, Garnett, Kelly, & Attwood, 2009).

Baron-Cohen (2001a, 2001b) suggested that developmentally appropriate tests are needed in order to reveal the manifestations of the ToM abnormalities in people with autism. In this paper we will describe the evolution of the instruments used to measure ToM abilities adequately in individuals with ASD. This methodological evolution started with the use of false-belief tasks in children with autism. As a second step these simple tasks were adapted, resulting in the "advanced" mind-reading tasks. Today, a more naturalistic design for measuring empathic abilities can be found in the empathic accuracy task that has been used primarily in adults with ASD.

FALSE-BELIEF TASKS

During the first years of research within the ToM domain, a lot of studies focused on the perspective taking abilities of children with autism, who obviously experience difficulties in their ToM competence (Baron-Cohen, 1995; Baron-Cohen et al., 1985; Leekam & Perner, 1991). In these studies, researchers mainly used standard laboratory first-order false-belief tasks, which only involve inferring one person's mental state (Baron-Cohen et al., 1985). These tasks require understanding that different people can think differently about the same situation and may therefore hold a false belief (Baron-Cohen, 2001b). The most popular task is the so-called changed-location false-belief task in which an object is relocated by one character during the absence of another character who knows the original location. While typically developing 4-year-old children are able to pass these tests, the proportion of children with autism found to fail these tasks varies from 40% to 85% (Happé, 1995). Many young children with autism, even in the absence of intellectual disability, apparently do not understand that another's mental representation of the situation is different from their own until their teens or even later (Baron-Cohen, 1995; Happé, 1995; Leekam & Perner, 1991; Leslie & Thaiss, 1992). Moreover, with the exception of somewhat older, high-functioning children (e.g., Bauminger & Kasari, 1999; Dahlgren & Trillingsgaard, 1996), they all fail second-order tests that involve the subject's reasoning about what one person thinks about another person's thoughts (Baron-Cohen, 1995). Second-order false-belief tests involve considering embedded mental states, e.g., what John thinks that Mary thinks (Baron-Cohen, 2001b).

Nevertheless, some individuals with high-functioning autism or Asperger syndrome (AS) even pass the second-order false-belief tasks in their teens or early adulthood (Bowler, 1992; Happé, 1994; Ozonoff, Rogers, & Pennington, 1991). Given the fact that typically developing children pass these tests around the age of 6 or 7, there is, however, no reason to conclude that social-cognitive understanding of adolescents or adults with ASD is intact. But the observation has given rise to a few more challenging so-called "advanced" ToM tasks, which make it possible to cope with potential ceiling effects in the simple ToM tasks (Happé, 1994).

ADVANCED TASKS

One of the first advanced ToM measures was the "Strange Stories Task" developed by Happé (1994). This task requires subjects to make inferences about the mental states of story characters. It includes concepts such as white lie and double bluff. Since these kinds of tasks appear to be highly correlated with verbal IQ (Kaland et al., 2002), their usefulness as a tool for the assessment of social cognition is probably rather limited.

Another influential task that has been proffered as an advanced ToM test is the "Reading the Mind in the Eyes" Test (Eyes Test), used in high-functioning adults with autism or AS (Baron-Cohen et al., 1997a). It involves inferring other people's mental states from a photograph of their eye region. The original adult Eyes Test was revised in 2001 (Baron-Cohen, Wheelwright, Hill, Raste, & Plumb, 2001a) and in the same year an adaptation of the test was used in a study of children with AS (Baron-Cohen, Wheelwright, Spong, Scahill, & Lawson, 2001b). Research in adults with ASD, using the Eyes Test, yielded mixed results. In some studies, adults with ASD showed deficits on this task (Baron-Cohen et al., 1997a; Baron-Cohen, Wheelwright, & Jolliffe, 1997b; Baron-Cohen et al., 2001a), while in other studies, where other facial pictures were used, adults with ASD performed as well as controls on the Eyes Test (Ponnet, Roeyers, Buysse, De Clercq, & Van der Heyden, 2004; Roeyers, Buysse, Ponnet, & Pichal, 2001). Two studies with children with ASD (10- to 14-year-olds in Back, Ropar, & Mitchell, 2007; 8- to 14-year-olds in Baron-Cohen et al., 2001b) showed impairment on the Eyes Task in the group of children with ASD. However, in a sample with slightly older children (11- to 15-year-olds), Back et al. (2007) found no evidence for inferiority in interpreting mental states from the eyes in children with ASD.

It can be questioned, however, whether the Eyes Task measures the ability to recognize mental states of others and to what extent the test relates to everyday social interaction (see Johnston, Miles, & McKinlay, 2008). The limitations that have been identified suggest that the test is not so advanced as originally thought and that it lacks ecological validity (Ponnet et al., 2004). The same is true for "single-modality" tests that require inferring people's emotions from their voice tone (Rutherford, Baron-Cohen, & Wheelwright, 2002) or providing mental-state explanations for the movement of geometric shapes such as triangles in animated cartoons (e.g., Castelli, Frith, Happé, & Frith, 2002).

Using dynamic facial stimuli may give a more accurate measure of mind-reading competence as it simulates the demands of daily social experience (Back et al., 2007; Klin, Jones, Schultz, Volkmar, & Cohen, 2002). In studies with typically developing persons, better performance on emotion-recognition tasks was found when dynamic faces were used, in comparison with static faces (Harwood, Hall, & Shinkfield, 1999; Wehrle, Kaiser, Schmidt, & Scherer, 2000). Similar findings were obtained with individuals with ASD (Back et al., 2007). This "dynamic advantage" has been attributed to additional information, typically for dynamic interactions, such as temporal cues (Back et al., 2007).

Making use of film fragments in mind-reading tasks is a first step towards meeting the shortcomings of the static or unimodal ToM tasks. Instruments such as the Awkward Moments Test (Heavey, Phillips, Baron-Cohen, & Rutter, 2000), the Reading the Mind in Films Task (Golan, Baron-Cohen, Hill, & Golan, 2006), the Movie for the Assessment of Social Cognition (MASC; Dziobek et al., 2006) and the Animated Theory of Mind Inventory for Children (ATOMIC; Beaumont & Sofronoff, 2008) use film scenes in a multimodal, dynamic task to assess recognition of a wide variety of complex emotions and mental states. On these tasks, both adults and children with ASD appear to exhibit difficulties in social cognition (Dziobek et al., 2006; Golan, Baron-Cohen, & Golan, 2008; Golan et al., 2006; Heavey et al., 2000). It should be noted that gains that were made with respect to increased approximation of everyday mind-reading, resulted in a decreased pureness of the tests since movies also inevitably involve executive functions and central coherence (Baron-Cohen et al., 1997a). Moreover, unlike in real-life situations, subjects are permitted to use as much time as they need to make inferences of other persons' thoughts and feelings. In addition, like in the Eyes Task, these mind-reading measures show acted emotions and mental states and no "real" interactions and as such they do not acknowledge the difference between genuine and posed expressions of mental states. In addition, the correct answers are generated by non-impaired judges by means of consensus. The impact of the test designers with their social norms and conventions may be substantial and is certainly a potential bias (Johnston et al., 2008).

EMPATHIC-ACCURACY TASK

A more ecologically valid and naturalistic way of measuring mind-reading ability was found in the social psychological research literature on social cognition. It is provided by the empathic-accuracy design of Ickes and colleagues (Ickes, 1993; Ickes, Stinson, Bissonnette, & Garcia, 1990). Good evidence for both the reliability and the validity of this method has been provided (Marangoni, Garcia, Ickes, & Teng, 1995). Empathic accuracy is the degree to which an individual is successful in the "everyday mind-reading" he or she does whenever he or she attempts to infer another person's thoughts and feelings (Ickes, 1997).

In the standard stimulus paradigm, individual participants each view the same standard set of videotaped interactions and try to infer the thoughts and feelings of the same set of target persons (Marangoni et al., 1995). Roeyers et al. (2001) used this paradigm with adults with ASD. They made two videotapes, in each of which two volunteer opposite-sex young adults participated in a genuine initial conversation between strangers. The interactions were covertly videotaped and after the session, each of the four young adults was instructed to make a complete log of all the unexpressed thoughts and feelings that he or she had during the interaction session. This resulted in two stimulus tapes and a whole range of thought/feeling entries for both tapes.

A group of young adults with ASD and an individually matched control group viewed both tapes. An experimenter interrupted the stimulus tapes at each of the points at which the targets had previously reported having had a thought or feeling. The participants' task was to record their own inferences about the nature of the specific thought or feeling being reported by the target at that point. Empathic accuracy scores were computed by comparing each participant's inference with the corresponding thought/feeling entry obtained from the targets on the basis of the logic and procedures developed by Ickes and his colleagues (Ickes, 2003). Subjects with ASD performed significantly worse than the control group on one of the two tapes.

Although it was not the intention to manipulate the videotapes, the conversation in the first videotape, where there was no difference in empathic accuracy between groups, was structured around one topic (a board game) and appeared to be more concrete and predictable than that in the second one. The findings were replicated in a second study using the same stimulus tapes with adults with Asperger syndrome (Ponnet et al., 2004). Again differences between the target and the control group were only found for the second, less structured, tape. IQ was measured in this study, but empathic accuracy of the clinical group was not related to intelligence.

In a next study, two new stimulus tapes were produced with "getting acquainted" conversations between two strangers. However, this time, the structure of both videotapes was manipulated in such a way that one tape was more structured than the other one. While in the first tape the naturally occurring initial conversation between two strangers was recorded, the participants in the second videotape were told that it was required that they got to know each other personally before starting the experiment in which they thought they would be involved. In order to become acquainted with each other in a decent and less stressful manner, the experimenter proposed to leave the room for a short period. Before leaving, he gave the targets an 8-point list with questions they surely had to ask each other. It was found that the structure of the situation clearly matters for the mind-reading abilities of subjects with ASD (Ponnet, Buysse, Roeyers, & De Clercq, 2008). The empathic-accuracy scores of young adults with ASD and typically developing controls were only significantly different when subjects had to infer the thoughts and feelings of other persons in the less-structured and more chaotic conversation in the first tape. There was no association between performance and IQ in the participants with ASD.

The abovementioned studies suggest that the standard stimulus empathic-accuracy paradigm is a promising and valuable way of studying the mind-reading abilities of adults with ASD (see also Beaumont & Sofronoff, 2008). However, this design is still different from everyday mind-reading since participants serve only as perceivers and not as targets and they infer thoughts and feelings of people with whom they do not interact. This is not the case when an alternative empathic-accuracy design is used: the dyadic-interaction design. In this paradigm, each participant is an active and interacting member of a dyad instead of being a passive observer. Ponnet, Buysse, Roeyers, and De Corte (2005) developed a study in which high-functioning adults with ASD, with above-average intellectual abilities were videotaped with a concealed camera during an initial conversation with a typically developing stranger. Afterwards, they had to infer the unexpressed thoughts and feelings of the other person in the dyad. The participants with ASD did not differ from the typically developing participants in the ability to infer the thoughts and feelings of their interaction partner. Further analyses revealed that this was not due to the fact that the participants with ASD had unusual or strange thoughts and feelings that were difficult to infer by their typically developing interaction partner. The finding that adults with ASD performed so well in this study is probably due to the fact that they were able, to some extent, to structure the conversation they were involved in. The level of performance was not related to the IQ of the participants.

Although the dyadic-interaction design is probably the most ecologically valid method that has been used up till now to measure mind-reading skills in ASD, it still differs from any real-life social situation in several ways. Most importantly, the participants had to infer the thoughts or feelings of their interaction partner while they were viewing the videotape of their own conversation for a second time and they were allowed to use as much time as needed. The demands of daily life do not permit us to review our interactions and expect us to make quick and immediate inferences about the thoughts and feelings of our interaction partners.

EMPATHIC ACCURACY IN ADOLESCENTS WITH ASD

While a lot of attention has been paid to school-aged children and, more recently, to adults, adolescents with ASD have been largely neglected in the mind-reading literature. This is also the case for their non-impaired peers. From a developmental point of view, however, information on mind-reading skills in youngsters is of great interest. Gleason and colleagues extended the standard stimulus paradigm of empathic accuracy by studying typically developing adolescents (Gleason, Jensen-Campbell, & Ickes, 2009). Their results revealed that teenagers who obtained higher empathic-accuracy scores were more likely to have better-quality friendships, and experienced lower levels of relational victimization. Additionally, adolescents who were at highest risk for internalizing and social problems had low scores on the empathic-accuracy task, and on peer dimensions such as number of friends and friendship quality. It was suggested that empathic accuracy in childhood relationships might be a buffering mechanism that protects children against the development of impaired peer relationships and adjustment problems (Gleason et al., 2009).

Demurie, De Corel, and Roeyers (2009), recently used the standard stimulus paradigm with adolescents with ASD between 11 and 17 years of age. They were compared with age-mates with ADHD and with a group of typically developing adolescents. The standard stimulus tape in this study consisted of 10 short fragments with interactions between 5 dyads of adolescents who were initially strangers to each other. Adolescents with ASD clearly experienced difficulties in inferring the thoughts and feelings of others. They performed significantly worse than typically developing adolescents. The difference with the group with ADHD was, however, not significant. Interestingly, the empathic accuracy of the adolescents in the ASD group was positively correlated with age, but not with IQ.

DISCUSSION AND CONCLUSIONS

Apparently the majority of young children with ASD fail traditional mind-reading tasks. High-functioning adults with ASD, on the contrary, show only difficulties when more advanced or naturalistic tasks are being used. Their mind-reading impairments appear to be more subtle than those of young children. Whether this means that mind-reading abilities improve spontaneously or through teaching and training when individuals with ASD grow older, is still unclear. Research in adolescents is scarce, but the available evidence usually reveals more pronounced difficulties than in adults. Together with the findings that empathic abilities are correlated with age in children and in adolescents with ASD (Begeer, Koot, Rieffe, Meerum Terwogt, & Stegge, 2008; Demurie et al., 2009), this may indicate an improvement of mind-reading skills with growing age. More studies with adolescents and especially longitudinal studies from adolescence or earlier to adulthood are needed to shed more light on this issue. The fact that a complex paradigm as the empathic-accuracy design was successfully used with adolescents with ASD, is promising for future research.

Although clear or somewhat subtle differences with typically developing persons were detected in studies with adolescents and adults with ASD, we should be well aware that these are all differences on a group level. In all the samples where the standard stimulus paradigm has been used, there were individuals with ASD who performed as well as their typically developing peers. Apart from age in the study with adolescents, however, we have not yet been able to detect a characteristic that clearly distinguishes the empathic persons with ASD from those with poorer mind-reading skills. Detailed analyses in the Ponnet et al. (2008) study revealed that, to a large extent, young adults with ASD use the same strategies as typically developing persons to infer other people's thoughts and feelings. This brings us to the unresolved issue as to whether the development of ToM in children with ASD is delayed, deviant or both (Serra, Loth, Van Geert, Hurkens, & Minderaa, 2002). In any case, some older individuals with ASD seem to have very similar mind-reading skills compared to typically developing adolescents and adults. This suggests that, at least for a subgroup of high-functioning individuals with ASD, ToM-development is delayed rather than deviant.

Different studies with adults with ASD have shown the importance of structure to the performance on a mind-reading task. It is well known that people with ASD prefer structured situations and activities with clear rules and that their symptoms are less obvious in a highly structured context (e.g., Howlin, 1997; Mesibov, 1992). Apparently it is also much easier for them to infer thoughts and feelings of people who are engaged in a structured, quite predictable conversation, than of those involved in an unstructured, more chaotic interaction. It can be considered that all participants are familiar with the script of the structured interactions in the different empathic accuracy studies (i.e., an initial conversation of the getting-acquainted type). This familiarity might be derived from experience or by having learned the script previously. Therefore, particular cues in the situation may lead to the retrieval of information from memory about similar situations to that of the target person, as well as social scripts or other socially relevant knowledge (see Karniol, 1995). Very little is known about the capabilities of subjects with ASD for using scripts, although script-fading procedures are increasingly being employed in interventions with children (e.g., Brown, Krantz, McClannahan, & Poulson, 2008). While a small study by Trillingsgaard (1999) suggested that children with autism have significantly fewer well-organized scripts for familiar social routines (such as celebrate a birthday or make a cake) than control children, the results of a study by Volden and Johnston (1999) suggested that the basic scriptal knowledge of children with autism appears to be intact. The question remains whether these results can be generalized to adults with ASD and to what extent scriptal knowledge of adults is related to their mind-reading performance.

The so-called advanced mind-reading tests have demonstrated that high-functioning adults with ASD should not be underestimated since they may have good, and in some cases very good, mind-reading skills. This does not imply, however, that they show appropriate social behaviour. Good mind-reading skills are often necessary but never sufficient for successful social functioning in everyday life (Astington, 2003).

Mind-reading impairments are most obvious when an unstructured, dynamic and naturalistic task is being used, which circumvents the use of non-social heuristic strategies (Frith et al., 1994). The empathic-accuracy tasks that have been described can be further developed to get a better insight into the nature and development of mind-reading in individuals with ASD. They have the advantage of working with genuine mental states and allow us to take into account and to manipulate contextual factors (Johnston et al., 2008). More recent work with typically developing adults suggests that empathic accuracy may depend more on the characteristics of the targets, than on those of the perceivers (e.g., Zaki, Bolger, & Ochsner, 2008). Our findings that the performance of adults with ASD is largely associated with the degree of structure of the conversation, rather than with IQ, may suggest that also in high-functioning ASD the focus should be more on dispositions of targets than on the identification of dispositions of accurate perceivers, although the role of scriptal knowledge should certainly be taken into account. The recent findings in typically developing adults that auditory, and especially verbal information is more critical to empathic accuracy than visual information and that target expressivity predicts empathic accuracy (Zaki et al., 2009) is in line with this view and offers testable hypotheses for future research with individuals with ASD. Examining whether more structured conversations provide clearer verbal cues to internal states and therefore allow perceivers with ASD to improve their empathic accuracy (see Zaki et al., 2009) is most probably the next step to take.

REFERENCES

American Psychiatric Association. (2000). *Diagnostic and statistical manual of mental disorders* (4th ed., text rev.). Washington, DC: American Psychiatric Association.

Astington, J. W. (2003). Sometimes necessary, never sufficient: False belief and social competence. In B. Repacholi & V. Slaughter (Eds.), *Individual differences in theory of mind: Implications for typical and atypical development* (pp. 13–38). Hove, UK: Psychology Press.

Back, E., Ropar, D., & Mitchell, P. (2007). Do the eyes have it? Inferring mental states from animated faces in autism. *Child Development, 2*, 397–411.

Baron-Cohen, S. (1995). *Mindblindness: An essay on autism and theory of mind*. Cambridge, MA: MIT Press/Bradford Books.

Baron-Cohen, S. (2001a). Theory of mind and autism: A review. *International Review of Mental Retardation, 23*, 169–184.

Baron-Cohen, S. (2001b). Theory of mind in normal development and autism. *Prisme, 34*, 174–183.

Baron-Cohen, S., Jolliffe, T., Mortimore, C., & Robertson, M. (1997a). Another advanced test of theory of mind: Evidence from very high functioning adults with autism or Asperger syndrome. *Journal of Child Psychology and Psychiatry, 38*, 813–822.

Baron-Cohen, S., Leslie, A. M., & Frith, U. (1985). Does the autistic child have a "theory of mind"? *Cognition, 21*, 37–46.

Baron-Cohen, S., Wheelwright, S., Hill, J., Raste, Y., & Plumb, I. (2001a). The "Reading the Mind in the Eyes" Test revised version: A study with normal adults and adults with Asperger syndrome or high-functioning autism. *Journal of Child Psychology and Psychiatry, 42*, 241–251.

Baron-Cohen, S., Wheelwright, S., & Jolliffe, T. (1997b). Is there a "language of the eyes"? Evidence from normal adults, and adults with autism or Asperger syndrome. *Visual Cognition, 4*, 311–331.

Baron-Cohen, S., Wheelwright, S., Spong, A., Scahill, V., & Lawson, J. (2001b). Are intuitive physics and intuitive psychology independent? A test with children with Asperger syndrome. *Journal of Developmental and Learning Disorders, 5*, 47–78.

Bauminger, N., & Kasari, C. (1999). Brief report: Theory of mind in high-functioning children with autism. *Journal of Autism and Developmental Disorders, 29*, 81–86.

Beaumont, R. B., & Sofronoff, K. (2008). A new computerised advanced theory of mind measure for children with Asperger syndrome: The ATOMIC. *Journal of Autism and Developmental Disorders, 38*, 249–260.

Begeer, S., Koot, H. M., Rieffe, C., Meerum Terwogt, M., & Stegge, H. (2008). Emotional competence in children with autism: Diagnostic criteria and empirical evidence. *Developmental Review, 28*, 342–369.

Bowler, D. M. (1992). Theory of mind in Asperger syndrome. *Journal of Child Psychology and Psychiatry, 33*, 877–893.

Brown, J. L., Krantz, P. J., McClannahan, L. E., & Poulson, C. L. (2008). Using script fading to promote natural environment stimulus control of verbal interactions among youths with autism. *Research in Autism Spectrum Disorders, 2*, 480–497.

Castelli, F., Frith, C., Happé, F., & Frith, U. (2002). Autism, Asperger syndrome and brain mechanisms for the attribution of mental states to animated shapes. *Brain, 125,* 1839–1849.

Dahlgren, S. O., & Trillingsgaard, A. (1996). Theory of mind in non-retarded children with autism and Asperger's syndrome. A research note. *Journal of Child Psychology and Psychiatry and Allied Disciplines, 37,* 759–763.

Demurie, E., De Corel, M., & Roeyers, H. (2009). *Empathic accuracy in adolescents with autism spectrum disorders and adolescents with attention-deficit/hyperactivity disorder.* Manuscript submitted for publication.

Dziobek, I., Fleck, S., Kalbe, E., Rogers, K., Hassenstab, J., Brand, M., et al. (2006). Introducing MASC: A movie for the assessment of social cognition. *Journal of Autism and Developmental Disorders, 36,* 623–636.

Frith, U., Happé, F., & Siddons, F. (1994). Autism and theory of mind in everyday life. *Social Development, 3,* 108–124.

Gleason, K. A., Jensen-Campbell, L. A., & Ickes, W. (2009). The role of empathic accuracy in adolescents' peer relations and adjustment. *Personality and Social Psychology Bulletin, 35,* 997–1011.

Golan, O., Baron-Cohen, S., & Golan, Y. (2008). The "Reading the Mind in Films" task (child version): Complex emotion and mental state recognition in children with and without autism spectrum conditions. *Journal of Autism and Developmental Disorders, 28,* 1543–1541.

Golan, O., Baron-Cohen, S., Hill, J. J., & Golan, Y. (2006). The "Reading the Mind in Films" tasks: Complex emotion recognition in adults with and without autism spectrum conditions. *Social Neuroscience, 1,* 111–123.

Happé, F. G. E. (1994). An advanced test of theory of mind: Understanding of story characters' thoughts and feelings by able autistic, mentally handicapped, and normal children and adults. *Journal of Autism and Developmental Disorders, 24,*129–154.

Happé, F. G. E. (1995). The role of age and verbal-ability in the theory of mind task-performance of subjects with autism. *Child Development, 66,* 843–855.

Harwood, N., Hall, L. J., & Shinkfield, A. J. (1999). Recognition of facial emotional expressions from moving and static displays by individuals with mental retardation. *American Journal of Mental Retardation, 104,* 270–278.

Heavey, L., Phillips, W., Baron-Cohen, S., & Rutter, M. (2000). The Awkward Moments Test: A naturalistic measure of social understanding in autism. *Journal of Autism and Developmental Disorders, 30,* 225–236.

Howlin, P. (1997). *Autism: Preparing for adulthood.* New York: Routledge.

Ickes, W. (1993). Empathic accuracy. *Journal of Personality, 61,* 587–610.

Ickes, W. (1997). *Empathic accuracy.* New York: Guilford Press.

Ickes, W. (2003). *Everyday mind-reading: Understanding what other people think and feel.* New York: Prometheus Books.

Ickes, W., Stinson, L., Bissonnette, V., & Garcia, S. (1990). Naturalistic social cognition: Empathic accuracy in mixed-sex dyads. *Journal of Personality and Social Psychology, 59,* 730–742.

Johnston, L., Miles, L., & McKinlay, A. (2008). A critical review of the Eyes Test as a measure of social-cognitive impairment. *Australian Journal of Psychology, 60,* 135–141.

Kaland, N., Moller-Nielsen, A., Callesen, K., Mortensen, E. L., Gottlieb, D., & Smith, L. (2002). A new "advanced" test of theory of mind: evidence from children and adolescents with Asperger syndrome. *Journal of Child Psychology and Psychiatry and Allied Disciplines, 43,* 517–528.

Kanner, L. (1943). Autistic disturbances of affective contact. *Nervous Child, 2,* 217–230.

Karniol, R. (1995). Developmental and individual differences in predicting others' thoughts and feelings: Applying the transformation rule model. In N. Eisenberg (Ed.), *Review of personality and social psychology: Social development* (Vol. 15, pp. 27–48). Thousand Oaks, CA: Sage.

Klin, A., Jones, W., Schultz, R., Volkmar, F., & Cohen, D. (2002). Visual fixation patterns during viewing of naturalistic social situations as predictors of social competence in individuals with autism. *Archives of General Psychiatry, 59*, 809–816.

Leekam, S., & Perner, J. (1991). Does the autistic child have a metarepresentational deficit? *Cognition, 40*, 203–218.

Leslie, A., & Thaiss, L. (1992). Domain specificity in conceptual development: Evidence from autism. *Cognition, 43*, 225–251.

Marangoni, C., Garcia, S., Ickes, W., & Teng, G. (1995). Empathic accuracy in a clinically relevant setting. *Journal of Personality and Social Psychology, 68*, 854–869.

Mesibov, G. (1992). Treatment issues with high-functioning adolescents and adults with autism. In E. Schopler & G. Mesibov (Eds.), *High-functioning individuals with autism* (pp. 143–156). New York: Plenum Press.

Ozonoff, S., Rogers, S. J., & Pennington, B. F. (1991). Asperger's syndrome: Evidence of an empirical distinction from high-functioning autism. *Journal of Child Psychology and Psychiatry and Allied Disciplines, 32*, 1107–1122.

Peterson, C. C., Garnett, M., Kelly, A., & Attwood, T. (2009). Everyday social and conversation applications of theory-of-mind understanding by children with autism-spectrum disorders or typical development. *European Child and Adolescent Psychiatry, 18*, 105–115.

Ponnet, K., Buysse, A., Roeyers, H., & De Clercq, A. (2008). Mind-reading in young adults with ASD: Does structure matter? *Journal of Autism and Developmental Disorders, 38*, 905–918.

Ponnet, K., Buysse, A., Roeyers, H., & De Corte, K. (2005). Empathic accuracy in adults with a pervasive developmental disorder during an unstructured conversation with a typically developing stranger. *Journal of Autism and Developmental Disorders, 35*, 585–600.

Ponnet, K. S., Roeyers, H., Buysse, A., De Clercq, A., & Van der Heyden, E. (2004). Advanced mind-reading in adults with Asperger syndrome. *Autism, 8*, 249–266.

Premack, D., & Woodruff, G. (1978). Does the chimpanzee have a theory of mind? *Behavioural and Brain Sciences, 4*, 515–526.

Roeyers, H., Buysse, A., Ponnet, K., & Pichal, B. (2001). Advancing advanced mind-reading tests: Empathic accuracy in adults with a pervasive developmental disorder. *Journal of Child Psychology and Psychiatry, 42*, 271–278.

Rutherford, M. D., Baron-Cohen, S., & Wheelwright, S. (2002). Reading the mind in the voice: A study with normal adults and adults with Asperger syndrome and high functioning autism. *Journal of Autism and Developmental Disorders, 32*, 189–194.

Serra, M., Loth, F. L., Van Geert, P. L., Hurkens, E., & Minderaa, R. B. (2002). Theory of mind in children with "lesser variants" of autism: A longitudinal study. *Journal of Child Psychology and Psychiatry, 43*, 885–900.

Sparrow, S. S., Balla, D. A., & Cicchetti, D. V. (1984). *Vineland Adaptive Behavior Scales: Interview edition, survey form manual.* Circle Pines, MN: American Guidance Service.

Trillingsgaard, P. (1999). The script model in relation to autism. *European Child and Adolescent Psychiatry, 8*, 45–49.

Volden, J., & Johnston, J. (1999). Cognitive scripts in autistic children and adolescents. *Journal of Autism and Developmental Disorders, 29*, 203–211.

Wehrle, T., Kaiser, S., Schmidt, S., & Scherer, K. R. (2000). Studying the dynamics of emotional expression using synthesized facial muscle movements. *Journal of Personality and Social Psychology, 78*, 105–119.

Zaki, J., Bolger, N., & Ochsner, K. (2008). It takes two. The interpersonal nature of empathic accuracy. *Psychological Science, 19*, 399–404.

EUROPEAN JOURNAL OF DEVELOPMENTAL PSYCHOLOGY
2010, 7 (1), 135–151

Ψ Psychology Press
Taylor & Francis Group

Thinking outside the executive functions box:
Theory of mind and pragmatic abilities in attention
deficit/hyperactivity disorder

Hilde M. Geurts and Mark Broeders

University of Amsterdam, Amsterdam, The Netherlands

Mante S. Nieuwland

*Tufts University, Medford, and Athinoula A. Martinos Center for Biomedical
Imaging, Charlestown, MA, USA*

An endophenotype for attention deficit/hyperactivity disorder (AD/HD) is executive functioning. In the autism and developmental literature executive dysfunctions has also been linked to theory of mind (ToM) and pragmatic language use. The central question of this review is whether deficits in ToM and pragmatic language use are common in AD/HD. AD/HD seems to be associated with pragmatic deficits, but not with ToM deficits. In this review we address how this pattern of findings might facilitate the understanding of the commonalities and differences between executive functioning, ToM, and pragmatic abilities. Based on the reviewed studies we conclude that ToM is not likely to be a potential endophenotype for AD/HD, while it is too early to draw such a conclusion for pragmatic language use.

Keywords: Autism; AD/HD; Executive functioning; Pragmatic abilities; Theory of Mind.

Correspondence should be addressed to Dr Hilde Geurts, Division of Psychonomics, Department of Psychology, University of Amsterdam, Roetersstraat 15, Amsterdam, NL-1018 WB, The Netherlands. E-mail: h.m.geurts@uva.nl

We want to thank the organizers of the ToM meeting "Theory of Mind: Module or Emergent property" (March 2007, Wageningen, The Netherlands) for the initiative for this special issue on ToM. Moreover, we thank Sander Begeer and two anonymous reviewers for their comments on an earlier version of this article.

http://www.psypress.com/edp   DOI: 10.1080/17405620902906965

Research regarding distinctive but related neurodevelopmental disorders such as attention deficit hyperactivity disorder (AD/HD) and autism,[1] is increasingly moving towards determining cognitive endophenotypes that can characterize the heterogenic nature of these disorders, instead of trying to pinpoint which single cognitive construct underlies all AD/HD or autism characteristics (e.g., Anderson, 2008; Castellanos & Tannock, 2002; Happé, Ronald & Plomin, 2006; Viding & Blakemore, 2007). These endophenotypes can be conceptualized on a neurophysiological, neuroanatomical and/or cognitive level, and they are the intermediate between the behavioural classification (i.e., AD/HD as phenotype) and the biological variables (i.e., genotypes and environment) that cause the disorder (Gottesman & Gould, 2003). One potential cognitive endophenotype for both AD/HD and autism is executive functioning (Durston, De Zeeuw, & Staal, 2009; Hill, 2004; Pennington & Ozonoff, 1996).

Executive functions (EFs) are cognitive control processes that enable us to monitor ongoing performance in a dynamically changing environment (Eslinger, 1996; Ridderinkhof, Van den Wildenberg, Segalowitz, & Carter, 2004). In recent reviews it has been discussed that executive functioning (or cognitive control) is a valid and reliable endophenotype for AD/HD (e.g., Doyle et al., 2005; Durston et al., 2009). However, these executive dysfunctions in AD/HD do not exist in isolation. Other potential endophenotypes have also been put forward to understand the aetiology of AD/HD (Castellanos & Tannock, 2002; Nigg, Willcutt, Doyle, & Sonuga-Barke, 2005; Rommelse et al., 2008; Sonuga-Barke, 2005). For example, evidence accumulates that deficient reward processing may be another likely endophenotype for AD/HD (Castellanos & Tannock, 2002; Luman, Oosterlaan, & Sergeant, 2005; Sonuga-Barke, 2005). Moreover, EFs do relate to other notions that are important in the cognitive developmental literature, such as theory of mind (ToM) and pragmatic language use. These two domains will be the focus of the current review.

Some researchers argue that the development of executive functioning is closely linked to the development of ToM (e.g., Hughes, 1998; Perner & Lang, 1999; Russell, 1997) and pragmatic language use (Martin & McDonald, 2003). Deficits in EFs (e.g., Hill, 2004), ToM (e.g., Baron-Cohen, Tager-Flusberg, & Cohen, 2000) and pragmatic language use (e.g., Bishop, 1998) are known to coexist in, for example, individuals with autism, but are there deficits in ToM and pragmatic language use in AD/HD?

In the theoretical debate on the relationship between EF and ToM (see, e.g., Fisher & Happé, 2005; Hughes & Ensor, 2007; Ozonoff, Pennington, & Rogers, 1991; Pellicano, 2007) there are three different viewpoints. It has

---

[1] We use the term autism to refer to autism spectrum disorders including autism, Asperger syndrome, and pervasive developmental disorders not otherwise specified (PPD-NOS).

been argued that EF deficits lead to ToM deficits (so EFs are a prerequisite to develop ToM; e.g., Hughes, 1998; Russell, 1997). However, the reverse argument that ToM deficits lead to EF deficits has also been made (e.g., Perner & Lang, 1999, 2000). Alternatively, it could even be the case that both EF and ToM deficits stem from some other cognitive deficit. If indeed EF deficits lead to ToM deficits or when both deficits stem from the same cognitive deficit, one would expect ToM deficits in individuals that are characterized by EF deficits. As executive dysfunction has been thought to underlie the key characteristics of AD/HD (Barkley, 1997; Nigg & Casey, 2005), AD/HD will be an interesting testing case as one would expect at least mild ToM difficulties in people with AD/HD due to their EF deficits (Sergeant, Geurts, & Oosterlaan, 2002; Willcutt, Doyle, Nigg, Faraone, & Pennington, 2005; Willcutt, Sonuga-Barke, Nigg, & Sergeant, 2008). This same line of reasoning can be followed for pragmatic language use as both EF and ToM are related to pragmatic language use (Martin & McDonald, 2003). Hence, even when no ToM deficits are present in individuals with AD/HD one could expect at least mild pragmatic deficits due to the presence of EF deficits.

In this paper we will argue that as EF deficits are a key characteristic of AD/HD it could be productive to study (1) ToM abilities in AD/HD, and (2) pragmatic language use in AD/HD. Studying these abilities in AD/HD will not just gain insight into what type of difficulties individuals with AD/HD encounter besides their well-described EF deficits (e.g., Willcutt et al., 2008), but might also shed some light on the relationship between three related constructs, EF, ToM, and pragmatic abilities. Moreover, if ToM and pragmatic language use deficits are indeed associated with AD/HD it might be fruitful to study in more detail whether these are also potential endopheno-types for AD/HD. First, we will define EF and ToM and explain why it is thought that these two cognitive domains are highly interlinked. Second, we will discuss AD/HD studies focusing on ToM. Third, the relationship between EF, ToM, and pragmatic language use will be introduced. Fourth, studies focusing on pragmatic language use in AD/HD will be discussed.

1. EXECUTIVE FUNCTIONS, THEORY OF MIND, AND THEIR POTENTIAL RELATIONSHIP

Various abilities are shared under the wings of EF (Eslinger, 1996) as EFs encompass the ability to change strategies (cognitive flexibility), to keep and manipulate information online (working memory), to plan ahead (plan-ning), and to suppress responses (inhibition). Hence, EFs are especially important when people need to exert effortful control to deal with novel, complex or ambiguous situations in everyday life. EFs have been studied with a broad range of tasks (see Table 1).

TABLE 1
Conceptual descriptions and commonly used tasks to study different domains of EF and ToM

EF/ToM	Concept	Description	Commonly used tasks/paradigms[1]
EF	Inhibition	To slow down or stop a particular activity or response because it is no longer appropriate	Stop Signal Task; Go–NoGo Task; Negative Priming Task; Stroop CWT; Eriksen Flanker Task
EF	Working memory	Maintaining and manipulating information across a given time interval	Memory span such as Reading span & Digit span backwards (WAIS); Numbers and Letters (WAIS); n-Back; SoP
EF	Planning	The ability to think ahead to reach future goals for which intermediate steps are needed. These steps need to be executed in a proper order and at the proper moment in time	ToL; ToH; Stockings of Cambridge; Rey CFT
EF	Cognitive flexibility	The ability to adjust ideas and responses in a dynamically changing environment	WCST; ID/ED; Task switching; TMT A/B
ToM[2]	1st order belief	Knowledge that other people's have other mental states and beliefs than yourself	False belief (ability to recognize that others can have beliefs about the world that are wrong) tasks; picture sequencing measure; transfer test; deceptive box test; appearance-reality task; "false-photograph" task, Smarties test
ToM[2]	2nd order belief	Knowledge of what people think of other ones thoughts and beliefs	Ice cream van test, 2nd order variants of the 1st order test mentioned above, SST, Irony test

Notes: [1]We selected some examples of tasks that are commonly used to measure each of the domains, but there are many variants of each of these tasks and different types of names are given. The list here gives a general idea of the tasks used in most of the papers we described in the current selective review. [2] Please note that there are also many ToM tasks that cannot be categorized as 1st or 2nd order belief. We refer to the comprehensive review of Baron-Cohen (2001) for a more detailed overview of the various ToM tasks. For example, the SST and the Irony test are not just 2nd order tests but also involve pragmatic language abilities (see text). EF = Executive Functions; ID/ED = Intra-Dimensional/Extra-Dimensional shift task; Rey CFT = Rey Complex Figure Test; SoP = Self ordered pointing task; SST = Strange Stories Test; Stroop CWT = Stroop Colour Word Task; TMT = Trailmaking A and B; ToH = Tower of Hanoi; ToL: Tower of London; ToM = Theory of Mind; WAIS = Wechsler Adult Intelligence Scale (similar tasks in children's version of this task); WCST = Wisconsin Card Sorting Test.

ToM involves the ability to attribute mental states to one's self and to others, and understanding how mental states influence human behaviour (e.g., Baron Cohen, 2001). A well-developed ToM is crucial for making social inferences and guiding social behaviour in everyday-life communicative interactions. In ToM research, distinctions are often made between tasks that require an understanding of false belief, 1st order belief, 2nd order belief, or of complex humour such as jokes and irony (see Table 1 for an overview of these different types of tasks). These ToM abilities are thought to be made up of the ability to decode mental states based on observable information (i.e., if a person is smiling, we assume he/she is happy), and on the ability to reason about others' mental states and to predict and explain human behaviour based on these mental states (Sabbagh, Xu, Carlson, Moses, & Lee, 2006).

The relationship between EF and ToM has received a great deal of attention (Fisher & Happé, 2005; Hughes & Ensor, 2007; Ozonoff et al., 1991; Pellicano, 2007) as these constructs seem to be highly interlinked (Frye, Zelazo, Brooks, & Samuels, 1996; Hala, Hug, & Henderson, 2003; Hughes, 1998; Perner & Lang, 2000; Sabbagh et al., 2006). For example, cognitive flexibility involves the ability to rapidly switch between multiple tasks, and may be crucial to changing strategies or perspective in ToM tasks or during everyday conversation. Moreover, ToM tasks require working memory (McKinnon & Moscovitch, 2007) as intermediate steps are needed to perform well on, for example 2nd order tasks. The intermediate steps need to be kept in mind, evaluated and perhaps adjusted, so more intermediate steps may require a larger involvement of working memory. In EF tasks such as classical cognitive flexibility tasks, ToM may play a role as the participants have to adjust their behaviour based on feedback given by the assessor of the task (Ozonoff, 1995). In most EF tasks the participants need to conceptualize (i.e., infer) what the experimenter wants them to do (see also Pellicano, 2007, for details), which is an important aspect of ToM. To put it differently, to perform adequately on these EF tasks one needs to have a representational understanding of mind (Perner & Lang, 2000). Hence, it is no surprise that EF and ToM deficits often go hand in hand.

2. THEORY OF MIND IN AD/HD

The cardinal features of AD/HD are inattentiveness, hyperactivity, and impulsivity (American Psychiatric Association, 2000). Although communication impairments and social impairments are not crucial for the diagnosis of AD/HD (American Psychiatric Association, 2000), people with AD/HD often show difficulties in these domains (Nijmeijer et al., 2007).

In the last decade, a plethora of studies focused on EF in AD/HD. This neurodevelopmental disorder is mainly associated with EF deficits in the domain of inhibition and working memory (see Willcutt et al., 2005, 2008, for overviews). However, to our knowledge, only five studies have examined ToM abilities in AD/HD. Three of these studies concluded that ToM abilities are intact in individuals with AD/HD (Charman, Carroll, & Sturge, 2001; Dyck, Ferguson, & Shochet, 2001; Perner, Kain, & Barchfeld, 2002), while the findings of two studies suggest that individuals with AD/HD might be challenged on ToM tasks (Buitelaar, Van der Wees, Schwaab-Barneveld, & Van der Gaag, 1999; Fahie & Symons, 2003).

Buitelaar and colleagues (1999) were the first to study ToM abilities in AD/HD. They reported that children with AD/HD and autism could not be differentiated on a composite score of 2nd order false-belief tasks while the clinical groups performed worse than the typically developing group. Based on these findings they concluded that children with AD/HD indeed have ToM difficulties. Although this study measured ToM abilities quite exhaustively (six 1st order and four 2nd order ToM tasks), it suffered from a very small sample size as it included only nine children with AD/HD. Moreover, no mention was made of whether participants belonged to a specific subtype of AD/HD. The EF account predicts executive dysfunctions in the predominantly combined subtype and the hyperactive/impulsive subtype, but not in the inattentive subtype (Barkley, 1997). Moreover, it is not clear whether these AD/HD children do have comorbid disorders or characteristics of comorbid disorders such as autism or specific language disorders that might also be associated with ToM deficits.

In contrast, ToM difficulties were not observed in two larger AD/HD studies (Charman et al., 2001; Dyck et al., 2001). In both these studies a well-known and broadly used ToM task, the Strange Stories Test (SST; Happé, 1994) was applied to measure ToM. The SST, which was not included in the Buitelaar study (1999), was developed as some people with autism are able to pass 1st order and 2nd order ToM tasks while showing difficulties in appreciating non-literal speech, such as indirect requests, sarcasm, irony, and metaphorical expressions (Happé, 1993, 1994). In the SST, participants read stories and are tested on whether they give mental-state explanations for the story characters' non-literal utterances (jokes, lies, or figures of speech). The SST is constructed in such a way that the motivation behind an utterance is interpreted in one specific way by most people. Studies using this task indeed showed that participants with autism that passed standard 2nd order ToM tasks had difficulties with the SST (e.g., Happé, 1994; Joliffe & Baron-Cohen, 1999). In both AD/HD studies the children with AD/HD passed the SST.

The Dyck et al. (2001) study only involved children with AD/HD of the inattentive subtype who are not expected to encounter EF deficits in the first place (Barkley, 1997). One would expect to observe ToM difficulties in children with AD/HD from the combined subtype as these children are known to encounter EF difficulties. Children with AD/HD of this specific subtype were included in the Charman study (2001) yet no ToM deficits were observed, even though these children failed on inhibition and planning tasks. It seems that when ToM is measured with the SST, children with AD/HD do not encounter ToM deficits (Charman et al., 2001; Dyck et al., 2001). The absence of difficulties on one specific ToM task does not imply that children with AD/HD will perform normally on other ToM tasks as ToM is a multi-faceted construct. Hence, children with AD/HD do not encounter difficulties on the SST, but might encounter deficits on other ToM tasks, which would be in line with the findings of Buitelaar et al. (1999) who found AD/HD-related ToM deficit on a composite score that included scores on various ToM tasks.

Also, Perner and colleagues (2002) included various ToM tasks (three 2nd order false-belief tasks) in their study. Participants in this community study were children at risk for developing AD/HD. None of these children showed any difficulties on a composite score of the ToM tasks whereas they showed difficulties in EF domains such as planning. Even when ToM performance was taken into account, the EF deficits were still present in the "at risk for AD/HD" group. A follow-up on these results is needed to determine whether these children indeed developed full-blown AD/HD later, but these findings suggest that AD/HD is not necessarily associated with ToM difficulties.

Interestingly, Fahie and Symons (2003) also included both ToM tasks (four false-belief tasks) and EF tasks (focusing on working memory). The participants in this study did not have clinical diagnoses of AD/HD, but showed attention and behavioural problems. These problems were similar to difficulties experienced by children with AD/HD and were so severe that referral to a clinic was needed. In these children, ToM ability (here, an aggregated score of the four false-belief tasks) was negatively related to both attention problems and impulsivity. Across all children working memory abilities were related to overall ToM performance. Working memory is an EF that is known to be dysfunctional in AD/HD and has been shown to be important for performances on various ToM tasks (e.g., Bull, Phillips, & Conway, 2008; McKinnon & Moscovitch, 2007). Please note that in this study it is also not clear whether other disorders next to AD/HD might explain the pattern of findings. Working memory is thought to be deficient in many other disorders besides AD/HD (Willcutt et al., 2008).

Based on the five aforementioned studies, it still seems premature to conclude whether or not children with AD/HD necessarily encounter ToM difficulties, but the evidence so far favours the idea that ToM deficits are not strongly present in these children. Hence, this would suggest that EF deficits do not automatically lead to ToM deficits.

3. EXECUTIVE FUNCTIONS, THEORY OF MIND, AND PRAGMATIC ABILITIES

Both EF and ToM are cognitive notions that are thought to be related to language deficits, especially pragmatic abilities (e.g., Martin & McDonald, 2003). Pragmatic ability refers to the appropriate use of language within a social communicative context (e.g., Rapin, 1996; Tannock & Schachar, 1996). It involves a broad array of social linguistic skills, such as using contextual information to interpret incoming utterances, the ability to comprehend non-literal/figurative expressions (such as jokes and irony), and inferring implicit messages. Pragmatic difficulties including, among others, overly literal language interpretation, impairments in production and comprehension of prosody, difficulties with understanding narrative-humour, making socially inappropriate comments, disorganization in the speech content, lie at the core of a neurodevelopmental disorder such as autism (American Psychiatric Association, 2000; Volkmar, Lord, Bailey, Schultz, & Klin, 2004). However, pragmatic deficits have also been observed in AD/HD, which will be discussed in more detail later on.

Under the EF account, pragmatic deficits are caused by executive dysfunction (McDonald, 1993). For instance, in order to interpret jokes, one must hold information in memory and, at the same time, flexibly evaluate and interpret this information, potentially in subsequent stages. It thus stands to reason that EFs such as cognitive flexibility and working memory are necessary for pragmatic language use (Ozonoff & Miller, 1996). Moreover, the ability to plan ahead during real-time conversation is important to retain a coherent story line, so failures in planning will negatively affect the discourse. So EF and pragmatic abilities seem to be interlinked. As AD/HD is associated with EF deficits one would expect pragmatic deficits in individuals with AD/HD.

According to the ToM account, pragmatic deficits in people with autism occur due to their inability to take someone else's perspective during communicative exchanges. Inferring the appropriate meaning of what your conversational partner is saying, requires taking into account his/her intentions, beliefs, and knowledge. Hence, pragmatic interpretation is considered by some as inherently metapsychological and involving the construction and evaluation of a hypothesis about the communicator's meaning, thus drawing upon processes that are also involved in ToM (i.e., social or communicative inference; see also Martin & McDonald, 2003; Sperber & Wilson, 2002). It is not clear how ToM and pragmatic abilities precisely relate to one another (see Sperber & Wilson, 2002, for a discussion) as a deficit in pragmatic abilities can occur for several reasons. For example, it might be due to some degree of mind blindness and/or a failure in use of context (see also Baron-Cohen, 2001). The general idea is that ToM is not needed for all pragmatic aspects of language (e.g., Sperber & Wilson, 2002). So, even absence of ToM deficits in AD/HD does not exclude the possibility of pragmatic language deficits in AD/HD.

4. PRAGMATIC ABILITIES IN AD/HD

Bishop and Baird (2001) showed that children with AD/HD had pragmatic difficulties: children with AD/HD showed more stereotyped conversations, had more problems with conversational rapport, and demonstrated more problems with social relationships compared to typically developing children, who show no deviances in their language development. A striking finding was that children with AD/HD hardly differed from children with autism. These observed pragmatic difficulties in AD/HD children have been replicated in various other studies (Bignell & Cain, 2007; Bruce, Thernlund, & Nettelbladt, 2006; Geurts & Embrechts, 2008; Geurts et al., 2004b; Norbury, Nash, Baird, & Bishop, 2004). The pragmatic difficulties in children with ADHD were, in general, less profound compared to those observed in children with autism for whom pragmatic language deficits are a key characteristic (American Psychiatric Association, 2000). Although each of these studies differed in the AD/HD subtypes that were included, the findings were consistent. To our knowledge, all studies to date have reported pragmatic language deficits in children with AD/HD.

In our most recent study, we even showed that parental reports of pragmatic difficulties in children with autism can partly be explained by the hyperactivity characteristics in these children (Geurts & Embrechts, 2008). The extent of pragmatic language difficulties was related to the hyperactivity characteristics, but not to the attention difficulties the parents reported. These findings were in line with the findings of Bignell and Cain (2007). These authors reported pragmatic language deficits in each of the three AD/HD subtypes, but the deficits were more profound in those children that were hyperactive and impulsive (irrespective of whether they also had attention deficits as for both groups large effect sizes were obtained) than in the children that had attention deficits only (as only small effect sizes were obtained). Interestingly, although only hyperactivity is related to pragmatic language abilities (Geurts & Embrechts, 2008), both attention problems and impulsivity are related to ToM abilities (Fahie & Symons, 2003).

One disadvantage of all studies that have focused specifically on pragmatic abilities in AD/HD is that they all relied on a parent questionnaire. The question is whether participants with AD/HD also encounter pragmatic deficits when pragmatic abilities are directly measured in the children themselves. As we mentioned before, children with AD/HD do not seem to have difficulties with the SST (Charman et al., 2001; Happé, 1994 in Dyck et al., 2001). Some might argue that the SST is a direct measure of pragmatic abilities instead of a broad ToM measure. As noted earlier, the SST was developed to detect ToM deficits in those participants with autism that pass other ToM tasks. This suggests that more advanced or subtle ToM abilities are needed for this task as compared to most other ToM tasks. If the earlier SST findings are interpreted as such we must conclude that children with AD/HD are not challenged on this advanced type of ToM. If we interpret the SST as a direct measure of pragmatic abilities, this would suggest that the findings are in contrast with the findings based on parent reports (Bignell & Cain, 2007; Bruce et al., 2006; Geurts & Embrechts, 2008; Geurts et al., 2004b; Norbury et al., 2004). A common finding in clinical language research is that the informant agreement between parents and other informants, even when very similar measures are used, is notoriously low (e.g., Bishop, 1998; Embrechts, Mugge, & Van Bon, 2005; Massa, Gomes, Tartter, Wolfson, & Halperin, 2008). We are not aware of any study that has directly tested pragmatic language use in participants with AD/HD. Hence, the inclusion of direct measures of pragmatic language use is needed in future studies to be able to draw strong conclusions regarding the pragmatic language abilities of children with AD/HD.

We focused on pragmatic language use as both EF and ToM are assumed to be related to pragmatic abilities. It seems that children with AD/HD do not encounter strong ToM deficits, even though they do encounter EF deficits (Sergeant et al., 2002; Willcutt et al., 2005, 2008). If we, for now, assume that they also encounter pragmatic deficits this would have some implications for the interpretation of findings on ToM tasks. The findings so far suggest that for every ToM task, it remains to be determined whether and to what extent task performance relies on EF and/or pragmatic abilities.[2]

5. CONCLUSIONS AND FUTURE DIRECTIONS

To serve as an endophenotype various criteria need to be met by the construct (such as EF, ToM, or pragmatic language use) under study (see De Geus & Boomsma, 2001; Durston et al., 2009; Viding & Blakemore, 2007, for details). For example, endophenotypes (such as EFs) need to be

---

[2]We calculated the pooled effect size by incorporating the number of participants for each of the effect sizes following the method described in the review paper of Willcutt and colleagues (2005). For the ToM studies this pooled effect size could not be calculated as most studies did not report all the necessary details (mean and standard deviation and number of participants per group). However, for the pragmatic language use studies, even though the studies sometimes differed in the reported dependent measures, the pooled effect size could be calculated. The pooled effect size (Cohen's d) for the pragmatic language measures is 0.14, which is small ($N_{AD/HD} = 266$ and $N_{controls} = 281$).

associated with the psychopathology (AD/HD) of interest (validity) and should represent a reliable characteristic. Moreover, the association between endophenotypes and specific behaviour must be theoretically meaningful (causality; De Geus & Boomsma, 2001). We know that EFs are related to AD/HD and the association between this potential endophenotype and the specific behaviour is theoretically meaningful (see Durston et al., 2009, for an extensive discussion). Moreover, we know that in other neurodevelopmental disorders such as autism, EF deficits go hand in hand with deficits in ToM and pragmatic abilities. In the current review we show that this is not the case for AD/HD. We argue that studying neurodevelopmental disorders such as AD/HD may help us in unravelling the complex relationship between EFs, ToM, and pragmatic abilities that is observed in individuals with autism and typical development. Based on this literature review, we will draw three major conclusions and give suggestions for future research. We think this might be helpful in both understanding the link between different cognitive domains and in determining whether ToM and pragmatic abilities might be additional endophenotypes to understand the aetiology of neurodevelopmental disorders such as AD/HD.

First, EF and ToM and pragmatic abilities are all multi-faceted constructs that need further clarification and specification, in particular with regard to the separability of its components and the validity and reliability of the different tasks that are used to measure these constructs. A more clear taxonomy of each of these three constructs is needed to improve understanding of how these domains relate to each other in typical and atypical development. The work of Bull and colleagues (2008) is a good example of how fractionating EF and ToM in separate subdomains can explain some of the discrepancies across earlier studies. In that study it was shown, by using a dual-task paradigm, that whereas different aspects of EF (inhibition, updating, and switching) commonly influenced the performance on a particular ToM task (SST), only inhibition had a specific effect on another ToM task (Mind in the Eyes Test). Clearly, more experimental work is needed to fractionate EF and ToM into subconstructs that allow for more specific hypothesis testing. Moreover, it is also important to develop measures of EF, ToM, and pragmatic abilities that are more similar in order to achieve a greater focus and convergence between the ideas related to these three constructs. For example, in most studies a ToM task is correlated to an EF task to determine how these two constructs relate to each other. However, the EF tasks chosen often differ in many aspects from the ToM task beside the fact that it is measuring EF instead of ToM as, for example, ToM tasks generally require verbal responses in contrast to EF tasks that often require non-verbal motor responses.

Second, as pragmatic functioning may partly draw upon similar inference processes as ToM, studies that focus on the relationship between EF and

ToM may also inform us on the relationship between EF and pragmatic functioning. This is especially the case when ToM tasks (e.g., the SST; Happé, 1994) also tap into pragmatic language ability. However, it is important to keep in mind that ToM is not needed to explain all aspects of pragmatic language use. So, the relationship between EF and pragmatic abilities might be only partly explained by the existing relationship between EF and ToM. Aside from addressing the relationship between all these three constructs simultaneously, future research that includes ToM tasks (including the SST) and pragmatic tests (both parental questionnaires as direct tests of pragmatic functioning) in typically developing children or adults might shed some more light on how ToM and pragmatic abilities relate to each other.

Third, the comparison of findings in related neurodevelopmental disorders can also enhance our knowledge about how different constructs might be related to each other. The discussion about the three different cognitive constructs (EF, ToM, and pragmatic abilities) stems from the autism research field. In this review we focused on a related neurodevelopmental disorder, AD/HD. We introduced AD/HD as a disorder that is associated with EF deficits, and we hypothesized, based on the suggested link between EF, ToM, and pragmatic abilities in the autism literature (e.g., Hughes & Ensor, 2007; Pellicano, 2007), that children with AD/HD would encounter deficits in ToM and pragmatic language use. However, no clear evidence for ToM deficits has been reported (e.g., Charman et al., 2001; Dyck et al., 2001; Perner et al., 2002), although children with AD/HD do show pragmatic deficits (Bignell & Cain, 2007; Bruce et al., 2006; Geurts & Embrechts, 2008; Geurts et al., 2004b; Norbury et al., 2004). From the current review we can conclude that EF deficits do not automatically lead to ToM deficits (which is in contrast with Hughes, 1998; Russell, 1997). Also, other neurodevelopmental disorders might be of interest to study the relationship between EF, ToM, and pragmatic abilities. For example, deaf children with delayed language acquisition ("late-signing") may have substantially delayed ToM development (Peterson, 2003), but do not always show the other social and pragmatic deficits that are characteristic of autism (Peterson & Siegal, 1995). This suggests that one can experience ToM difficulties without having pragmatic difficulties. The studies with children with AD/HD already suggest that one can also experience pragmatic deficits without having ToM deficits, but another interesting group to study the relationship between ToM and pragmatic abilities are children with specific pragmatic language impairments. These children hardly have any difficulties in processing language form but show specific pragmatic impairments in language use (e.g., Bishop, 1998), whereas they show no difficulties involving the other components of the autism triad (difficulties in non-verbal communication, lack of sociability, or showing repetitive behaviours).

Although specific pragmatic language impairments children are known for their pragmatic difficulties, it is not evident whether these children have ToM and EF difficulties (Bishop, 1998; Bishop & Norbury, 2005; Botting & Conti-Ramsden, 2003; Shields, Varley, Broks, & Simpson, 1996). We believe that by focusing on distinct but overlapping disorders, a better understanding can be achieved about the relationship between EF, ToM, and also pragmatic abilities, and, therefore, future studies in this area are warranted.

One such future study might, for example, include both children with AD/HD and autism to test more specific hypotheses. It is known that these groups of children both have difficulties in working memory (Willcutt et al., 2008), whereas difficulties in cognitive flexibility seem the most prominent EF deficit in children with autism (Hill, 2004; Willcutt et al., 2008; but see Geurts, Corbett, & Solomon, 2009), and inhibition deficits lie at the core of AD/HD (Sergeant et al., 2002; Willcutt et al., 2005, 2008). As described earlier, these different EF domains seem to relate to different aspects of ToM. Hence, the two disorders might be associated with different type of both EF and ToM deficits. Although speculative, difficulties with inhibition and working memory might lead to subtle difficulties in pragmatic abilities but not in ToM as seen in children with AD/HD, while difficulties in both cognitive flexibility and working memory possibly lead to more severe ToM and pragmatic difficulties as seen in autism. So, we would predict that there might be both quantitative and qualitative differences between these two disorders in the EF, ToM, and pragmatic difficulties they encounter. For example, if inhibition measures predict conversational turn-taking abilities but cognitive flexibility measures predict perspective-taking abilities, then one would expect children with AD/HD to have more severe difficulties in turn taking while children with autism might have more severe difficulties in perspective taking. Even though some studies have focused either on EF or ToM in both AD/HD and autism (e.g., Buitelaar et al., 1999; Geurts, Verte, Oosterlaan, Roeyers, & Sergeant, 2004a; Happé et al., 2006), research has yet to be done that examines both these domains simultaneously in these two partly overlapping neurodevelopmental disorders.

In sum, there is a clear need for longitudinal studies that simultaneously focus on several developmental domains in related disorders, in order to disentangle why some children end up with severe difficulties in one domain (e.g., EF) but manage to perform well in another related domain (e.g., ToM). EF might indeed be a valid and reliable endophenotype for AD/HD and may point to those genotypes that are related to AD/HD but also to autism (see Ronald, Simonoff, Kuntsi, Asherson, & Plomin, 2008). Combining different endophenotypes such as EF, ToM, and pragmatic abilities might help us in explaining the overlap and differences between neurodevelopmental disorders in general, and more specifically in AD/HD and autism. However, as argued in this review, it has become clear that ToM is not likely to be a potential endophenotype for AD/HD, while it is too early to draw such a conclusion for pragmatic language use.

REFERENCES

Anderson, G. M. (2008). The potential role for emergence in autism. *Autism Research, 1,* 18–30.

American Psychiatric Association. (2000). *Diagnostic and statistical manual of mental disorders* (4th ed., text rev.). Washington, DC: Author.

Barkley, R. A. (1997). Behavioral inhibition, sustained attention, and executive functions: Constructing a unifying theory of AD/HD. *Psychological Bulletin, 121,* 65–94.

Baron Cohen, S. (2001). Theory of mind and autism: A review. In L. M. Glidden (Ed.), *International review of research in mental retardation: Autism* (Vol. 23, pp. 169–184). San Diego, CA: Academic Press.

Baron Cohen, S., Tager-Flusberg, H., & Cohen, D. J. (2000). *Understanding other minds: Perspectives from developmental neuroscience* (2nd revised ed.) Oxford, UK: Oxford University Press.

Bignell, S., & Cain, K. (2007). Pragmatic aspects of communication and language comprehension in groups of children differentiated by teacher ratings of inattention and hyperactivity. *British Journal of Developmental Psychology, 25,* 499–512.

Bishop, D. V. M. (1998). Development of the Children's Communication Checklist (CCC): A method for assessing qualitative aspects of communicative impairment in children. *Journal of Child Psychology and Psychiatry, 39,* 879–891.

Bishop, D. V. M., & Baird, G. (2001). Parent and teacher report of pragmatic aspects of communication: Use of the Children's Communication Checklist in a clinical setting. *Developmental Medicine and Child Neurology, 43,* 809–818.

Bishop, D. V. M., & Norbury, C. F. (2005). Executive functions in children with communication impairments, in relation to autistic symptomatology 2: Response inhibition. *Autism, 9,* 29–43.

Botting, N., & Conti Ramsden, G. (2003). Autism, primary pragmatic difficulties, and specific language impairment: Can we distinguish them using psycholinguistic markers? *Developmental Medicine & Child Neurology, 45,* 515–524.

Bruce, B., Thernlund, G., & Nettelbladt, U. (2006). AD/HD and language impairment: A study of the parent questionnaire FTF (Five to Fifteen). *European Child & Adolescent Psychiatry, 15,* 52–60.

Buitelaar, J. K., Van der Wees, M., Schwaab-Barneveld, H., & Van der Gaag, R. J. (1999). Theory of mind and emotion-recognition functioning in autistic spectrum disorders and in psychiatric control and normal children. *Development and Psychopathology, 11,* 39–58.

Bull, R., Phillips, L. H., & Conway, C. A. (2008). The role of control functions in mentalizing: Dual-task studies of theory of mind and executive function. *Cognition, 107,* 663–672.

Castellanos, F. X., & Tannock, R. (2002). Neuroscience of attention-deficit/hyperactivity disorder: The search for endophenotypes. *Nature Review of Neuroscience, 3,* 617–628.

Charman, T., Carroll, F., & Sturge, C. (2001). Theory of mind, executive function and social competence in boys with AD/HD. *Emotional and Behavioural Difficulties, 6,* 31–49.

De Geus, E. J. C., & Boomsma, D. I. (2001). A genetic neuroscience approach to human cognition. *European Psychologist, 6,* 241–253.

Doyle, A. E., Faraone, S. V., Seidman, L. J., Willcutt, E. G., Nigg, J. T., Waldman, I. D., et al. (2005). Are endophenotypes based on measures of executive functions useful for molecular genetic studies of ADHD? *Journal of Child Psychology and Psychiatry, 46,* 774–803.

Durston, S., de Zeeuw, P., & Staal, W. G. (2009). Imaging genetics in ADHD: A focus on cognitive control. *Neuroscience & Biobehavioural Review, 33,* 674–689.

Dyck, M. J., Ferguson, K., & Shochet, I. M. (2001). Do autism spectrum disorders differ from each other and from non-spectrum disorders on emotion recognition tests? *European Child and Adolescent Psychiatry, 10,* 105–116.

Embrechts, M., Mugge. A., & van Bon, W. (2005). *De Nijmeegse Pragmatiektest [the Nijmegen Pragmatics Test].* Amsterdam: Harcourt Test Publishers.

Eslinger, P. J. (1996). Conceptualizing, describing, and measuring components of executive function. In G. R. Lyon & N. A. Krasnegor (Eds.), *Attention, memory, and executive function* (pp. 263–277). Baltimore: Paul H. Brookes.

Fahie, C. M., & Symons, D. K. (2003). Executive functioning and theory of mind in children clinically referred for attention and behavior problems. *Journal of Applied Developmental Psychology, 24,* 51–73.

Fisher, N., & Happé, F. (2005). A training study of theory of mind and executive function in children with autistic spectrum disorders. *Journal of Autism and Developmental Disorders, 35,* 757–771.

Frye, D., Zelazo, P. D., Brooks, P. J., & Samuels, M. C. (1996). Inference and action in early causal reasoning. *Developmental Psychology, 32,* 120–131.

Geurts, H. M., Corbett, B., & Solomon, M. (2009). The paradox of cognitive flexibility in autism. *Trends in Cognitive Science, 13,* 74–82.

Geurts, H. M., & Embrechts, M. (2008). Language profiles in ASD, SLI, and AD/HD. *Journal of Autism and Developmental Disorders, 38,* 1931–1943.

Geurts, H. M., Verte, S., Oosterlaan, J., Roeyers, H., Hartman, C. A., Mulder, E. J., et al. (2004b). Can the Children's Communication Checklist differentiate between children with autism, children with AD/HD, and normal controls? *Journal of Child Psychology and Psychiatry, 45,* 1437–1453.

Geurts, H. M., Verte, S., Oosterlaan, J., Roeyers, H., & Sergeant, J. A. (2004a). How specific are executive functioning deficits in attention deficit hyperactivity disorder and autism? *Journal of Child Psychology and Psychiatry, 45,* 836–854.

Gottesman, I. I., & Gould, T. D. (2003). The endophenotype concept in psychiatry: Etymology and strategic intentions. *American Journal of Psychiatry, 160,* 636–645.

Hala, S., Hug, S., & Henderson, A. (2003). Executive function and false-belief understanding in preschool children: Two tasks are harder than one. *Journal of Cognition and Development, 4,* 275–298.

Happé, F., Ronald, A., & Plomin, R. (2006). Time to give up on a single explanation for autism. *Nature Neuroscience, 9,* 1218–1220.

Happé, F. G. E. (1993). Communicative competence and theory of mind in autism: A test of relevance theory. *Cognition, 48,* 101–119.

Happé, F. G. E. (1994). An advanced test of theory of mind: Understanding of story characters' thoughts and feelings by able autistic, mentally handicapped, and normal children and adults. *Journal of Autism and Developmental Disorders, 24,* 129–154.

Hill, E. L. (2004). Evaluating the theory of executive dysfunction in autism. *Developmental Review, 24,* 189–233.

Hughes, C. (1998). Executive function in preschoolers: Links with theory of mind and verbal ability. *British Journal of Developmental Psychology, 16,* 233–253.

Hughes, C., & Ensor, R. (2007). Executive function and theory of mind: Predictive relations from ages 2 to 4. *Developmental Psychology, 43,* 1447–1459.

Joliffe, T., & Baron Cohen, S. (1999). A test of central coherence theory: Linguistic processing in high-functioning adults with autism or Asperger syndrome: Is local coherence impaired? *Cognition, 71,* 149–185.

Luman, M., Oosterlaan, J., & Sergeant, J. A. (2005). The impact of reinforcement contingencies on AD/HD: A review and theoretical appraisal. *Clinical Psychology Review, 25,* 183–213.

Martin, I., & McDonald, S. (2003). Weak coherence, no theory of mind, or executive dysfunction? Solving the puzzle of pragmatic language disorders. *Brain and Language, 85,* 451–466.

Massa, J., Gomes, H., Tartter, V., Wolfson, V., & Halperin, J. M. (2008). Concordance rates between parent and teacher clinical evaluation of language fundamentals observational rating scale. *International Journal of Language and Communication Disorders, 43,* 99–110.

McDonald, S. (1993). Pragmatic language skills after closed head injury: Ability to meet the informational needs of the listener. *Brain and Language, 44,* 28–46.

McKinnon, M. C., & Moscovitch, M. (2007). Domain-general contributions to social reasoning: Theory of mind and deontic reasoning re-explored. *Cognition, 102,* 179–218.

Nigg, J. T., & Casey, B. J. (2005). An integrative theory of attention-deficit/hyperactivity disorder based on the cognitive and affective neurosciences. *Development and Psychopathology, 17,* 785–806.

Nigg, J. T., Willcutt, E. G., Doyle, A. E., & Sonuga-Barke, E. J. (2005). Causal heterogeneity in attention-deficit/hyperactivity disorder: Do we need neuropsychologically impaired subtypes? *Biological Psychiatry, 57,* 1224–1230.

Nijmeijer, J. S., Minderaa, R. B., Buitelaar, J. K., Mulligan, A., Hartman, C. A., & Hoekstra, P. J. (2008). Attention-deficit/hyperactivity disorder and social dysfunctioning. *Clinical Psychology Review, 28,* 692–708.

Norbury, C. F., Nash, M., Baird, G., & Bishop, D. (2004). Using a parental checklist to identify diagnostic groups in children with communication impairment: A validation of the Children's Communication Checklist – 2. *International Journal of Language & Communication Disorders, 39,* 345–364.

Ozonoff, S. (1995). Reliability and validity of the Wisconsin Card Sorting Test in studies of autism. *Neuropsychology, 9,* 491–500.

Ozonoff, S., & Miller, J. N. (1996). An exploration of right-hemisphere contributions to the pragmatic impairments of autism. *Brain and Language, 52,* 411–434.

Ozonoff, S., Pennington, B. F., & Rogers, S. J. (1991). Executive function deficits in high-functioning autistic individuals: Relationship to theory of mind. *Journal of Child Psychology and Psychiatry, 32,* 1081–1105.

Pellicano, E. (2007). Links between theory of mind and executive function in young children with autism: Clues to developmental primacy. *Developmental Psychology, 43,* 974–990.

Pennington, B. F., & Ozonoff, S. (1996). Executive functions and developmental psychopathology. *Journal of Child Psychology and Psychiatry, 37,* 51–87.

Perner, J., Kain, W., & Barchfeld, P. (2002). Executive control and higher-order theory of mind in children at risk of AD/HD. *Infant and Child Development, 11*(2), 141–158.

Perner, J., & Lang, B. (1999). Development of theory of mind and executive control. *Trends in Cognitive Sciences, 3,* 337–344.

Perner, J., & Lang, B. (2000). Theory of mind and executive function: Is there a developmental relationship?. In D. J. Cohen, S. Baron Cohen, & H. Tager-Flusberg (Eds.), *Understanding other minds: Perspectives from developmental cognitive neuroscience* (2nd ed., pp. 150–181). New York: Oxford University Press.

Peterson, C. C. (2003). The social face of theory of mind: The development of concepts of emotion, desire, visual perspective and false belief in deaf and hearing children. In V. Slaughter & B. Repacholi (Eds.), *Individual differences in theory of mind: Implications for typical and atypical development* (pp. 171–196). New York: Psychology Press.

Peterson, C. C., & Siegal, M. (1995). Deafness, conversation and theory of mind. *Journal of Child Psychology and Psychiatry, 36*, 459–474.

Rapin, I. (1996). Practitioner review: Developmental language disorders: A clinical update. *Journal of Child Psychology and Psychiatry, 37*, 643–655.

Ridderinkhof, K. R., van den Wildenberg, W. P. M., Segalowitz, S. J., & Carter, C. S. (2004). Neurocognitive mechanisms of cognitive control: The role of prefrontal cortex in action selection, response inhibition, performance monitoring, and reward-based learning. *Brain and Cognition, 56*, 129–140.

Rommelse, N. N., Altink, M. E., Oosterlaan, J., Buschgens, C. J., Buitelaar, J., & Sergeant, J. A. (2008). Support for an independent familial segregation of executive and intelligence endophenotypes in ADHD families. *Psychological Medicine, 38*, 1595–1606.

Ronald, A., Simonoff, E., Kuntsi, J., Asherson, P., & Plomin, R. (2008). Evidence for overlapping genetic influences on autistic and ADHD behaviours in a community twin sample. *Journal of Child Psychology and Psychiatry, 49*, 535–542.

Russell, J. (1997). *Autism as an executive disorder*. New York: Oxford University Press.

Sabbagh, M. A., Xu, F., Carlson, S. M., Moses, L. J., & Lee, K. (2006). The development of executive functioning and theory of mind: A comparison of Chinese and US preschoolers. *Psychological Science, 17*, 74–81.

Sergeant, J. A., Geurts, H., & Oosterlaan, J. (2002). How specific is a deficit of executive functioning for attention-deficit/hyperactivity disorder? *Behavioural Brain Research, 130*, 3–28.

Shields, J., Varley, R., Broks, P., & Simpson, A. (1996). Social cognition in developmental language disorders and high-level autism. *Developmental Medicine and Child Neurology, 38*, 487–495.

Sonuga-Barke, E. J. S. (2005). Causal models of attention-deficit/hyperactivity disorder: From common simple deficits to multiple developmental pathways. *Biological Psychiatry, 57*, 1231–1238.

Sperber, D., & Wilson, D. (2002). Pragmatics, modularity and mind-reading. *Mind and Language, 17*, 3–23.

Tannock, R., & Schachar, R. (1996). Executive dysfunction as an underlying mechanism of behavior and language problems in attention deficit hyperactivity disorder. In M. M. Konstantareas, R. Tannock, J. H. Beitchman, & N. J. Cohen (Eds.), *Language, learning, and behavior disorders: Developmental, biological, and clinical perspectives* (pp. 128–155). New York: Cambridge University Press.

Viding, E., & Blakemore, S. J. (2007). Endophenotype approach to developmental psychopathology: Implications for autism research. *Behaviour Genetics, 37*, 51–60.

Volkmar, F. R., Lord, C., Bailey, A., Schultz, R. T., & Klin, A. (2004). Autism and pervasive developmental disorders. *Journal of Child Psychology and Psychiatry, 45*, 135–170.

Willcutt, E. G., Doyle, A. E., Nigg, J. T., Faraone, S. V., & Pennington, B. F. (2005). Validity of the executive function theory of attention-deficit/hyperactivity disorder: A meta-analytic review. *Biological Psychiatry, 57*(11), 1336–1346.

Willcutt, E. G., Sonuga-Barke, E. J. S., Nigg, J. T., & Sergeant, J. A. (2008). Recent developments in neuropsychological models of childhood psychiatric disorders. *Advances in Biological Psychiatry, 24*, 195–226.

For Product Safety Concerns and Information please contact our EU
representative GPSR@taylorandfrancis.com
Taylor & Francis Verlag GmbH, Kaufingerstraße 24, 80331 München, Germany

www.ingramcontent.com/pod-product-compliance
Lightning Source LLC
Chambersburg PA
CBHW050529270326
41926CB00015B/3138